Dialogue Rejoined

Theology and Ministry in the United States Hispanic Reality

With a Foreword by Donald Senior, C.P.

Moisés Sandoval
Carlos B. Córdova
Dominga Zapata, S.H.
Guillermo Fernández-Toledo
Barbara E. Reid, O.P.
Gary Riebe-Estrella, S.V.D.
John E. Linnan, C.S.V.
Paul J. Wadell, C.P.
Ana María Pineda, R.S.M.
Mark R. Francis, C.S.V.
Robert Schreiter, C.PP.S.

Edited by

Ana María Pineda, R.S.M.
Robert Schreiter, C.PP.S.

A Liturgical Press Book

THE LITURGICAL PRESS
Collegeville, Minnesota

Cover design by David Manahan, O.S.B.

1   2   3   4   5   6   7   8   9

Library of Congress Cataloging-in-Publication Data

Dialogue rejoined : theology and ministry in the United States Hispanic
    reality / with a foreword by Donald Senior ; Moíses Sandoval . . . [et al.] ;
    edited by Ana María Pineda, Robert Schreiter.
        p.   cm.
    Includes bibliographical references.
    ISBN 0-8146-2206-2
    1. Church work with Hispanic Americans.   2. Hispanic Americans—
Religion.   3. Hispanic Americans—Social conditions.   4. Church and
social problems—Catholic Church—History.   5. Sociology, Christian
(Catholic)   6. Hispanic American Catholics—History.   I. Sandoval,
Moises.   II. Pineda, Ana María.   III. Schreiter, Robert J.
    BV4468.2.H57D52   1995
    277.3′082′08968—dc20
                                                                95-7432
                                                                CIP

Contents

Acknowledgments

We are indebted to many colleagues who have guided our effort in rejoining the dialogue. We have been assisted in this endeavor in a variety of ways.

We are grateful to María Pilar Aquino, Assistant Professor of Theology at the University of San Diego; Roberto Goizueta, Associate Professor of Theology at Loyola University in Chicago; Ninfa Garza, M.J., Diocesan Director of Basic Church Communities in the Diocese of Brownsville, Texas, and Dolorita Martínez, O.P., Director of the Hispanic Pastoral Planning Office of the Archdiocese of Omaha, Nebraska; Arturo Bañuelas, Director of the Tepeyac Institute in El Paso, Texas; Rev. Ricardo García of the Diocese of San Jose, California; Antonio Medina of Chicago; members of the Executive Committee of the Conference of Religious for Hispanic Ministry (CORHIM): Clemente Barrón, C.P., Cathy García, R.S.H.M., Verónica Méndez, R.C.D., Ana María Pineda, R.S.M., Gary Riebe-Estrella, S.V.D., and Elisa Rodríguez, S.L., for mentoring the contributors to this publication in writing their manuscripts.

The final draft of the manuscripts were refined and enriched by the insights of the Hispanic respondents and participants who were present at the sessions of the Hispanic Faculty Seminar where the manuscripts were initially presented. We thank the respondents, Dominga Zapata, S.H., Rev. Arturo Pérez, and Rev. Juan Huitrado, for their constructive appraisal of the initial drafts of the manuscripts. We are grateful to the Hispanic leaders and to representatives of Chicago Educational Institutes who joined the CTU faculty in the year-long Hispanic Faculty Seminar: Virgilio Bonifazi, Angelina Márquez, Alicia Gutiérrez, S.H., Rev. Arturo Pérez, José Castillo, Alvaro Dávila, Enrique Alonso, Rev. Wayne Prist, Judy Connolly, S.S.N.D., Carol Frances Jegen, B.V.M., and Dan Eckelkamp-Baker.

Our gratitude to the faculty and administration of Catholic Theological Union for the invaluable contribution they offered during the presentation of these manuscripts at the Hispanic Faculty Seminar and for their ongoing support. Our debt of gratitude to Olga Pavisich-Ryan, Linda Wanner, S.S.N.D., and Lissa Romell, who have assisted in preparing the typescript for publication. Finally, we wish to thank the Lilly Endowment for the generous financial support that made this project possible.

Foreword

Hospitality is a strong biblical virtue, one prized not only by Israel with its covenant responsibility to the "sojourner" but also by the early Christian community that recognized the risen Christ in the face of the unexpected stranger. Hospitality as a Christian virtue, therefore, is not simply a matter of being kind to strangers in need; it means being open to learn from and even be inspired by God's truth, which comes to us in ways beyond the familiar.

One might also make the case that "hospitality" is part of the founding mythology of the United States. On these shores the stranger, the victim, and peoples seeking new opportunity and freedom were to be welcome. We were not to be a state in which one culture, one race, or one way of worship would dominate. The hard realities of limited economic resources and the difficult art of understanding and appreciating cultures very different from one's own have made this both America's appeal and its most glaring failure. In our own day, for example, border patrols and racist politics cannot be easily reconciled with the famed beacon of liberty and tolerance that is planted in New York Harbor.

The Church has not been exempt from these struggles. In the great wave of immigration that swept through North America at the turn of the century, local Churches often served as both lifeboat and entry port for new peoples, and they still do. But the dominances and prejudices of the surrounding culture have also been played out within the life of the Church. Nowhere is that more evident than in the case of Hispanic Catholics. As the essays in this volume document, the Hispanic communities in the United States are diverse, rich in tradition, and composed both of new immigrants and of generations who were at home in the Americas long before the Pilgrims arrived. They are a people of extraordinary, tenacious faith and a devotional life full of exuberance and reverence. Yet Hispanic Catholics have often been left at the margins of formal Church life to a degree that rivals their political and economic deprivations in national life.

But a new consciousness within the Church at large and within the Hispanic communities themselves is changing the equation. As the second millennium approaches the Church in North America has become more aware that Hispanic Catholics are a substantial and growing part of the community, a reality that is bringing fresh life and enormous pastoral challenge. If the Church is to live up to the gospel, it will need to revive the virtue of hospitality—being open to the beauty and wisdom of the "other" and finding there the face of the risen Christ.

The need to be hospitable extends as well to theological education. In the seminaries and schools of theology the future is now: the priests and ministers of the second-millennium Church are already in our classrooms. Yet with few exceptions our schools of theology have not adequately adapted to the realities of Hispanic Catholics. There are a minimal number of Hispanics on our faculties and few Hispanic seminarians and even fewer Hispanic lay ministers in our student bodies. This reflects in part the scandals of our national life: Hispanics have had little opportunity for graduate education in the United States and still stand at the bottom of the list of minorities in this regard. But the dearth of Hispanic students and faculty is also due to a lack of hospitality. Many Hispanics simply do not feel at home in the world of graduate theological education. Their culture and traditions are not respected or alluded to. Their proud heritage is subject to stereotype and not considered as a source of wisdom for the Church. In many dioceses, even ones with sizable Hispanic populations, Hispanic leaders are not taken seriously.

No crystal ball is needed to realize that the future of American Catholicism depends in large part on preparing a new generation of leaders that will include Hispanics, as well as Anglos who not only know the language but are at home in Hispanic contexts.

I had the privilege of being president of Catholic Theological Union as it worked hard to be more hospitable to Hispanic Catholics. The essays in this volume are one expression of that hard work. Through a series of gifted speakers we learned more about the diversity of Hispanic culture in the United States. And through the commitment of our faculty, working in collaboration with Hispanic colleagues across the country, we began to consider how the theology and pedagogy of our own classrooms could be enriched by attention to Hispanics as well as representatives of other cultures within the rich diversity of North America.

I am most grateful to Sr. Ana María Pineda, R.S.M., director of Hispanic ministry at CTU, for her leadership at the school and in helping this project come to fruition. The response of those involved in these programs was extraordinarily positive, and seldom have I witnessed a faculty seminar with more energy than the one that sparked this volume. Hopefully, some of what we have learned in the process will be of use to others. As anyone who aspires to build a diverse Christian community knows, the work is never dull and never finished, but every attempt to welcome the other has the wonderful risk of discovering the risen Christ in our midst.

Donald Senior, C.P.
Catholic Theological Union

Introduction

Ana María Pineda, R.S.M.

In the history of evangelization in the "New World," the Franciscan friars who had accompanied Fr. Martín de Valencia from Spain would be considered the first official missionaries who would begin a formal and organized process of Christianization. They had been sent at the request of the Holy See and the emperor. *Los Doce* had been chosen with great care, since the task of evangelization in the New World was deemed so important. They had received their philosophical and theological preparation at the most prestigious universities of Spain and were held in great esteem because of their wisdom, knowledge, and virtue.

In the process of this beginning missionary endeavor, these Twelve, the chosen wise men, were to enter into dialogue with the wisemen of the Aztec-Nahuatl world. This historical encounter was to be documented in the valuable work of Fray Bernardino de Sahagun, *Colloquies and Christian Doctrine with which the Twelve Friars of Saint Francis sent by Pope Adrian VI and Emperor Charles V converted the Indians of New Spain, in the Mexican and Spanish Languages.* The *Colloquies* recorded the original dialogues and discussions that transpired between *Los Doce* and the native people. It is significant because it records the efforts of *Los Doce* to catechize the religious leaders of the conquered Aztec world. In the exchange *Los Doce* used translators for purposes of communicating the Christian doctrine to the leaders and learned members of the people. Despite the assistance of the translators it soon became evident that the Nahuatl language could not accommodate itself to a religious understanding that proceeded from a world foreign to their own.

After listening respectfully to the logically crafted proclamation of the Christian doctrine, one of the principal leaders arose and with great courtesy, calm, and self-composure manifested their complete disgust at having their customs and beliefs as had been handed to them by their grandparents and ancients attacked by the foreigners. The spokesman for the group confessed that he was not a wiseman but that there were still some among them who were truly wise and could adequately refute the lessons of the friars.[1] The spokesperson continued to make it known to the friars that they had not understood the gods of their ancestors. It was through them that they had received life. It was impossible for the native people to deny all that their ancestors had given them. It was impossible for them to accept the teaching of the friars. In the end he made it known that as a people they had lost life itself. Their government had been defeated, their women violated, and their temples destroyed. Were they now being asked to give up their gods? The response could be no other than to insist that they would not abandon their gods. Death was preferable. They were determined not to leave their service and adoration: "For our ancestors before us, who lived upon the earth, were unaccustomed to speak thus. From them have we inherited our pattern of life which in truth did they hold, in reverence they held, they honored, our gods. They taught us all their rules of worship, all their ways of honoring the gods."[2] With that final word, silence fell between the first missionaries and the native people.

The conversation ended, the friars continued in their evangelization of the people. History documents the intense activity of those years devoted in large part to the instruction and baptizing of the native converts. Any trace of the religious tradition of the people was destroyed to assure the permanency in the Christian faith of the new converts. Every manifestation of their religiosity was suspect and could not be tolerated. To this end, the temples, idols, and painted codices of the indigenous world were destroyed by the religious themselves or by the *conquistadores*. The prophecy declared in the *Chilam Balam de Chumayel*, the sacred book of the Maya of Mesoamerica had been fulfilled:

> In the Eleventh Ahau there begins the counting of the time. . . .
> It was only because of the mad time, the mad priests, that sadness came
> among us, that Christianity came among us; for the great Christians came
> here with the true God; but that was the beginning of our distress, the
> beginning of the tribute,
> the beginning of the alms, what made the
> hidden discord appear,
> the beginning of the fighting with firearms,
> the beginning of the outrages,
> the beginning of being stripped of everything,
> the beginning of slavery for debts,
> the beginning of the debts bound to the shoulders,
> the beginning of the constant quarrelling,
> the beginning of the suffering.[3]

In the end, while the Twelve had directed words of instruction to the learned ones of the Aztec-Nahuatl world, dialogue had not occurred. Both had predispositions that made dialogue at this level impossible.[4] The encounter between *Los Doce* and the native people of the "New World," as documented in the *Colloquies,* is not only one of a historical nature, but above all it is one of methodology. The missionaries had confronted a mission reality that in their experience had no historical antecedent. They had been selected carefully for this important task of evangelization in the New World because they fulfilled the requirements of excelling in wisdom, knowledge, and virtue. Many had been prepared in the University of Alcalá, established by Cardinal Cisneros in response to the spirit of the Renaissance. Spain valued truth, and that was defined in the measure of intellectual achievements acquired in the humanities, theology, and linguistics. Wisdom and intellectual achievement were synonymous. Since the indigenous population was the conquered one, they were placed under submission to the Spaniards' criteria of what it meant to be human. From all observations it was doubtful whether the newly conquered could be considered human. They did not accept the logical Christian doctrine and they did not read or write, even in their own language. Thus the initial exchange between *Los Doce* and the learned ones of the Aztec-Nahuatl world had ended not in dialogue but in a violent disjuncture of worlds. Neither was capable of entering into the theological worldview of the other. Neither grasped the theological truth that was articulated by the other.

Today we are attempting to undertake a new dialogue in this era of the New Evangelization. It is a dialogue that is mindful of the debts of the past and one that is conscious of the need to create new models for evangelization. This requires that a respectful climate for dialogue be created in which both the agents and the *destinatarios* can participate in the mutual discovery of how God is revealed through their respective histories and cultural symbols. This new dialogue requires a mutual engagement as equals and an openness to how each experiences God and what symbolic language is used to express that profound relationship.

This collection of essays is the result of a modern-day effort to establish such a dialogue. It is a well-known fact that the Hispanic population in the United States, which is traditionally Catholic, is projected to comprise more than 50 percent of the Catholic Church by the year 2000, a statistic that is being questioned by the success of evangelical fundamentalist sects with Hispanics as reflected in the results of a 1990 survey conducted by the NCCB/USCC Secretariat for Hispanic Affairs, which indicated that half of the dioceses surveyed expressed a grave concern regarding the impact that proselytism is having on Hispanic Catholics and how this endangers their traditional affiliation to the Roman Catholic Church. In what pertains to the presence of Hispanic leadership within diocesan structures, the survey revealed that less than 1 percent of Hispanics are found in significant diocesan positions where they can influence and shape pastoral policies. In 1988, "In My Father's House: Part II," a forum on Hispanic priestly formation, was held in Denver, Colorado, as part of an NCCB-sponsored project studying how best to respond to the phenomenon that while a significant number of Hispanic candidates began study for the priesthood, few persevered to ordination or final profession. The results of the forum confirmed the need for theological education and formation to seriously acknowledge the role of culture in the shaping of appropriate formation programs in the Hispanic context. This recommendation had repeatedly been articulated over the last twenty years during the process of pastoral assessment initiated by the national convocation of Hispanic lay and religious leaders known as the *Encuentro Nacional Hispano de Pastoral* (1972, 1977, 1985) and had found support in the 1983 NCCB pastoral letter on Hispanic ministry, *The Hispanic Presence: Challenge and Commitment.* These indicators and many others insistently pointed to the fact that other approaches had to be taken in the pastoral attention given to Hispanics in the United States and to the preparation of the ministers for those communities. This reality raises questions for the world of theological education, which is faced with the challenge of how best to prepare ministers to serve the U.S. Hispanic communities and how to grapple with the methodological and pedagogical issues this implies. What new approaches to evangelization need to be considered in the process of theological education and formation of ministers? What is required of theological educators in the New Evangelization?

These were issues that the Catholic Theological Union in Chicago sought to explore in 1989 with the assistance of a grant from the Lilly Endowment. The goal of the proposed project was to investigate ways of appropriately preparing ordained and nonordained to minister in the U.S. Hispanic communities. From the beginning it seemed imperative to engage pastoral and theological resource persons on a national level representative of the multifaceted U.S. Hispanic reality as equal dialogue partners in the exploration of the issue. Subsequently, during the winter of 1990 Catholic Theological Union hosted a lecture series open to the wider theological and Church community addressing the diverse multicultural reality of the urban Hispanic communities in the United States. The lectures were given by Hispanic/Latino resource persons with expertise in the articulation of the diversity of Hispanic culture in the United States. This was followed by two major events. The first was a convocation of a national consultation between U.S. Hispanic pastoralists and theologians and theological educators from graduate theological institutions in the country entitled "Graduate Theological Education for Ministry to Hispanics." The second was a year-long seminar at Catholic Theological Union in which CTU faculty prepared and presented papers in consultation with Hispanics in ministry on various areas of theology, exploring how the Hispanic reality reshaped the articulation of theological formation in preparing ministers for ministry in U.S. Hispanic communities. In each instance, the primary value was to engage Hispanic resource persons as equal dialogue partners in this modern day *"Colloquios."*

The collection of essays offered in this book are the fruits of this effort to establish a mutually enriching dialogue between the world of theological education and the U.S. Hispanic reality. The first section addresses the diverse Hispanic realities in an attempt to broaden the general perception of who the Hispanic is. Moíses Sandoval provides an overall look at the current U.S. Hispanic reality: a history marked by a process of conquest as well as the ongoing struggle to attain liberation in the sociopolitical and religious arenas of U.S. society. The social, cultural, and religious experiences of Central American migrant communities in the United States and the challenges these pose for Church ministers and community organizers in the United States are addressed by Carlos B. Córdova. Dominga Zapata follows with a description of the Puerto Rican experience in the United States, linking it to its Taíno, African, and Spanish heritage and its present unresolved political relationship with the United States. Zapata surfaces how the presence of Puerto Ricans in the United States brings cultural, racial, economic, political, and religious challenges to the dominant culture and to Church ministry. Finally, Guillermo Fernández-Toledo explores the religious idiosyncracy of the Cuban immigrant population in the United States as well as the history of the Cuban experience of evangelization, a history marked by a significantly different political experience than that of other Latino national groups.

The second section addresses the Hispanic reality and how the resources of theological education might be reshaped to help prepare both Hispanic and non-Hispanic ministers for ministry within the Hispanic communities. The essays contained in this section are the result of a year-long seminar that engaged faculty members of Catholic Theological Union and theological resource persons of Hispanic background in a dialogue concerning how particular theological and pastoral disciplines can be presented in the context of Hispanic culture. The interaction was intended to heighten the awareness of CTU faculty of the assumptions and the cultural and spiritual values operative in the Hispanic communities, these values being essential to the development of an appropriate theological process of education, in order to meet the present challenges and realities. This section opens with Barbara E. Reid's essay exploring the significance of the Bible in the lives of Hispanic women, the contribution that liberation theology has made in the last three decades to biblical interpretation, the fundamental dynamics of biblical exegesis from a liberation perspective, and how the method is used by U.S. Hispanics. This is followed by an essay by Gary Riebe-Estrella, who addresses the issue of developing a praxis-oriented methodology in a theological curriculum that acknowledges the historical and cultural location of the theologian, the sources of each communion of faith, and each culturally distinct faith-tradition. John E. Linnan explores the ecclesiological significance of the concrete realities of basic Church communities in the Mexican-American and Mexican community and explores the ecclesiological issues and questions that their existence raise. Paul J. Wadell's essay examines the distinctive approach to ethics of Hispanics, which focuses not on theories of human nature or arguments for a common rationality but on the pivotal narratives experienced in a history marked by conquest and oppression. Wadell develops the inseparable connection between the sense of morality that Hispanics possess and their constitutive life-narrative. Mark R. Francis examines the relationship between Hispanic popular religion and the official worship of the Church and the need not only to consider the norms enunciated in the official liturgical books but also to be attentive to the rites and practices of popular religion. A refusal to enter into an honest dialogue between Hispanic popular religion and the official worship of the Church can result in compromising the Church's ability to speak to Hispanic religious experience and to celebrate that experience in the Liturgy. Finally, Ana María Pineda takes a look at some of the historical reasons responsible for the general absence of Hispanic religious and lay leadership in the Church and points to a distinct style and understanding of ministry that is emerging, particularly among Catholic Hispanic lay leadership. The implications of this model of ministry invite those involved in the theological education and formation of ministers to dialogue with wisepersons of the Hispanic community.

The insights reflected in this collection of essays are an initial attempt on our part to rejoin the dialogue with the Hispanic peoples in the United States. We have been mentored and accompanied in this endeavor by Hispanic colleagues who have shared with us their experience of life and faith with great generosity, kindness, and patience. We hope that this contribution offers a new approach to establishing a mutually enriching and respectful dialogue between the world of theological education and that of the diverse Hispanic realities in this country—a dialogue that breaks through the silence and historical misunderstanding experienced in the exchange between *Los Doce* and the wisepersons of the native peoples of this land.

Notes

1. Virgilio P. Elizondo, *La Morenita: Evangelizer of the Americas* (San Antonio: Mexican American Cultural Center, 1980) 50.

2. Ibid., 50.

3. Quoted in Miguel Leon-Portilla, *El reverso de la conquista* (Mexico, 1978) 86.

4. Elizondo, *La Morenita,* 54.

PART ONE

Hispanic Realities and Ministry Today

1

Hispanics in the United States:
Between Conquest and Liberation

Moisés Sandoval

Introduction

Hispanics are a separate people in the United States. That means they have been kept apart, for human nature being what it is, they would otherwise have merged long ago. Other ethnic groups, with a few exceptions, progressively incorporated into the general society until they became indistinguishable from it. This was possible because society put no barriers in their way. Though there may have been resistance in the beginning, these groups were eventually accorded equal economic and political opportunity and social equality. That is the essence of integration. Hispanics have remained distinct at least in part because they had no choice. A 1992 poll undertaken by several foundations found, for example, that even those on the margins of society have a desire "to gain access to mainstream America."[1] Perhaps one could argue that Hispanics are at fault because, by choice or accident of geography, they have clung to their language and culture, but these are not the real causes of their separation. Hispanics have, in fact, learned English and accepted the values of society that should lead to successful integration. The causes of their isolation lie elsewhere.

Hispanics, like blacks and Asians, are an identifiable minority, and it is precisely the characteristics or stereotypes attributed to them that make them, in the eyes of their detractors, less than ideal Americans. When the United States invaded Mexico and seized one-half of its territory in 1846, political philosopher John Calhoun said that only the "free white race" should be added to the Union, a view that was widely shared.[2] Hispanics were rejected because they were of mixed race—"mongrel" was the pejorative applied to them—and because they were from a culture long despised by the English-speaking people. They were also held in low account because, next to the Indians, they were the only other people incorporated by conquest. As a result they were expected to live a life apart, on the periphery of the economy and of political and social institutions. Public attitudes and institutional policies and practices still reflect at least vestiges of some of these views.

In part because of that lack of welcome, Hispanics have never lost their sense of culture. In fact, since the 1960s there has been a revival. They want bilingual and bicultural education. Spanish can be heard on the streets of major cities, and those speaking it are not only immigrants but also American-born citizens who have relearned it in recent years. Mass is celebrated in Spanish in Catholic churches throughout the nation. Also, a sense of nationhood has been rising. Social scientists say that this group constitutes the fifth largest Latin nation in the world (after Mexico, Spain, Argentina, and Colombia). No other group in the United States is seen in that same way. Blacks, for instance, are not considered a black nation.

What that means is that Hispanics have regained some sense of being a people. They are trying to recover their history, which has been neglected or suppressed. The sense of brotherhood with Latins in other nations is growing. In recent years, for example, leaders of the Mexican American community have met with leaders of other Latin nations. That, however, should not be alarming; it is the same bond that exists among Jews around the world. It does not mean that Hispanics are in the process of establishing a separate country in the United States. On the contrary, paradoxical as it may seem, the recovery of culture is necessary to successful participation in American society.

The identity of Hispanics in the United States has been shaped by the historical process they have lived. Over nearly 150 years, Hispanics in the United States have experienced what social scientists have defined as a process of conquest. At the same time, they have been involved in a struggle for liberation. Because Church leaders have either been unaware or uninterested in what was happening, they have often taken positions that militated against the common welfare of Hispanic people, leading to the perception that the Church has not been a true mother. Therefore, there can be no greater need than to study these processes of conquest and liberation if future leaders, either Anglo or Hispanic, are to serve Hispanics well. Otherwise, the Church, having failed to learn from the past, will be condemned to keep making the same mistakes, and not with an insignificant minority but with a people destined to be the majority of its members in the early part of the twenty-first century.

Demographic Characteristics

In 1950, according to estimates, Hispanics in the United States numbered 4 million; in 1960, 6.9 million; in 1970, 10.5 million. In 1980, the first time a serious attempt was made to count them, the Census Bureau determined that they totaled 14.6 million, not counting the 3.5 million inhabitants of the Commonwealth of Puerto Rico. Between 1980 and 1990 Hispanics increased fifty-three percent, reaching 22.4 million, according to the 1990 census. By the year 2013, according to projections by demographers, Hispanics will number 42 million.[3] By then they will not only have surpassed blacks as the largest minority but they will also be the majority of the Catholics in the nation, assuming that the attrition due to proselytizing by other denominations does not increase.

Though the majority live in the Southwest, with 55 percent living in California and Texas, the Hispanics are a highly urbanized people, concentrated in the largest cities. A million or more live in the metropolitan areas of New York, Chicago, and Los Angeles, and hundreds of thousands in each of at least a dozen other cities. But every major city in the nation has a sizable community. Furthermore, Hispanics have been spreading in recent years to smaller cities of the Northeast, Southeast, and Northwest, even to Hawaii and Alaska. The growth will continue because of both high fertility rates and a steady flow of immigrants. Research by Wayne Cornelius of the Center for U.S.–Mexican Studies at the University of California, San Diego, shows that Mexicans, who are the largest Hispanic ethnic group, are now coming from Mexican states that in the past did not contribute migrants or immigrants.[4] Nevertheless, the Hispanics are not, in the main, an immigrant population. More than three-quarters are native-born or legal residents.

Thirty-four percent of Hispanics (6.8 million) live in California, and 21 percent (4.2 million) in Texas. Colorado, New Mexico, and Arizona together have another 1.6 million. Two million live in the New York area, 1.6 million in Florida, and about a million in Chicago and its suburbs.

Though there are representatives of all the Spanish-speaking nations of Latin America and Spain in the United States, those of Mexican origin are the largest group: 12.6 million. Next come people from Central and South America, the fastest-growing group in the 1980s, with 2.5 million, followed by Puerto Ricans at 2.3 million, Cubans at 1.1 million, and those who designate themselves as being of other Hispanic origin at 1.6 million.

The Economics and Politics of Hispanic Communities

Hispanic poverty has increased significantly in the past decade. The number of Hispanics living below the poverty line increased from 21.6 percent in 1978 to 28.2 percent in 1987. At that time a total of 5.5 million Hispanics lived in poverty. Since then the trend has not only not been reversed but poverty has increased. Conditions are worse in some areas than the national figures above. In 1989 the 300,000 Hispanics in Massachusetts (55 percent of whom are Puerto Rican) had an unemployment rate of 50 percent.[5] Of families headed by one parent, 78 percent lived below the poverty line.

In 1988, six in ten Hispanic families fell into the poorest two-fifths of all U.S. families, while only one in ten was in the wealthiest fifth. In 1978, the income of the typical Hispanic married family was 75 percent of the income of the typical white family; in 1987, it was only 69.9 percent.[6] Thus the gap between Hispanics and society as a whole has been widening. After the end of the 1982 recession, the income of the typical white family increased 11.4 percent; that of the black family, 13 percent; but that of the Hispanic family, only 6.3 percent. Furthermore, the poverty of the poor has been getting worse. In 1978, the average poor Hispanic family was $4,043 below the poverty line; in 1987, $4,775.

The immediate cause of low income is that most Hispanics work in blue-collar or other low-paying jobs. Data for 1987 show that 28 percent of Hispanic males worked as laborers, manufacturers, and operators; 21 percent in precision production and crafts; 10 percent in farming, forestry, and fishing. Only 10.8 percent (as opposed to 26.5 percent for the non-Hispanics) had managerial or professional positions.[7] Other factors, including the 1986 Immigration Reform and Control Act, also tended to impoverish them. A 1988 study of the New York metropolitan area showed that twenty-two thousand Hispanics who were citizens or immigrants with work permits were denied employment because they looked foreign. The act levies criminal and civil penalties against employers who hire undocumented immigrants.

In New York Hispanics entering the engineering profession decreased from 5 percent in the 1970s to 1.9 percent in the 1980s, according to the State Board of Regents. Of 14.4 million businesses in the country, only 300,000 are owned by Hispanics.

A major cause of poverty among Hispanics is lack of education. Only half of all Hispanics over twenty-five years of age have graduated from high school in comparison with 60 percent of blacks and 75 percent of whites. Only one in ten have graduated from college in comparison with one in five for whites. Dropout rates from high school range from 30 to 50 percent. In Massachusetts 53.8 percent of Hispanics fail to complete high school. Moreover, those who stay in school often do not get a good education; 76 percent, for example, score in the lower half of standardized tests, according to the National Commission of Secondary Education for Hispanics. Their reading scores are in the lower 25 percent. Fifty-seven percent of Hispanic males and 54 percent of females drop out of college. In contrast, only 34 percent of both male and female whites in college fail to graduate.

There are many reasons why Hispanics do not perform well in school. Immigrants often do not speak English. Of 3.5 million children in the United States whose primary language in 1980 was other than English, 70 percent of them were Spanish-speaking.[8] Children who come from Puerto Rico, where the language of instruction is Spanish, also experience problems.

Poverty traditionally forces many to go to work early to help support themselves and their families. Some leave school simply because their families have no tradition of education; the benefits of staying in school are not clear to them. The children of illegal immigrants often stay away from school out of fear of being deported or because they cannot afford to buy clothes or school supplies.[9] Sometimes, too, the violence encountered in school, such as gang fights, causes some to drop out.

Poverty, however, is the most important cause of failure in school—not just the poverty of the students and their families but of the communities in which they live. Good education is a function of wealth. The best schools are in the most affluent neighborhoods, with the highest expenditure per student, the best facilities, and the best teachers. In the wealthy Alamo Heights section of San Antonio, children have access to computers; in the poor Edgewood district across town, they have only pictures of a keyboard. The worst schools are found in poor areas, especially those where the minorities live. These areas lack the tax base and adequate state aid to make up the difference. The public is indifferent because these poor schools often serve only minority students. In 1972, 56 percent of Hispanic students attended predominantly minority schools; by 1980 segregation had increased to 70 percent.[10] In Texas and California the educational experience of Hispanics is as segregated as that of African Americans who live in Alabama or Mississippi, according to a study cited by Sojourners.[11]

Poor performance by Hispanics in school is also the legacy of prejudice, attitudes, and policies that have been in place for generations. For a long time Hispanic students read or heard nothing in school that would enhance their self-image. A Mexican American girl in East Los Angeles said in the 1970s: "We look for others like ourselves in the history books, for something to be proud of being a Mexican, and all we see in books, magazines, films, and TV shows are stereotypes of a dark, smelly man with a tequila bottle in one hand and a dripping taco in the other." Wittingly or unwittingly, the schools have continually insinuated the idea that Hispanics are inferior.

"The public school system as a whole has neither welcomed Hispanic children nor been willing to deal with their learning problems in an effective way," said Alan Pifer, president of the Carnegie Corporation, in 1980.[12] Teachers and administrators have never held high expectations for their

Hispanic students. Many think that such students are there only to prepare for low-skilled jobs, not for higher education, Tomás Arciniega, president of California State University, said in 1988.[13] The premise behind such views is that Hispanics have a place only on the fringes of society. In the San Luis Valley in Colorado in the 1970s some teachers actually encouraged Hispanics to drop out, figuring they did not need much schooling to work in the fields—their place in that society. The Chicano Education Project in Colorado found that Hispanics were often urged to drop out of high school to join the Armed Forces.

In politics, Hispanics have been largely spectators. No other minority has had so little voice in the legislative chambers of government—national, state, or local. Few Hispanics hold elective or appointive offices at any level. They were only marginally better represented in 1990 than twenty years before. In 1970 there were three Hispanics in the House of Representatives and one in the Senate; in 1990, seven representatives and no senators. After the 1992 general election, however, there were seventeen Hispanics in the House. Nevertheless, in proportion to their numbers, there should have been thirty-five. In 1978, Jews, a much smaller group, had twenty-two representatives; blacks, who total about thirty million, had sixteen.

The same disparities apply at local levels. In 1988 only one governor (Florida) and three big-city mayors (Miami, Denver, and San Antonio) were Hispanics. Hispanics in the California Legislature were underrepresented by two-thirds, in Texas by one-third. The same pattern held for county commissions, boards of education, and city councils.

Many gains have been made in recent years in changing election structures so that Hispanics can have a political voice. Poll taxes have been eliminated in the South and Southwest. Changes from at-large to district voting have given Hispanics a voice in cities like San Antonio and Denver. Anglos, who traditionally have refused to vote for Hispanics, elected Federico Peña mayor of Denver, a city where Hispanics are only 20 percent of the voters. Leticia Quezada, a Mexican immigrant who did not speak a word of English when she immigrated to the United States at the age of thirteen, was elected to the Los Angeles Board of Education in 1987; in 1992, at the age of thirty-nine, she was elected president of the board. Similarly, Gloria Molina was elected in 1991 as the first Hispanic member of the Los Angeles County Board of Supervisors. In another encouraging note, President Bill Clinton chose two Hispanics, both former mayors, to serve on his cabinet: Federico Peña of Denver as secretary of transportation and Henry Cisneros of San Antonio as secretary of housing and urban affairs.

Nevertheless, some people still think that Hispanics should be denied a political voice. Late in 1989 the Republican Party of Orange County,

California, settled for $400,000 a lawsuit charging that it had attempted to intimidate Hispanic voters at twenty polling places in the 1988 election. The party had hired uniformed guards who carried signs in English and Spanish warning that noncitizens cannot legally vote.[14] Though prejudice has diminished in some ways, the institutions of discrimination often remain.

Hispanics and Their Cultures

Socially, Hispanics experience vexing problems. Though they are only 8 percent of the population, they represent 14 percent of the AIDS cases. In Massachusetts, a Hispanic woman is ten times as likely to have AIDS as a white woman. In many Hispanic poor neighborhoods across the nation there is a high incidence of crime and drug abuse. Nearly one of every four Hispanic families is headed by a female, twice the proportion of white families.

Sometimes Hispanics who have been here longer are those least able to cope. Having suffered the slights and defeats of a despised minority, they lack a secure self-image. They have been told that to succeed in this society they must reject their own culture, an action that leads to self-hate.

In the past Church leaders thought Hispanics had to reject their cultural values to become better Catholics. As one historian put it, "Church leaders viewed religious conversion as intimately linked to the American way of life."[15] But if one looks at Hispanics today, those who are most successful in the Church or in society are those who have retained their culture. The Church's programs, which until recently made Americanization a goal, have therefore been a tragic mistake: they have contributed to a process that tends to defeat the Hispanic people.

In the Church today Hispanic leadership comes largely from two groups who have been least affected by American culture. One consists of immigrants and the other of people who, though rooted here, have escaped being overwhelmed by American ways. Ten of the twenty-one Hispanic bishops in the United States are immigrants: two from Mexico, two from Cuba, two from Spain, two from Puerto Rico,[16] one from Ecuador, and one from Venezuela. Most of the remainder are the sons of immigrants. Of some 1,954 Hispanic priests in the United States, fewer than 200 are native born. The proportion of native-born among the estimated 1,300 Sisters and Brothers is similar.[17] Furthermore, if one looks at the seminarians now studying, one finds that most of them are immigrants or the sons of immigrants. A few years ago, at the Southwestern Youth Congress, most of the young people were in the same category.

Many important offices in the Church are headed by Hispanic immigrants. For example, Mario Paredes, a Chilean, heads the Northeast

Regional Office for Hispanics; Fr. Mario Vizcaíno, a Cuban, the Southeast Regional Office; Fr. Ricardo Chávez, son of Mexican immigrants, headed the West Coast Office; Araceli Cantero, a Spaniard, is editor of *La Voz*, the highly successful Spanish edition of the archdiocesan newspaper of the Archdiocese of Miami; Julio Alejandro Escalona, a Mexican, edited the Spanish edition of the *Chicago Catholic*. That pattern holds throughout the rest of the nation.

Other Hispanic leaders in the Church tend to come from areas in this country that are havens for Hispanic culture: New Mexico, parts of Texas, Arizona, South Florida, southern California, and a few other pockets throughout the nation. These are places where U.S. culture has not overwhelmed Hispanic culture. New Mexico is the home of Pablo Sedillo, director of the bishops' Secretariat for Hispanic Affairs until 1991, and of Archbishop Robert Sánchez, Bishop Arturo Tafoya, and many of the native-born Hispanic clergy and religious. San Antonio, Texas, nurtured Fr. Virgil Elizondo, leading Mexican American theologian, and Communities Organized for Public Service (COPS), the Church federation based on the principles of Saul Alinsky, which has become a model throughout the nation. These areas have also provided political leaders like Texas' U.S. representative Henry B. González and New Mexico's Manuel Luján, secretary of the interior during the Bush administration, among others.

What is common to all these persons, immigrants and citizens alike, is a rich Hispanic culture. This means much more than that they speak Spanish, eat ethnic foods, and have their own music. They have a strong sense of identity, of self-worth. They have high self-expectations. They are connected with a past of which they are proud. They have a long religious tradition. They are part of a community rather than isolated individuals, and that community has had a strong influence over their lives. And, not unimportantly, they have power.

I was born in such a culture in northern New Mexico, sometimes described by writers as having been at least a century behind the times. In those rural foothills on the eastern side of the Sangre de Cristo Mountains, some eighty miles north of Santa Fe, the people were poor farmers. I began my academic career in a one-room school for eight grades. But our teacher let us know that we were special, that we could have great aspirations. And we dared to dream big. Some of the boys and girls who attended that school went on to earn doctorates in chemistry, education, dentistry. One became a Sister. Others became successful businessmen. Some became teachers and professors in colleges.

Though we spoke English only in school, we were not handicapped when we moved out of that haven into a tougher, crueler world, where we were continually told we were inferior. Our self-image had already been firmly established.

In contrast, some Hispanics show characteristics associated with conquered people: apathy, apparent indifference, passivity, and lack of motivation in relation to the objectives of the dominant society.[18] In areas that have borne the full brunt of the process of conquest, most typically the urban *barrios*, Hispanics have experienced a continual erosion of their culture, which is another way of saying they have lost their identity. With loss of identity has come a disorientation as to destiny and purpose. These Hispanics have lost their myths, their heroes, and their history. Joaquín Murieta, the so-called Chilean bandit—really, a guerrilla fighter of the nineteenth century—said, "I never guessed that my nationality would be divided, my personality diminished."

As a youth growing up in Colorado, I looked in vain for heroes from my own people in the movies and in society. For some, that search has ended in self-hate or hate of their culture. Many of the Hispanic priests were so trained by our seminaries that when they were ordained they did not want to serve their people.

The alienated are the people who most challenge the Church today, not the immigrants or the citizens from enclaves of strong Hispanic culture. These alienated are most numerous in the native-born population that has endured a full measure of conquest: Chicanos, Puerto Ricans, others who have been here a long time. The Church, including the specialized Hispanic ministries, is not reaching them very well. Because these Hispanics do not speak Spanish well, the *Encuentro* did not touch them. They are the Church's biggest challenge.

The Church and a Legacy of Conquest

Conquest, the cross carried by Hispanics in the United States since that country seized the Southwest from Mexico in 1846, has gone through different phases. At times it has been open warfare against an entire people; at others, violence, intimidation, and discrimination against individuals. The Treaty of Guadalupe Hidalgo ending the Mexican-American War was followed by violence, dispossession, and intimidation of the inhabitants of the captured lands. At first the objective was to extirpate Hispanic culture; later, it was to keep the people in their place: subservient, isolated in certain menial occupations, and in the *colonias* or *barrios*.

The definitions of conquest have also varied with the times. The Protestant Churches called it regeneration; the Catholic Church called it evangelization, of which Americanization was an essential part. It stripped Hispanics of their culture but did not welcome them into the culture of the majority. Even those who thought they had assimilated were unable to evade the stigma of being second class. Conquest continues today with the exploitation of the farmworkers and undocumented immigrants. It continues with the English-only movement, immigration laws that deny human beings the basic right to work for a living, and the unprovoked discourtesy and violence Hispanics suffer at the hands of those charged with enforcing the law. A study by the Diocese of Las Cruces, a See that is heavily Hispanic, showed that forty percent of the people, active Catholics who are not only law abiding but usually the most productive people in the community, had had contacts with the police. One of every five complained of "abusive or unprofessional behavior."[19]

For a long time the Churches participated in the process of conquest in other ways. The clergy accepted the stereotypes about Hispanics— that they were inferior people lacking in initiative or work ethic, prone to crime, lacking future orientation, and constituting a culture unable to overcome poverty. They did not oppose the social scientists who saw the causes of that putative inferiority as cultural, or others who said it was genetic, the product of the mongrelization of Spaniard and Indian.

On one occasion Archbishop Edward Hanna, who headed the Archdiocese of San Francisco from 1915 to 1935, wrote to the California congressional delegation asking that immigration from Mexico be limited. The Mexicans, he said, "drain our charities; they and their children become a large portion of our jail population, affect the health of our community, create a problem in our labor camps, require special attention in our schools and are of low mentality, diminish the percentage of our white population and remain foreign."[20] "We have shut out the European immigrant and have accepted the uncivilized Mexican in his place," a priest in Gary, Indiana, said during that same period. He charged that there were 560 communists in Gary and that most of them were Mexicans and Russians.

Church leaders were either not aware of what was happening to the Hispanic people or did not see that what they were saying and doing was contributing to the conquest. When confronted with having to defend the Hispanics, they demurred on the basis that the mission of the Church was spiritual. They did dispense charity, but what the Hispanics needed was a voice to defend their rights.

In their own sphere the bishops, clergy, religious orders, and congregations carried out their own type of discrimination. For generations Hispanics were not considered qualified for the priesthood or the religious life. They were seen only as subjects of evangelization, not as agents of ministry. The tradition of priesthood already beginning when the Southwest came under the control of the United States in 1846 was quashed. Nearly a century passed before Hispanic vocations were welcomed, and not by all bishops. The late Archbishop Urban J. Vehr of Denver said publicly in the 1950s that he did not have Hispanic seminarians because they did not meet his standards. Almost a hundred years passed between the appointment of the first black bishop in the United States and the appointment of the first Hispanic bishop in 1970.

Thus a major consequence of the process of conquest in the Church has been the lack of Hispanic leaders. Church leaders have claimed that the vocations weren't there, but in my travels throughout this country I have found evidence that many were either turned away or discouraged.

Despite the eloquent statements of recent years, there is evidence that many Church leaders have not become fully aware of the historical process Hispanics have undergone. Consider the following paragraph from a prestigious two-volume history on the Catholic parish, published in 1987:

> Besides being out of touch with the American Church, the Mexican American has found other elements of American culture difficult to accept. The Mexican sense of alienation has been increased by his or her inability to relate to the American work ethic. Nor was the ambition to succeed highly prized. Satisfaction was found in one's family and friends. To outsiders, this was often interpreted as sloth. The lack of initiative made many Anglos assume that the Mexican was best suited for menial labor. Neither did the Mexican family place much emphasis on formal education.[21]

Any Hispanic knows that the premises behind such a statement are false. No one works harder and for less remuneration than poor people. My father used to get up at dawn to get to the employment office of the sugar factory in Brighton, Colorado, before anyone else. But then he was forced to wait until all Anglos behind him were hired before his application was taken. As a result, he never got a job there. The grower for whom my brothers and I worked when we were teenagers insisted that Hispanics were suited only for menial labor. That was how discrimination was rationalized. Prejudice, not lack of ability, condemned us to toil as farmworkers, janitors, construction laborers, and shepherds. When the labor shortages of World War II provided new opportunities, we proved we were capable of doing many other kinds of work. Many Hispanic families make great sacrifices to educate their children.

Hispanics, like blacks, have been changed definitively by the historical processes they have experienced in the United States. John López, a psychotherapist at the Center for Mental Health at Montrose, Colorado, said that Hispanics have been drugged by hurt and anger. Some are excessively passive, with low expectations and a pessimistic outlook; others are excessively aggressive, angry, and distrustful, often with good cause. A study made in the Gardiner District of San Jose, California, in the late 1970s, stated: "A kind of paranoia afflicts some of the residents here who see the dog-catcher call at their home, but not at their Anglo neighbor's, their boy roughed up and held in a holding cell all night, while the Anglo friends, with whom he was picked up, are treated courteously and allowed to wait in the auditorium for their parents."[22] These are the same kinds of feelings people in formation are likely to encounter in Hispanics in the seminary.

In one seminary today where knowledge of Spanish and Hispanic culture is required for ordination, people responsible for formation have found that some of the Chicanos are hostile to their culture and have no desire to serve their own people. To qualify for continuing in the seminary, they have to enroll in special courses so that they will learn to value their heritage.

Between Conquest and Liberation

The history of Hispanics in the United States has been marked not only by a process of conquest but by a struggle for liberation. The imperatives for learning about this process of liberation and becoming involved in it are just as urgent as becoming aware of conquest and avoiding participating in it. Like conquest, the struggle for liberation has gone through different stages. Each generation, upon experiencing the process of conquest, has responded in its own way. Some were passive; others struggled. Silence, the protective coloration of oppressed peoples, was for a long time a dominant characteristic. Since World War II active struggle has been more common. Like blacks, Hispanics had their civil rights movement, which they called the *Movimiento*. But while blacks were led by their clergy in their marches and confrontations, Hispanics had no such luxury. They were led by laypersons or, in northern New Mexico, by a Protestant minister, Reies López Tijerina. They tried to recover land grants taken from them by questionable means, to gain economic and political control of their *barrios* in the cities, to gain a stronger voice in politics, and to improve the performance of their schools.

Hispanics also confronted the Church because it was one of the institutions that had oppressed them. They charged that the Church had not been a true mother to her Hispanic sons and daughters. Instead, as Bishop Patricio Flores expressed it at the first *Encuentro,* she was like a prostitute who had abandoned her children. Besides their grievance about being only objects of evangelization, they were angry because none of their priests had been ordained bishop, because their priests and religious were seldom given the opportunity to minister to their own people, because their culture had been disparaged by their shepherds. The *Encuentros* provided the forum for Hispanics to vent that anger in constructive ways, leading to the crafting of the *National Pastoral Plan for Hispanic Ministry.* They demanded that the Church become an authentic mother for them. Much progress has been made in recent years, but much remains to be achieved. Just as conquest has not been totally successful, the struggle of Hispanics for liberation is still incomplete.

Yet there are grounds for optimism. A major study by sociologist David Hayes-Bautista of the UCLA Chicano Studies Research Center shows that even though Hispanics have the highest poverty rate and lowest education rate of any ethnic group in California, they (1) smoke, drink, and use drugs less than Anglos and African Americans and as a result have a higher life expectancy; (2) are more likely to form family units consisting of two parents with children; (3) have the lowest rate of low-birth-weight babies among all groups even though they are less likely to be covered by health insurance; and (4) participate in the labor force in a higher proportion than any other group.

As the noted Mexican writer Carlos Fuentes writes, the Hispanics, by retaining their culture, add to the diversity of North American society. He suggests that the encounter of North American and Hispanic cultures means birth, even rebirth. "More and more often," Fuentes says, "people are starting to understand that speaking more than one language does not harm anyone."[23] He suggests that the greatest gift Hispanics bring to the United States and to the Church is their culture, with all its values on faith, family, and community. Slowly, the Church has come to the same conclusion.

Notes

1. Roberto Suro, "Hispanic Pragmatism Seen in Survey," *The New York Times*, December 15, 1992.

2. Edwin Sylvest, Jr., "Hispanic American Protestantism in the United States," *Fronteras: A History of the Latin American Church in the USA Since 1513*, ed. Moíses Sandoval (San Antonio: Mexican American Cultural Center, 1983) 285.

3. Robert Pear, "New Look at the U.S. in 2050: Bigger, Older, Less White," *The New York Times*, December 4, 1992.

4. Wayne A. Cornelius, "Los Migrantes de La Crisis: The Changing Profile of Mexican Labor Migration to California in the 1980s," a paper presented at the conference "Population and Work in Regional Settings" at El Colegio de Michoacán, Zamora, Michoacán (November 28–30, 1988) 9.

5. Constance L. Hays, "Hispanic Population Suffering Along with Massachusetts Economy," *The New York Times*, December 25, 1989.

6. "Shortchanged: Recent Developments in Hispanic Poverty, Income, and Employment," Center for Budget and Policy Priorities, November 1988.

7. Fran Gillespie, "Hispanics in the U.S. Labor Force: A Briefing Presented to the U.S. Catholic Conference," February 5, 1988.

8. "Bilingual Education," *America* (September 6, 1980) 83.

9. "Illegal Aliens Stay Out of School," *Newsweek* (December 8, 1980) 19.

10. Danny Colburn and Wendy Melillo, "Hispanics a Forgotten Health Population," *Washington Post*, June 16, 1987.

11. Aaron Gallegos, "Unity in Diversity: The New Reality of the Latino Community," *America's Original Sin, A Study Guide on White Racism* (Washington: Sojourners) 148.

12. "Bilingual Education," Op. cit.

13. Edward B. Fiske, "Colleges Are Seeking to Remedy Lag in Their Hispanic Enrollment," *The New York Times,* March 20, 1988.

14. "Republicans Settle Suit over Guards at Polls," *The New York Times,* December 25, 1989.

15. Jay P. Dolan, *The American Catholic Experience: A History from Colonial Times to the Present* (New York: Doubleday, 1985) 373.

16. Puerto Ricans, since they have been U.S. citizens since 1917, are not technically immigrants, but their experience on the mainland has been the same as if they had been foreigners.

17. Figures derived from various studies by the Bishops' Committee on Vocations, the Bishops' Committee for Hispanic Affairs, and the Secretariat for Hispanics.

18. Andrés Guerrero, *A Chicano Theology* (Maryknoll, N.Y.: Orbis, 1987) 23, citing the U.S. Commission on Civil Rights, *Stranger in One's Land,* Publication No. 17, 25–26.

19. Diocese of Las Cruces, *Study of Social Concern: A Framework for Analysis and Report of Findings,* ed. Antonio Luján, James D. Williams, and Celia Geck Anchondo (1985).

20. Manuel Gamio, *Mexican Immigration to the United States: A Study of Human Migration and Adjustment* (New York: Dover, 1971) 118.

21. Jeffrey M. Burns, "Building the Best: A History of Catholic Parish Life in the Pacific States," *The American Catholic Parish: A History from 1850 to the Present,* vol. 2, ed. Jay P. Dolan (New York: Paulist, 1987) 87.

22. "The Gardiner District," unpublished paper (1978) 1.

23. Carlos Fuentes, *The Buried Mirror: Reflections on Spain and the New World* (New York: Houghton Mifflin, 1992) 347.

2

The Social, Cultural, and Religious Realities of Central American Immigrants in the United States

Carlos B. Córdova

Central American Migrations to the United States

Since the early 1900s Central Americans have often migrated to the United States as a result of political and economic conditions. The economic crisis and political instability that affected Latin America in the 1930s created the right conditions for the first large-scale Central American migration to the United States. During the 1930s the military began to ascend to higher levels of control in Central American governments and began to share the political power with the oligarchic families that had ruled most of those countries since the 1860s. In Nicaragua, for example, the military, under the leadership of Anastasio Somoza García, created one of the most repressive dictatorships in Central America and forced many people to leave the country. A significant number of Nicaraguans escaped the political persecution and lack of personal freedom and arrived in the United States during the period from 1930 to 1940 and resettled in San Francisco, Los Angeles, Houston, and New Orleans. This marked the beginning of a new migration network that established the social and economic foundations of the ethnic immigrant community of future generations of Central Americans who would be arriving later in the United States.

A few decades later, during the 1960s, Central American immigration to the United States increased as a direct result of the policies of the Immigration Act of 1965. These new immigration policies allowed for the granting of immigrant quotas to countries that historically had not been included in U.S. immigration policies. The 1965 law encouraged professionals and skilled laborers to migrate to the United States and permitted the resettlement of large numbers of young working-class and middle-class families from Latin America. That was specifically the case for Central Americans at that time. Many U.S. cities had Latin American immigrant neighborhoods and communities that attracted Central Americans to their municipalities. Newcomers settled in the Latin American neighborhoods because of the familiar cultural traditions and support systems maintained there. The new Central American arrivals further developed the economic, social, and cultural foundations of the Latin American ethnic networks and economic enclaves in San Francisco, Los Angeles, Houston, New York, and Washington.

The influx of Central American immigrants to the United States has sharply risen since the late 1970s. At the present time Central America contributes the second largest number of Latin American migrants to the United States. Before the 1970s most Central American immigrants arrived with legal immigration status as permanent residents or with student visas. In the 1980s migration patterns changed as a direct impact of adverse sociopolitical and economic conditions present in the Central American region, and the final results were large numbers of Salvadoreans, Guatemalans, and Nicaraguans who entered the United States without legal immigration status or as political asylum applicants. The pre-1979 migrations were mostly economic in nature, while the post-1979 migrations were generated by the economic and political realities faced by the nations in the region (ACLU; Córdova, 1986, 1987).

Demographic Characteristics of 1970–1990 Central American Immigrants to the United States

The Latin American population in the United States has increased to more than 20 million people in 1989 and has demonstrated an increase of 5.5 million people since the 1980 census. The Census Bureau reported in October 1989 that there were approximately 12,567,000 people of Mexican origin in the United States. The fastest growing population were Central and South Americans, who added up to 2,545,000 people. These demographic statistics reflecting the Central American population appear to be low, as they do not include the figures of undocumented people residing in the United States.

The actual numbers of legal and undocumented Central American immigrants in the United States are not available. The demographic statistics calculated by the Immigration and Naturalization Service (INS) estimate that there are approximately two million Central Americans in this country. These figures are not exactly accurate, because the majority of Central Americans who arrived in the United States after 1979 entered the country as undocumented workers or as political asylum applicants and have not been included in the demographic surveys conducted by the U.S. government (ACLU).

The demographic figures of the Central American immigrant population in the United States have sharply increased since the 1970s as a consequence of the socioeconomic and political instability and the guerrilla wars in Central America. The region suffers from widespread poverty, and the various economic systems are internally controlled by interrelated oligarchic families and the military hierarchy. Their economies are unstable because of the lack of diversification of agricultural exports and their extreme dependency on the monocultivation of agricultural cash crops, the international trade markets, and foreign economic aid.

The Central American sociopolitical and economic crises are the most important determinants for the present migrations to the United States. Guatemala, El Salvador, and Nicaragua have been affected by armed insurgency against the established sociopolitical systems. Since 1980 more than 200,000 people have been assassinated by right-wing paramilitary death squads and the armed forces in El Salvador and Guatemala. During this time of war and persecution the most common targets for assassination are labor leaders, Indian leaders, intellectuals, community organizers, Catholic priests, lay preachers, catechists, agricultural workers, and students.

It is important to consider the entire spectrum of cultural, social, and political factors when analyzing the demographic makeup of Central American communities in the United States because of the complex nature of those communities and their migration determinants. It is imperative to first look at the conditions in the various countries to avoid stereotyping the different Central American nationalities. Central American communities have divergent political ideologies, ranging from conservative right-wing views to orthodox Marxism. Thus, a Central American immigrant community in a specific geographical area in the United States may manifest a wide diversity of political views; such is the case in San Francisco and Los Angeles. Or, a Central American community may hold a unified political position, as is the case in Miami. There are more similarities in socioeconomic class status than in national identity issues among the populations in Central American countries. For example, the upper classes in the different countries have often intermarried and have close social, business, and cultural relations among themselves.

In the urban centers of the United States, such as Florida and California, one also finds such upper-class individuals and groups of individuals. The reality remains, however, that the majority of Central Americans in the United States are middle- or working-class individuals. In their home countries, they were teachers, high school and university students, secretaries, accountants, housewives, domestic workers, office workers, and skilled factory workers.

Guatemalans in the United States

During the early 1980s in Guatemala, especially in areas of conflict, numerous Mayan Indian communities were destroyed and their entire populations forcibly relocated in strategic villages; others had no option but to flee to refugee camps in Mexico or to migrate to the United States as a result of the intensive military repression and the anti-insurgency campaigns carried out by the armed forces. Those who remained in the strategic villages were forced to participate in civilian patrols. These civilian patrols were used by the military to lead the army patrols into conflictive territories, thereby exposing civilians to crossfire between guerrillas and the army. The refugees were subjected to repressive government military actions that resulted in massacres of elderly, women, and children, who make up the vast majority of the refugee population (ACLU; Amnesty International; Camarda; Manz).

During this period, Catholic priests and lay workers became direct targets of the repressive actions of the Guatemalan army. Many of them were abducted, tortured, killed, or forced into exile. As part of this campaign of terror, the Guatemalan government did not allow Catholic priests into the conflictive areas or the strategic villages. These actions were characteristic of the military government of General Efraín Ríos Montt, a Christian Fundamentalist and a preacher. He allowed only the participation of Christian Fundamentalist preachers in the areas controlled by the government and had set himself the goals of changing the religious traditions of the Guatemalan people. He took a strong anti-Catholic position by stating that priests were responsible for creating the revolutionary movements against the government in Guatemala.

Indian people were suddenly in a situation in which they no longer had Catholic religion and ritual available in their communities and were abruptly introduced to a new religious perspective that was not totally acceptable to them. What developed out of this experience was a new resurgence of the traditional Mayan religious practices, in which the Indian shamans have taken the religious leadership in numerous Indian areas of Guatemala. The Mayan movement is gaining members at a very fast pace as a response to aggression, repression, and censorship in the Guatemalan highlands.

In rural areas in the U.S. Southwest, the Central American population is composed mostly of indigenous rural people who had made a living from traditional agricultural activities in Central America. The indigenous culture is governed by the rhythm of the corn agriculture and the seasons, and the people prefer rural over urban lifestyles. The majority of Guatemalan Indian immigrants are unskilled young people with low educational backgrounds who are employed as seasonal migrant workers in the agricultural farms throughout the Sunbelt states. There are numerous Guatemalan Mayan people working in the agricultural fields of Florida, Texas, Arizona, Oregon, Washington State, and California.

The situation of Guatemalan Mayan Indians in the United States is very difficult because they hold non-Western cultural values and often speak only their Mayan languages. The majority of Guatemalans working in Florida are Kanjobal-speaking people who originate from the town of San Miguel Acatlán, located in the northern province of Huehuetenango. In addition to the language difficulties, they have also encountered a major cultural problem that creates disruption in their culture and religion: the discontinuation of their rituals and traditions related to the cultivation of corn. The Mayan refugees in Florida work in the harvesting of the citrus fields and no longer engage themselves in the cycle of corn agriculture.

In the U.S. urban centers the majority of Guatemalans are of urban backgrounds; these people originate from middle- and working-class backgrounds in Guatemala. They are mostly *mestizo,* Spanish speaking, and have higher levels of education. They are more skilled and better prepared to cope in the U.S. culture and society than the Mayan Indians.

Salvadoreans in the United States

The Salvadorean immigrant population in the United States is not a homogeneous group. They come from different socioeconomic and cultural backgrounds. In the 1970s and 1980s members of the ruling classes could foresee the developing political crisis, and so they left El Salvador and resettled, mostly in Florida and California, to safeguard their fortunes and livelihood. These upper-class individuals already had economic, cultural, and political ties in the United States; for decades, they had taken their fortunes out of Central America and deposited them in U.S. banks. Many of them were educated in U.S. universities and were fluent in English. The combination of their economic and educational status, bilingual skills, and their legal residency or U.S. citizenship helped them adjust to their new life in this country. A similar phenomenon was observable in the case of upper-class families from Cuba and Nicaragua after the revolutions there.

In contrast, the more recent Salvadorean immigrants arriving in the United States are undocumented and come from middle- and lower-class backgrounds. They lack the economic and social support available to upper-class Salvadoreans. They do not have the educational, occupational, and linguistic skills needed to succeed in this country. The working-class populations of the various countries in Central America have strong similarities among themselves in their social and cultural experiences and have little in common with the upper-class social and cultural experiences.

As in the case of Guatemalan immigrants, the majority of Salvadoreans in the United States have left their country in an attempt to escape the civil war and to search for personal safety and a new life. Salvadorean society has been severely affected by a long history of political corruption, and the impact of the civil war has been multidimensional. The judicial system does not offer protection to civilians, and threats and intimidation prevent justice and freedom from existing in El Salvador (ACLU). As in Guatemala, the civilian population in areas of conflict was forcibly removed and relocated in refugee camps throughout the country. Often the refugees were subjected to military actions that resulted in massacres of women and children. The definition of political affiliation and association is narrow: one is either a subversive or a government sympathizer. Civilians get caught in the crossfire—they are abducted, disappeared, or tortured by paramilitary groups because of their political, social, or religious activities.

Many priests and catechizers were forced to leave the country because of the unsafe conditions and repression. As in the rest of the region, Catholic priests and lay workers, following a theology of liberation and working among the poor, have been persecuted by the right-wing governments. In many rural communities in El Salvador those individuals who believe and practice liberation theology are considered subversive and communists, thereby becoming the targets of attacks by paramilitary death squads and the armed forces. Their religious beliefs and practices are closely associated with the hope and struggle for better social and human conditions in society, and their activity is marked by participation in community advocacy and development.

Since the early 1980s Salvadoreans have made up the largest of all of the Central American groups in the United States; but, as previously stated, the actual demographic figures are not readily available because of the undocumented immigration status of a large percentage of this population (Córdova, 1992; Melville). Salvadorean immigrants have relocated in areas where there is an already established Salvadorean population: San Francisco, Los Angeles, Houston. Salvadorean migrations to the United States began at the turn of the century, but the largest and most significant began in 1979. Many of these new immigrants arrived in this country as a result of already established ethnic and family networks.

Nicaraguans in the United States

The Nicaraguan migrations to the United States began in the early 1930s and have continued up to the present time. Nicaraguans have migrated for diverse reasons over the years and have resettled in different areas throughout the country. The 1930s migration was characterized by a flow of people escaping the Somoza government, many of whom settled in San Francisco and Los Angeles. During the 1940s, Nicaraguans entered the United States in search of economic opportunities and developed the solid foundations for the immigrant community, although many of them eventually returned to their country to become part of a new entrepreneurial class. During the 1960s, the Nicaraguan immigration was the largest of all Central American groups, and at this time many middle-class Nicaraguans arrived in this country. During the mid-1970s the political tensions escalated into armed conflicts and Nicaraguans fled their country to seek refuge in the United States. After the fall of Somoza and the Sandinista victory, many of the original immigrants or their descendants returned to Nicaragua to be part of the new society.

At the same time, other groups of Nicaraguans associated with the former government arrived in the United States. Some of the first Nicaraguans to arrive during the early 1980s were members of the upper class fleeing the country because of their ties with the former Somoza dictatorship and their disagreements with the new Sandinista government. Some were businessmen who had direct economic ties to Somoza and his government, while others were former members of the National Guard escaping the wrath of the Sandinista army. The majority of Nicaraguans resettled in Florida and brought with them their wealth and their conservative political ideology. More recently, Nicaraguan immigrants have been young working-class people who left to escape the contra war and the military draft.

Hondurans and Costa Ricans

There is an extreme scarcity of academic studies of the Honduran and Costa Rican immigrant communities in the United States because their populations are not very large. The majority of Hondurans reside on the East Coast, from Florida to New York. Their social and cultural experience has not been studied in depth. One can assume that not many Costa Ricans live in the United States or have left their country because of the long history of political stability and democratic traditions in this Central American country.

The Structure of Central American Communities in the United States

Central Americans arrive in the United States metropolitan centers following already established ethnic and family networks. Friends or relatives may give recent arrivals a temporary place to live. The new arrivals use ethnic or family contacts to secure employment, housing, and to meet immediate needs. Once the person settles down and is able to save money, other relatives begin to arrive. After a few years of living in the Latin American neighborhoods many Central American immigrants adapt socially to the U.S. lifestyle and acquire the necessary employment skills and education to participate fully in the mainstream economic life. Some may relocate in other ethnically mixed neighborhoods or in suburban centers; others take advantage of economic opportunities to develop business enterprises in the Latin American neighborhoods, utilizing the immigrant labor force to maximize their profits.

The ethnic enclave is where the immigrant first becomes familiarized with a new social environment. Latin American enclaves maintain the culture, language, religion, foods, and traditional festivities of the arriving immigrant. There are concrete features that illustrate the clear distinctions between an ethnic enclave and ethnic immigrant communities. As a rule, immigrants initially relocate in ethnic communities while developing a few small business enterprises to meet local consumption demands. However, these ethnic neighborhoods lack the sophisticated economic structure and the extensive division of labor of the enclave (Portes and Bach).

The Central American enclaves in San Francisco, Los Angeles, Washington, and Houston, among others, demonstrate a well-diversified economic base and division of labor. The economic structure of the enclave makes bilingual professional services available to the community. The ethnic enclave allows the immigrant to receive a wide variety of services: legal, educational, immigration, medical, dental, accounting, income tax consulting, counseling, employment training, and referrals. This sector is made up not only of immigrants but of first- and second-generation Central Americans and other Latin Americans who provide these professional services. Mainstream professionals and merchants also provide services in Spanish within the enclave.

The enclave provides for the development of regional associations that support the immigrant with cultural, social, and recreational activities. Regional associations and the enclave provide new immigrants with support structures and resources that develop cultural identification, security, and a sense of belonging in the host society. Regional associations allow the preservation of cultural traditions and the retention of a strong cultural and national identification as a Central American. Many regional associations are named after towns, cities, states, or regions from where the immigrant populations originate in Central America. Some organizations are affiliated with religious societies, sports clubs, artistic or cultural organizations, or social service organizations as they exist in Central America. Some of the most popular regional associations are identified with soccer or baseball clubs that participate in Latin American or mainstream sports leagues. These associations have well-structured organizations and large memberships. Their members pay dues and usually rent a small place as a recreation center. Other regional associations are dedicated to the religious cult of a patron saint or other special Catholic figure. Such are the examples in the Nicaraguan community with groups dedicated to Our Lady of the Immaculate Conception (La Purísima) and Saint Dominic (Santo Domingo). Salvadoreans have regional associations dedicated to El Salvador del Mundo.

The Empowerment of Central American Communities

Given the socioeconomic and political diversity of the Central American communities, one may surmise that they have limited political power and influence within the United States political structure. The Central American communities are divided on issues related to national identity and origin, political affiliations in Central America and the United States, ethnicity, and socioeconomic status. These divisions do not allow the necessary social cohesion needed to transform this population into a strong political body able to seek viable political solutions to the problems and realities they encounter in this society. There is a need to develop responsible and accountable political and social activists within the Central American community in order to critically confront the wide range of problems they face in this country.

Another drawback to empowerment in Central American communities is the common belief among some immigrants that their stay of residence in the United States will be of a temporary nature. Because of this, these immigrants become isolated and neglect to participate in political affairs at the community, municipal, state, or national levels. With the exception of those who have some degree of political sophistication or experience, most Central Americans show signs of apathy toward U.S. political and social issues. Community activists have attempted to persuade Latin American immigrants to become U.S. citizens and to register to vote. These efforts have generally been fruitless because many Latin Americans believe that to become U.S. citizens would be a betrayal of their own national identity and citizenship.

The Paulo Freire Model of Community Empowerment

The Freire method of community empowerment is based on the pedagogical and organizational strategies that bring about critical consciousness in individuals and the community. Paulo Freire's methodology has been widely used in Latin America by the Catholic base communities in the empowerment of political activists, union leaders, lay preachers, *campesinos,* and students. These base communities are modeled after Freire's Brazilian experiences with his pedagogy during the early 1960s.

Freire's methodology teaches basic literacy skills to adults while providing them with basic notions of political awareness in order to develop praxis and community social action. These pedagogical strategies are implemented by base community organizations and educational centers in the United States, while teaching English language skills to those speaking only Spanish. Basic concepts of social and political awareness are introduced within language lessons as the means of empowering new immigrants.

Influenced by the Second Vatican Council, Catholic priests and nuns trained laypeople to reinterpret the teachings of the Bible and to apply those teachings to their social and political environments. The new goal of the Catholic Church in Latin America was to look at religion from a holistic perspective and to teach people not only about spirituality but also about their socioeconomic and political realities (McKiernan). The new vision of the Catholic Church expressed support for the poor in their struggles against the rich and against economic and political exploitation. The "Church of the Poor," or the popular Church, was born out of the organizational efforts of the base communities. Eventually the rich and the military took a strong position against base communities and the Church of the Poor and accused them of being communists. Governments in Central America carried out repressive campaigns and spread terror throughout the region in their attempt to stop social change (Martín-Baró). Many priests, nuns, and lay workers were killed, abducted, tortured, or exiled during the late seventies and eighties.

Refugee self-help committees located in various U.S. cities have been successful in the implementation of the above-mentioned methodologies. It is noteworthy to mention two refugee organizations that are effective in the internal affairs of the Central American communities while representing the refugees in the mainstream society and local political structures. They are the Comité de Refugiados Centro Americanos (CRECE), which provides legal and immigration services and advocacy for Central American refugee rights, and the Central American Refugee Center (CARECEN), which provides refugees with social services.

In these organizations the refugees themselves empower other refugees. They are designed after the organizational models of Freire's "Critical Consciousness" and the Central American Catholic base communities. Because of their organizational structure, history, philosophy, and empowerment efforts, these community groups are recognized as representing the leadership in the Central American refugee community. They address issues affecting the social experiences and cultural adaptation of Guatemalan and Salvadorean immigrants and refugees. CRECE provides the refugee community with basic survival services such as food and clothes distribution, emergency housing, medical services, job referrals, and skills development workshops. It also provides educational information to mainstream communities by making presentations at schools, universities, churches, and home meetings, where speakers give testimonies of their experiences in Central America. CRECE is an active advocate of refugee rights in Central America and is actively involved in the repopulation of refugees in El Salvador. CARECEN provides legal representation to refugees in political asylum hearings, gives health referral services, trains health promoters, and produces literature for the Central American refugee community. CARECEN played an important role in the formation of the Central American National Network (CARNET), which includes thirty-eight refugee agencies and grass-roots organizations in the United States.

CARECEN and CRECE demonstrate a strong commitment to empowering the Central American community. The development of local leadership is an important priority in the selection and training of low-income refugees, who work as refugee rights promoters and refugee advocates. The promoters provide services to the refugee community, speak in public forums, and monitor and attempt to impact legislation affecting the Central American refugee community at the municipal, state, and national levels. Their achievements include the declaration of cities of refuge in which local governments and law enforcement agencies do not cooperate in Immigration and Naturalization Service (INS) raids against undocumented workers. These organizations work closely with the network of Churches associated with the sanctuary movement, the Baptist ministries, the Quakers, and others. They receive funds and direct services from religious organizations and private foundations like Catholic Charities.

What Needs to Be Done in the Near Future

Further theoretical and practical research studies are necessary to comprehend and resolve more fully the acculturation issues faced by Central American immigrants in the United States. Specific areas in need of a greater scope of examination are legal, medical, psychological, educational, professional and occupational skills-retraining, nutrition, counseling, and religious issues affecting this population. There is a need for studies in the major metropolitan and rural centers where the Central American populations are resettling. It is imperative for mainstream professionals, researchers, and religious organizations to develop critical awareness in order to address effectively the needs of Central Americans in the United States.

Institutions of higher education must implement broad curricular offerings across the various disciplines addressing the cultural, socioeconomic, and historical backgrounds as well as the basic needs of this rapidly growing population. In cities with high numbers of Central Americans, universities must include specific curricular offerings and training programs for students enrolled in undergraduate and graduate studies. Course offerings must develop in students a critical understanding of the ethnic, cultural, economic, religious, and sociopolitical backgrounds of Central Americans residing in their geographical areas.

The Role of the Catholic Church in U.S. Central American Communities

The Catholic Church needs to develop comparative studies on the religious practices in Central America and the local religious practices, beliefs, and attitudes of Central American immigrants and refugees. It is important that the Church become acquainted with the cultural and religious beliefs of Central Americans and that these belief systems be incorporated into the religious practices of the Central American community as the means of providing continuity, a feeling of belonging, and familiarity.

Recent Latin American immigrants often feel a sense of disorientation in the Catholic religious practices in the United States. These feelings may result from the difference in ritual practices, the physical appearance of the church, the lack of faith in the cult of the saints, and the lack of Latino priests. The Catholic Church must continue to study the problem of Latin Americans changing religions in this country as a means of preventing large segments of this population from abandoning Catholicism. A number of studies recently conducted make an attempt to understand the variety of reasons Latin American immigrants are leaving Catholicism and converting to Protestantism (Deck, 1985, 1988, 1989; Greeley; Vilar; Marín and Gamba).

These studies employ different strategies and methodologies to analyze the problem of Latino Catholics converting to Protestantism and have reached various conclusions in their research. They analyze the immigrant expectations of the Church, the role of the priests, and the nature and structure of religious services. Marin and Gamba find of particular significance the high degree of dissatisfaction with U.S. Catholicism that recent Latin American immigrants expressed in their research study. It is important to note that this high level of dissatisfaction leads to the conversion of these individuals to other Churches. Furthermore, they found that the lower the levels of acculturation to the U.S. culture, the higher the levels of dissatisfaction this population demonstrated. Their research also explains some important factors that lead to this level of dissatisfaction, such as the fact that Protestant Churches provide a feeling of family and community and are sensitive to the immigrant's cultural experiences.

Protestant ministers take very seriously their role as missionaries by actively walking and targeting the Latino *barrios* and ethnic immigrant communities. They also place a high degree of importance in their work among youth by taking on challenging issues such as drug abuse, gang violence, and education among young Latin American immigrants. In most cases these ministers, who are recruited from the ranks of the local populations, are fluent in Spanish and are competent in the immigrants' cultural experience (Deck, 1985).

Many Latin American immigrants also feel that the U.S. Catholic Church does not provide an adequate level of training in the faith and the teachings of the Bible, while the Protestant Churches place a great deal of importance in these areas (Marín and Gamba; Vilar). It is important to mention that a significant number of the most recent Central American immigrants worked very closely with and were active participants in the Church of the Poor and liberation theology in their home countries. Liberation theology places emphasis on the critical analysis of the Scriptures and their direct applications to the family, the community, and society at large. The philosophical views of liberation theology state that the relationship between humans and God is horizontal and extends outward from self to others, views different from those of U.S. Catholicism.

The popular Church in Central America took a radical approach by incorporating the traditional culture and the socioeconomic realities of the majority of the population into their rituals. Culture was expressed through the Mass and included the musical accompaniment of guitars and songs that represented cultural traditions and criticisms of the political and socioeconomic realities of Central America. Many priests incorporated artistic murals into their church buildings that represented historical scenes or themes associated with the liberation of the poor from the oppression of the rich and the military. The Church has demonstrated a high level of commitment and support for the poor and the oppressed in Central America for the past three decades; thus, when Central American immigrants arrive in the United States they have a high level of expectation from the Church.

Scholars have also addressed the issue of Church rituals and teachings and have concluded that U.S. Catholicism gives importance to guidance in personal life and in understanding the faith. Latin American Catholics are also looking for spiritual growth as they attempt to understand the rituals and religion. The problem arises with the nature of U.S. Catholicism in the sense that it may be too complex to understand on the part of recent immigrants manifesting low levels of acculturation to U.S. culture and society (Deck, 1985; Marín and Gamba).

As previously stated, Central American immigrants and refugees have said that one reason for their conversion to other religions is their lack of understanding of U.S. Catholic ritual practices and the cultural differences between Catholicism in Central America and in the United States (Córdova, 1986). The religious practices in Central American Catholicism are quite different from those in the United States. The popular religion in Central America combines the religious experiences brought to the region by the Catholic missionaries during the sixteenth century as they blended with the indigenous religious structure, tradition, and ritual practice through five hundred years of colonization. The religious rituals and traditions of Central Americans include a strong devotion to the saints, who in numerous instances have syncretized personalities with the native indigenous deities. The ritual traditions are dynamic and vibrant; they involve the community in religious worship that includes personal and collective religious activities, for example, fiestas, offerings, processions, and penance (Córdova, 1981).

Scholars have suggested that Latin American immigrants are also leaving the Catholic Church in search of a supportive community. Priests must learn to speak Spanish and must become competent in the immigrant's culture in order to be effective in their interaction with this population (Deck, 1989; Greeley; Marín and Gamba). There is a serious need for Latin American priests and bishops as well as a need to incorporate the laity into roles of prominence and importance within the Church. This is an area in which Protestant Churches have been extremely successful.

The Catholic Church has traditionally provided services to underserved populations and must now develop a critical awareness of the reality of Central American immigrants in the United States. The Church must continue in a position of leadership, providing legal and survival services through the office of Catholic Charities. One interesting reaction took place in the Central American community in San Francisco when the name Catholic Social Services changed to Catholic Charities. During that time many immigrants refused to seek help because of negative associations with the term "charities." Central Americans are a proud people and will first exhaust all possible avenues for self-help before seeking charity from the Church. Others feel that there is a contradiction in the name when the Church charges for legal services if these are "charity." In Latin America the support systems originate in the family; what we know in this country as "social services" are almost unknown in Latin America. Charity is given by the government, the Church, and benevolent associations only in extreme cases and to individuals who cannot provide for themselves. The common attitude is that if you are physically able and can work, then you must provide for yourself without expecting society to support you. The name "Catholic Charities" creates a negative feeling in the Latino community, and for this reason the usage of the term should be reconsidered.

The Need for Counseling Services

It is important to reframe the immigrants' perceptions regarding counseling and social services. In Latin America the extended family and the Church provide the economic, emotional, spiritual, and social support to individuals. Family cohesion and support are strong, providing security and stability to the individual and the community. Social services are seen as charity in the traditional Central American culture, and to receive charity is not considered a positive communal action. People must work to make a living; only those who are lazy or disabled are expected to receive charity. This attitude may create complications for immigrants in the United States. For instance, individuals may not seek medical help until an illness or other problem becomes a life-threatening emergency. It is a common belief that if an able-bodied person cannot afford to pay for a medical service, then he or she seeks home remedies or assistance from family or friends but not from the government or the Church.

It is essential to inform undocumented Central Americans of available social services. They must know their legal rights as well as the legal implications of their undocumented status. Although there are community agencies providing information and referral services, organizations need budget increases to provide more efficient services. Financial support is needed to expand available facilities and services and to effectively train professional staff.

There is a need to develop culturally sensitive counseling and social services, at low cost or free of charge, that provide support to Central Americans in their relocation and acculturation experiences. Community organizers must offer classes or workshops that provide cultural, social, and political awareness as well as survival skills. Workshops must include an orientation to U.S. cultural, legal, and social systems to ensure understanding and familiarity with the societal dynamics of the United States.

Basic cultural differences must be explained to newcomers so they develop a clear understanding of the host society. It is important for the newcomer to acquire understanding of and competency in cultural attitudes, values, and laws of the United States. For example, concepts of time and punctuality are themes to discuss with newly arrived immigrants. In Central America the pace of life is slower, and punctuality is not considered as important as it is in this country. Individuals need to be acquainted with proper procedures and expected behavior such as scheduling and canceling appointments.

Other important subjects for community organizers and school professionals to discuss with recently arrived immigrants are the values, attitudes, and laws related to child rearing practices and child abuse. For example, it is expected in the Central American culture that parents discipline children by using corporal punishments—spanking, belting, forcing a child to kneel on the floor for prolonged periods of time. If a parent does not punish a child as expected in a particular situation, people might feel that the parents are too permissive, allowing the children to run their lives. What is accepted behavior in Central America, however, might be seen as child abuse in this country. In the United States corporal punishment is not a widely accepted child-rearing practice; spanking a child on the buttocks might be accepted only in extreme situations.

A high incidence of child abuse by undocumented Central Americans is reported by community agencies, clinics, hospitals, and schools. Parents must be aware of the different values, attitudes, and laws dealing with child rearing to prevent legal problems for the family. It is imperative to develop cultural awareness and sensitivity on the part of school administrators and teachers, community organizers, doctors, and other professionals who frequently interact with and treat Central Americans.

A problem was brought to the author's attention by a high school counselor in San Francisco when a Salvadorean father had belted a young teen student on the legs. The child showed several bruises from the punishment, and the school administrators called the father to a meeting to discuss the problem. The father was upset with the school administrators for threatening to report him to the authorities for child abuse. In anger the father told the principal that if he was expected not to discipline the child in the traditional ways, then the child would be the responsibility of the school officials and that they would have to assume the cost of bringing up the son. There are also instances in which children threaten to report their parents to the authorities for child abuse. This situation creates discord within the family: the parents see their traditional roles challenged by what they consider disrespectful children.

The majority of family problems encountered by this population arise from conflicts between the values and cultural systems of the U.S. society and the contrasting nature of Central American values and traditions. Children and adolescents, especially girls, are given more rights and privileges in this country. This practice is considerably different from the traditional family values held in the Central American society. Problems often develop in the family, resulting in intergenerational conflict between parents and children. Conflicts often develop when children and adolescents find part-time employment to meet the family's financial responsibilities. Emotional problems are created for the father because of the disruption of the traditional image of the father as financial provider for the family.

Other family problems may arise because young people usually acculturate faster than older adults and learn English at a more rapid pace. Children used as interpreters assume more responsibilities for the family. When the parents interact with the mainstream society the children serve as interpreters for the family business affairs, including interactions with utility companies, school officials, landlords, and the like. These interpreting responsibilities empower the children, placing them in a bargaining situation with the parents. Children begin to negotiate with parents for privileges as well as for access to more of the material things they desire for their social activities.

Medical and Mental Health Care Needs

The Central American population in the United States is in great need of culturally sensitive health care services, especially in the areas of health and nutrition. Recent immigrants suffer from a variety of tropical diseases—parasites, gastroenteritis, malnutrition, tuberculosis—as well as from high mortality rates. Further academic research is needed on the incidence of psychosocial trauma and post traumatic stress disorders (PTSD) in Central Americans in this country, which until recently has been studied by only a small number of researchers. More scientific and psychological studies are needed to understand and develop successful treatment for these disorders.

Many Central Americans are not familiar with Western mental health concepts and psychological treatment. It is common belief in Central America that healthy and sane individuals do not need the services of psychologists and that only the mentally ill do. The incidence of mental health problems, including psychosocial trauma, post traumatic stress disorders, alcoholism, and abuse of pharmaceutical drugs, are reportedly high among Central American immigrants, many of whom suffer psychological and physiological stresses created by the civil war and their relocation experiences. These stresses are categorized as various forms of psychosocial trauma by Latin American psychologists (Martín-Baró).

Psychological stresses common to political refugees in general are also manifested in Central Americans. Individuals may suffer from PTSD related to the environment of violence and the effects of the civil war. They are reported to suffer anxiety and acute depression, which may result in hospitalization and intensive psychiatric treatment. Those individuals who were victims of political violence in Central America often manifest various forms of psychological problems upon their arrival and settlement in the United States. Torture victims suffer from PTSD symptoms, exhibited as severe depression, guilt, nightmares, hyperalertness, insomnia, suicidal tendencies, and withdrawal. Because of the high incidence of torture cases reported among recent Central American immigrants and refugees, a national coalition of medical and mental health professionals and organizations has been created to treat survivors of torture. Increased efforts are needed to provide adequate treatment to individuals who have suffered psychological and physical torture (Córdova, 1986). Psychiatric evaluations of Central Americans conducted by refugee centers in the San Francisco Bay Area have concluded that a significantly large number of their clients suffer from psychosocial trauma and PTSD. Reports documenting the impact of psychological disorders on immigrants and their families suggest that marital and family relationships are negatively affected by these problems. Conflicts, depression, alcohol and drug abuse, frustration, physical abuse to wife and children, separation, and divorce are the recurring consequences.

The medical profession has the moral and social obligation to develop competency in the cultural perspectives of health and disease within the Central American population. Psychologists, psychiatrists, doctors, nurses, and hospital staff need to understand the traditional healing concepts and methodologies used by Central Americans in order to treat their medical and mental health problems more effectively. Workshops and curricular offerings need to be developed by universities, hospitals, and clinics to give professionals a critical awareness of the socioeconomic, political, and cultural backgrounds of undocumented Central Americans.

Culture-bound diseases in Central American patients are often reported by doctors in hospitals and clinics. Many illnesses are perceived by Central Americans to be of supernatural or magical origins. These patients often do not respond to Western medical methodologies unless they undergo the necessary rituals or take remedies according to the traditional cultural beliefs in Central America. In California, efforts are being made to develop effective methodologies and programs to treat Central American patients in hospitals and community agencies.

Conclusion

The spectrum of problems faced by Central Americans may dishearten Church leaders and community organizers in the United States. The challenges and responsibilities are many and range from the development of a body of knowledge about and an understanding of immigration issues to educational concern, housing, and the broad dynamics of acculturation. Added to these responsibilities are the cultural sensitivity and critical awareness required for successful community action.

Since there is a scarcity of literature on organizing with Central Americans, community and religious organizers must modify and adapt existing methods of practice and strategies. Social action models, with the exception of the sanctuary movement, the Paulo Freire model, and the Catholic base communities, are the least favored because of the attention drawn to the people involved in the process. The social action models usually bring a negative outcome, since police or immigration officials become aware of the individuals and their possible undocumented immigration status. Furthermore, since many Central Americans live marginally in our society, they have a strong reluctance to engage in this level of social change and advocacy. Traditionally, the poor and disenfranchised tend to be conservative in nature and are reluctant to engage in direct confrontation tactics.

Community and economic development models are more acceptable and effective in working with Central Americans in this country. They are more status quo in their orientations and offer more real material gains such as employment, housing, and the development of an economic exchange market that may exist parallel to the traditional mainstream market systems. The utilization of Paulo Freire's methods for developing critical awareness and empowerment are especially relevant in organizing with Central Americans, since they do not posit false expectations and they emphasize very real material and educational rewards. Furthermore, many Central American immigrants are already familiar with Freire's methods because they were implemented in the Central American Catholic base communities. The challenges are obvious; the strategies have to be determined on a day-by-day basis as we work with and learn to develop a critical understanding of the communities.

Bibliography

American Civil Liberties Union. *Salvadorans in the United States: The Case for Extended Voluntary Departure.* National Immigration and Alien Rights Project, Report No. 1. Washington: April 1984.

Amnesty International. *Annual Report.* Washington: 1983.

Burgos, Elisabeth. *I . . . Rigoberta Menchu.* New York: Schocken Books, 1984.

Camarda, Renato. *Forced to Move: Salvadorean Refugees in Honduras.* San Francisco: Solidarity Publications, 1985.

Chernow, Ron. "The Strange Death of Bill Woods: Did He Fly Too Far in the Zone of the Generals?" *Mother Jones.* Vol. 4, no. 4 (May 1979).

Córdova, Carlos B. "The Role of Sorcery Prayers in El Salvador, Central America." Master's thesis, San Francisco State University, 1981.

__________. "Migration and Acculturation Dynamics of Undocumented El Salvadoreans in the San Francisco Bay Area." Ph.D. diss., University of San Francisco, 1986.

__________. "Undocumented El Salvadoreans in the San Francisco Bay Area: Migration and Adaptation Dynamics." *Journal of La Raza Studies* 1(1) (Fall 1987) 9–37.

__________. "The Mission District: The Ethnic Diversity of the Latin American Enclave in San Francisco, California." *Journal of La Raza Studies* 2 (1) (Summer/Fall 1989) 21–32.

__________. "Organizing in Central American Communities in the United States." *Community Organizing in a Diverse Society.* Ed. Felix G. Rivera and John L. Erlich. Boston: Allyn and Bacon, 1992.

Deck, A. F. "Fundamentalism and the Hispanic Catholic." *America* (January 25, 1985).

__________. "Proselytism and Hispanic Catholics: How Long Can We Cry Wolf." *America* (December 10, 1988).

__________. *The Second Wave: Hispanic Ministry and the Evangelization of Cultures.* New York: Paulist, 1989.

Fallows, James. "The New Immigrants: How New Citizens and Illegal Aliens Are Affecting the United States." *The Atlantic* (November 1983) 45–106.

Freire, Paulo. *Pedagogy of the Oppressed.* New York: Seabury, 1970.

__________. *Education for Critical Consciousness.* New York: Seabury, 1973.

Greeley, A. M. "Defection Among Hispanics." *America* (July 30, 1988).

Manz, Beatriz. *Refugees of a Hidden War: The Aftermath of Counterinsurgency in Guatemala.* Albany, N.Y.: State University of New York Press, 1988.

Marín, Gerardo, and Raymond Gamba. *Expectations and Experiences of Hispanic Catholics and Converts to Protestant Churches.* San Francisco: University of San Francisco, Social Psychology Laboratory, Hispanic Studies. February 1990.

Martín-Baró, Ignacio. "Political Violence and War as Causes of Psychosocial Trauma in El Salvador." *Journal of La Raza Studies* 2 (1) (Summer/Fall 1989) 5–15.

McKiernan, Kevin. "Shrines and Slogans: The Divided Church in Nicaragua." *Mother Jones.* Vol. 9, no. 3 (April 1984).

Melville, Margarita B. "Hispanics: Race, Class, or Ethnicity." *The Journal of Ethnic Studies* 16 (1) (1988) 67–84.

Muller, T., and T. Espenshade, with D. Manson and others. *The Fourth Wave: Californias Newest Immigrants.* Washington: The Urban Institute Press, 1985.

National Lawyers Guild. *Immigration Law and Defense.* New York: Clark Boardman, 1981.

Portes, Alejandro, R. Nash Parker, and J. A. Cobas. "Assimilation or Consciousness: Perceptions of United States Society by Recent Latin American Immigrants to the U.S." *Social Forces* 59 (1) (September 1980) 200–224.

Portes, Alejandro, and Robert L. Bach. *Latin Journey: Cuban and Mexican Immigrants in the United States.* Berkeley: University of California Press, 1985.

Rivera, Felix G., and John L. Erlich. "Neo-Gemeinschaft Minority Communities in the United States: Implications for Community Organizing." *Community Development Journal* 16 (3) (October 1981) 189–200.

__________. *Community Organizing in a Diverse Society.* Boston: Allyn and Bacon, 1992.

United Nations Human Rights Commission. *Report on the Situation of Human Rights in El Salvador.* Washington: 1983.

Vilar, J. J. D. "The Success of the Sects Among Hispanics in the United States." *America* (February 25, 1989).

3

The Puerto Rican Experience in the United States: A Pastoral Perspective

Dominga Zapata, S.H.

Introduction

The Hispanicization of the United States has been a concern for many for various reasons. Institutions at all levels have been affected by increase in population. Corporate America has rediscovered the Hispanic market and has targeted advertising and productivity to them. The mass media seem also to be profiting from the Spanish-language audience. Educational, social service, and religious institutions are no less affected by the Hispanicization of the United States.

The states that lead in the number of Hispanics reflect the plurality of the Hispanic community throughout the country. California, with 34 percent of the Hispanic population and a large number of Mexican Americans, has seen an increase of Central Americans during the past ten to fifteen years. Texas, with 21 percent, is nearly homogeneous, with an almost totally Mexican American population. New York, with 10 percent, is primarily Caribbean, with people coming from Puerto Rico, the Dominican Republic, and Cuba. Florida, with an almost all-Cuban population, and Arizona, Colorado, and New Mexico, all predominantly Mexican American, rank fourth, with 8 percent each of the Hispanic population. These and the rest of the fifty states witness to the Hispanicization of the United States, as reflected in the Census Bureau figures of 22.4 million in 1990. These figures represent Hispanics from twenty-one countries (Schmidt, 1990, 14–15).

The Churches are looking into this reality from their pastoral perspective: Who are the Hispanics? What are the religious practices and values inherent in their cultural patterns? How are they to be pastorally served, welcomed, and integrated into the existing Church structures? What changes are going to be necessary to do so?

As part of an attempt to respond to these questions, I will here present a general historical background of the Puerto Ricans so we might better understand their situation as immigrants in the United States and the challenges this reality can present to pastoral responses by religious institutions. Even when I am not speaking directly on religious matters, my presentation will always be from the pastoral perspective.

Identity

Cultural

The identity of the Puerto Rican people is intimately related to the island's history; the name "Puerto Rico" reveals the various stages of that history. For the indigenous Indians, the Taínos, the island was Boríken, land of the valiant lord. The first Spaniards, conquistadors, named it San Juan Bautista, and then, through a mistake in a document, it became Puerto Rico. In 1898, when it became a possession of the United States, Puerto Rico's name was Anglicized, "Porto Rico," until the insistence of the independence movement brought back the name of "Puerto Rico" in 1932. Despite all the changes of its name, "Borínquen" has remained the familiar name of the island and the source of identity for the Borícuas (Wagenheim, 1975, 92).

The geographical position of the island is also part of its identity. Its cultural identity is both from the north and from Latin America. Puerto Ricans consider Puerto Rico their country and the United States their nation. The roots of the cultural identity are found in the Taíno, African, and Spanish heritages.

The cultural roots of the indigenous people were almost totally extinguished by the Spaniards. Silén points out the three arms used by the conquistadors to wipe out the Taínos:

> 1. "repartimiento"—private property was foreign to the Taíno culture and it created a class society.
> 2. "encomienda"—dominion and lordship over the Indians broke their sedentary habits, destroyed their independence, and caused them to rebel.
> 3. religious indoctrination—part of the ideological violence that created the assimilation to European values and the loss of the Taíno identity. It is the beginning of a moral life that exalted humility, submission, and meekness. The Hispanic heritage of the language and the religion diminished the indian (Silén, 1973, 24–25).

The dominant culture became Spanish even though the Spaniards were never the majority. The African slaves were the majority of the population by 1530. For the first 405 years of the Spanish colonization, Puerto Rico underwent constant attacks by the French, Dutch, British, and finally, by the United States.

There were various demonstrations in search of independence by the Indians and the African slaves. Later the *criollos*, children of the Spaniards, joined them. The most significant rebellion was the Grito de Lares on September 23, 1868. It resulted in the abolition of slavery in 1873 and the elimination of the booking of the daily workers, and in the future autonomy. It was also the inspiration for the first Puerto Rican flag and the national anthem, even though these did not become official until colonization by the United States.

The political and economic situation of the island created four types of people characteristic of the colonization period of Puerto Rico (Silén, 1973, 74):

> 1. the military—for the defense of Spain in the Caribbean.
> 2. the hacendado—production at the cost of the farm worker and the slave and with the defense of the military.
> 3. the daily worker—agricultural worker, future proletariat of Puerto Rico.
> 4. the pirate—outside the law; supplied the goods and the slaves; key in the economic development.

Christianity had a great influence in all the aspects of the colonization. Even though Spain did not practice it to perfection, it had posed to itself the ethical question of the indigenous peoples and the slaves. The cross and the sword created a different racial experience from that of North America.

Spain offered emancipation to the Indians in 1517, to the slaves in 1873, and autonomy to the island in 1897. In 1898 Puerto Rico was expecting the United States to help in its autonomous development as it had done with Cuba. Soon Puerto Rico discovered that all it had gained was another form of suffering as it became a U.S. colony (Figueroa, 1979, 49).

Pedro Mejía, the first mulatto, with *cacica* Luisa became the parents of the new people of three different cultures. The blacks were a majority on the island from the end of the sixteenth century until 1950, when integration had reduced them to only 20 percent of the population of Puerto Rico. The African influence is present in the language, crafts, music, religion, entertainment, cooking, herbs, and healing practices. It is the African who made the Spanish music typically Puerto Rican in the waltz *(danza)* and the *plena*. Their music, musical instruments, and dances became part of the communal celebrations of the island.

Thus the identity of the Puerto Rican is mulatto racially and Hispanic culturally (Alvarez, 1974, 28–34). This core identity has been enriched by various influences of other peoples throughout history. During the nineteenth century a great influx of Spaniards and Latin Americans, and later French from Louisiana (U.S.A.), slaves from Haiti, workers from China (1840), Italians, Lebanese, Germans, Scottish, and Irish all contributed to the island's cultural identity. Then came the North Americans (1898),

Cubans (1959), Dominican Republicans (1965), and Argentineans. Through all of this the Borícuas claim only one identity without the division of black and white. It is the best combination of the spirit of Spain and of America.

The *jíbaro* learned the love, the suffering, and the death of the Indian, the Spaniard, and the African. The Puerto Rican expresses this identity in music, dance, and poetry. The *décima,* a melancholic song, is the best popular form of the being and the feeling of the *pueblo Borincano.* María Teresa Babín states that the collective psychology of the Borícua is reflected in the combination of the three characters of the popular stories of the *jíbaro*: Juan Bobo, who makes believe that he is stupid before the wise; Juan Animala, who makes fun of the powerful; and Juan Cuchilla, who is destined to evil and fraud (Babin, 1970, 84). The rich cultural heritage has developed primarily through music, stories, poetry, and the theater. Many of these traditions are passed on orally and through the circle of the family.

The family circle embodies both the deepest cultural values of the island and the seeds of cultural weakness. The home is the haven of personalism, relationships beyond social classes, the family responsibility, the primacy of the spiritual, the authority of the family over the individual, hospitality, and generosity. It also exerts strong control over relationships, especially for the woman: domination of the male over children and women, masculinity based on physical strength, aggressivity, freedom and sexual dominion over the woman, and the inferiority of the woman (Fitzpatrick, 1971, 83). It is the family that represents also the desires of the people in general, the proper balance between the economic development and the traditional values of human dignity.

Political

The political history of Puerto Rico is another important element to consider in the understanding of the Borícua who migrates to the United States. All the thrust of autonomy developed prior to 1898 was wiped out by the military force of the United States on July 25, 1898. Not until 1946 was Puerto Rico again to see one of its own named as governor, with proper elections to follow in 1948. In 1952 Puerto Rico became a Commonwealth (Estado Libre Asociado) with its own flag and national anthem alongside those of the United States. But these concessions have not been sufficient to stop the desire for autonomy.

The political status of the island continues to be the central feature of the life of Puerto Rico. In a letter of January 1989 all the Puerto Rican political parties said to President George Bush, "The people of Puerto Rico have not been formally consulted by the United States of America as to their choice of their ultimate political status." In its February 1990 *Report,* the 8th Day Center for Justice summarized the meaning of colonialism for the Puerto Rican: 13 percent of Puerto Rico is controlled and used by the U.S. military (Puerto Rico has become the home of thirteen military bases and two nuclear satellites); 90 percent of the industry is U.S. owned and operated without the protection of U.S. environmental laws, and all profits are tax free; any decision made by the Puerto Rican people is subject to veto by the U.S. Congress; though bound by U.S. laws, Puerto Ricans cannot vote in presidential elections (*8th Day Report,* 1990, 44–45). A constant declaration of independence has been the resistance to English becoming the official language of the island.

Linguistic

The Taíno influence in the language of Puerto Rico is minimal. Most of the Indian words are the names of cities like Mayagüez, Yauco, Arecibo. The African influence may be lessened by the Afroespañol of those who already had integrated their language into that of the Andaluz, Canarian, and Catalán who came to the Caribbean (Alvarez, 1974, 28–48). Despite the strong resistance to English as the official language of the island, it was imposed from 1898 to 1948. English continues to be the teaching language in most of the private educational institutions in the island. The reverse migration is also a factor in the language struggle. The Puerto Rican seems to refuse to become the "American of the Caribbean." The language has become the root of the cultural identity. Luis Muñoz Marín echoed his father's inspiration (Rodríguez, 1965, 9): "We are not North Americans, we are Puerto Ricans because God so willed it and thus we also desire it."

Economic

Up to 1898 the economy of the island was dependent on decentralized agriculture. With the transfer of possession from Spain to the United States, Puerto Rico became economically dependent on its new colonizer. By 1936, coffee production had been converted into sugar and tobacco. *Jalda arriba* was the theme of the industrialization project of the 1950s of then Governor Luis Muñoz Marín, with little lasting success. Tourism also became an important part of the economic development of the island. But the pace of development could not keep up with the population growth. In 1970, 70 percent of the people were under the age of thirty-five. The government's response to the problem of economic development was to curtail fertility and to channel surplus population out of Puerto Rico. In 1959 family planning became a confrontation issue with the Catholic Church in Puerto Rico. The unemployment and the large family created extreme poverty areas such as La Perla next to El Morro.

These families migrated to the mainland to face similar situations all over again. A third of Puerto Rico's population migrated to the United

States (Noriega, 1984, 16). These economic problems are augmented by others such as the nuclear experimentation by the U.S. army in Puerto Rico's best fishing areas, thus obliging the island to import 95 percent of the fish it consumes. The means of economic production are not yet in the hands of Puerto Ricans. We are strangers in our own land! Migration is the direct result of the cultural, political, and economic crisis of the Puerto Ricans in their own land. Educational progress in the 1980s has not been matched with professional opportunities; thus the flow of professionals to the mainland. They are part of the 40 percent unemployment rate of the island and made up the "new migration" of the 1980s. Many professionals were affected by President Reagan's cuts on government and federal jobs in Puerto Rico. Unemployment combined with a high cost of living has made it harder for both the poor and those professionals beginning their careers to be able to stay in Puerto Rico (Vice; Beardsley; Friedman, 1983).

This type of emigration affects in turn the economy of the island, since it results in the departure of the most productive members of society and, as Noriega calls it, the most precious natural resource of any people.

Migration Experience

Hispanic Community in the United States

Puerto Ricans have become part of the larger Hispanic population in the United States and its struggle to overcome oppression. Like many others, Puerto Ricans come to the United States in search of a better human life. They have helped make the United States the fifth largest Spanish-speaking country, outranked only by Mexico, Spain, Argentina, and Colombia. In 1990 the number of Hispanics in the United States reached 22.4 million, an increase of 53 percent. Even though they are spread throughout the country, New York has 65 percent of the Puerto Rican community; Texas has 46 percent of the Mexican; Florida has 53 percent of the Cuban; and California has 53 percent of the other Hispanics (cf. Schmidt, 1990, 14).

Hispanic immigrants come from the borders of the United States. Only a few hours by jet, ground transportation, or merely a walk can take them home. This access to their homeland makes them feel that they are "neither from here nor from there." Their cultural identity, their language, and their religion become more important in their immigrant situation. The American dream is not yet realized among them.

Puerto Rican Migration

The journey. Puerto Ricans are the second largest Hispanic group in the United States, making up 14 percent of the Hispanic population. They are the only massive migration of U.S. citizens with a different culture and a different language. With home only a few hours away, 82 percent of them were born on the island. The migration flow of Puerto Ricans has been in three key periods: 1920–38, before World War II; 1941–45, during the war; and 1945–60, immediately after the war. The largest number came between 1950 and 1960. As stated previously, the flow has a direct relationship with the economic development in the island. As long as the Boricuas are able to manage on the island, they will not migrate. This is confirmed by only two periods of economic progress and employment in Puerto Rico; in 1961–63 and 1970–74, there were more Puerto Ricans returning to the island than coming into the mainland.

The government of the island has been directly involved in helping the flow of migration as part of the economic development. Most of the initial efforts were for agricultural workers, and thus the concentration of the Puerto Rican community in the United States has been in farming areas or in large urban cities near the agricultural settings: New York, Connecticut, Pennsylvania, Massachusetts, and Chicago. The textile and garment industries in New York, the electronic industries in Illinois, the foundries in Wisconsin, and the steel mills in Ohio, Indiana, and Pennsylvania have been sources of attraction for employment for Puerto Rican migrants. During the 1980s a significantly low percentage of Puerto Ricans settled in New York: only 30 percent compared with 65 percent in 1955–60, due to the lack of employment possibilities. While the majority remains around the northeast region (New Jersey, Connecticut, Pennsylvania, Massachusetts, and New York), 12 percent of the Puerto Rican community has settled in Florida, and there was a significant increase in the states of Texas and California during the 1980s (Commonwealth, 1975; 1983).

The migrants of the 1980s had greater possibilities of moving in search of employment because people had more skills to offer and a better educational background. According to the 1983 Report of the Division of Migration of the Commonwealth of Puerto Rico, 51 percent of those migrating to the New York area had an educational background ranging from a high school diploma to three years of college education. But their limited knowledge of English (47 percent) continued to prevent them from adequate positions of employment (Commonwealth, 1983).

Puerto Ricans have been U.S. citizens since 1917, but they still do not enjoy equal rights and opportunities. Only in 1973 was it possible to have bilingual electoral possibilities in New York that would allow the Puerto Rican community to participate. Strong stereotypes of Puerto Ricans have been developed that perpetuate prejudice and racial discrimination, for example, that all Puerto Ricans carry knives and come to the United States to live off the welfare system.

The Puerto Rican family system has suffered the most in the migration experience. The migration is an ongoing process—a little time here, a little time there. This constant mobility primarily affects children's education: the dropout rate is the highest among all Hispanics. In 1970, 55 percent of Puerto Ricans between the ages of 16 and 21 were not in school. Only 8 percent graduated from college in 1980. This is reflected in the high percentage of unemployment and the low income of the Puerto Rican family. A great number are obliged to depend on the welfare system for subsistence as a consequence of their poverty. An image of the Puerto Rican as welfare recipient has been projected as if it were part of the personality rather than the result of the oppressive system. According to the 1985 census report on the poverty status of all families, 42 percent of Puerto Rican families lived below the poverty level (U.S. Bureau of the Census, 1970, 1980).

With the goings from and comings to the island, the use of the Spanish language and the cultural identity remain strong in the extended family and the *barrios*. Sixty percent of the Puerto Rican community claims to be bilingual. In 1980, 14 percent of the total population of Puerto Rico had lived on the mainland for six months or more.

There are factors that contribute to this migrant status of Puerto Ricans. As U.S. citizens they have no need for migration documents or foreign currency; New York is only three and a half hours from Puerto Rico, placing Puerto Ricans in a different position regarding their home country as compared with other immigrants who could never think of returning to their country. Another factor is the involvement in the ongoing political question of the status of Puerto Rico as a Commonwealth of the United States. The frequent presence on the island keeps alive the interest in the question of identity and relationship to the United States.

Within this socioeconomic situation, the positive values of Puerto Ricans and their contributions pass unnoticed. The extended family circle continues to be centered on the dignity of the person rather than on possessions or achievements. There is a fidelity to these relationships that supports qualities of love, justice, and faithfulness. The Puerto Rican family is distinguished by its hospitality. "Where one eats, many can eat" is the guiding rule. This common interdependence can be labeled laziness, dependency, and lack of maturity by a dominant world that values competition and shrewdness.

Despite these difficulties, a number of Borícuas have found ways to make larger contributions to the culture. Among these are Pedro Pietri, Puerto Rican poet who, even with limited Spanish, has been able to express the sentiments of his people; René Marqués, who portrays vivid reality through the pessimism of Puerto Rican literature; José García, honored for his film "Down These Mean Streets" about the destiny of the young

Puerto Rican obliged to walk the painful streets of oppression in the city of New York; Jesús María Sanroma, famous soloist of the Boston Symphony Orchestra; and many others who through their literary talents have contributed to the cultural development and have awakened the consciousness of a people seeking their identity from the reality of the mainland (*The Rican,* 1973, 15).

The political contribution, though small, has been significant. A Puerto Rican was mayor of Miami for many years. In 1961 President Kennedy named the first Puerto Rican ambassador, José Teodore Moscoso, to Venezuela and later to the position of coordinator of the Alliance for Latin American Progress. And in 1970, New York elected its first Puerto Rican congressman.

Organizations such as Aspira, Development Project of the Puerto Rican Community, Puerto Rican Legal Defense Forum, the National Puerto Rican Forum, Center of Study and Analysis of the Puerto Rican Reality, the Puerto Rican Woman Conference, and many others identified with the Puerto Rican community have a consistent commitment to the sociocultural development of the people and their contribution to the general society.

The Puerto Rican migration is unique. The United States has never before had a massive immigration of its own citizens from outside its borders, with a culture and language of its own, many of whom are of the black race. The Puerto Rican presence challenges the principles of the U.S. Constitution based on equality for all—an equality that has yet to be accorded to Puerto Ricans.

After more than thirty years of migration, the Puerto Rican continues to claim Puerto Rican identity, with its Hispanic language and culture, its racial *mestizaje,* and the island as home.

The Puerto Rican migration is a generation in progress. The major results of its struggles will have to wait for several years, since the median age of the second generation is only nine years old. This makes its future as uncertain as the promise of its hopeful youth.

One thing seems to be certain: "There is a Puerto Rican way of viewing life, death, love, eternity, and authority," testifies *The Rican* (1973, 18). The Puerto Rican immigrant tries to do it from "here" (the United States).

Relationships. Chicago is the most heterogenous of the places in which Hispanics in this country reside. In addition to the cultural diversity of the non-Hispanic ethnic groups, the Hispanics of Chicago represent twenty countries from Latin America and Spain.

The Puerto Rican people are primarily linked with the rest of the Hispanic community by culture and Hispanic roots. Despite the fact that Puerto Rico has been a possession of the United States since 1898 and its people U.S. citizens since 1910, Puerto Rico has its own Hispanic identity. But this same history gives its own specific characteristics. Although a U.S. citizen, the Puerto Rican continues to behave, speak, think, and feel as a Hispanic. This has caused an insecurity, reflected perhaps most of all in the Puerto Rican relationship with other Hispanics. The Puerto Rican Hispanic culture has been challenged and Americanized throughout its sociopolitical history. This is not the reality of any other Hispanic people.

As was shown in the sociocultural analysis, the majority of Puerto Ricans who migrated to the United States, until recently, had less formal education and fewer professional skills. This determines the level of integration into the dominant society. In some instances Puerto Ricans are considered inferior by other Hispanic groups. The U.S. citizenship of Puerto Ricans does not provide any privileges; on the contrary, they seem to have less than other Hispanics who do not have any political status in this country. Puerto Ricans do not seem to have any better image among other Hispanics than they do among the larger society. They are at times considered as those who speak Spanish badly, who are easily satisfied with the minimum, who are aggressive trouble makers. These stereotypes among Hispanics are mutual; some of the negative relationships began at home, for example, when the Cubans arrived on the island of Puerto Rico and began to occupy business positions of influence while the Puerto Ricans lacked jobs or opportunities for employment development.

This experience with the Cuban community can exemplify the core of the difficulties in relationship. Each group is competing for the same limited opportunities; thus relationship become a struggle for survival. What results follows the familiar pattern experienced by those oppressed, that is, to oppress the other group as if this would expand one's own opportunities. Thus history proves again the effectiveness of the oppressive technique of "divide and conquer!"

The geographical settings of the different groups in cities like Chicago, where each Hispanic group is to be found in a specific geographic area, also contribute to separatist and nationalistic relationships rather than a united front. Each group seems to fight its own battles as if these pertain only to itself.

Since the late 1970s or early 1980s, political coalitions and organizations have increased among Hispanics. Organizations like The Puerto Rican Forum and Aspira are among the leading Puerto Rican organizations contributing to a new image of relationships of Puerto Rican and other Hispanics. Such efforts of solidarity have brought political results in the election of Hispanic candidates at various levels in addition to common projects benefiting all the communities.

These results also include a solidarity with African Americans. Perhaps Puerto Ricans are the Hispanic group who can best understand the situation of African Americans, since they also experience racial discrimination as well as ethnic discrimination. But in many instances, in order to avoid the racial discrimination of the dominant society, the Puerto Rican stresses the ethnic identity, as though the black Puerto Rican were better than the African American. In many neighborhoods Puerto Ricans share the community with them. For economic reasons Puerto Ricans cannot leave these areas as they once did and as the white community did previously. Thus the relationship with African Americans also includes the common situation of poverty. Again, competition for survival marks this relationship. Frequently these two groups must compete for government positions, especially in socially oriented programs for minorities.

The lack of communication within the communities because of language barriers adds to this difficulty. But language is not a problem among most of the leaders, who could be the means to help the rest of the community understand the need for unity and solidarity among the two groups. Some results from such efforts were experienced in the 1980 elections when, in Chicago, the solidarity of the two groups contributed to the election of a African American mayor. The main cause of separation between Puerto Ricans and African Americans may be the lack of mutual awareness of their common oppressive situation. Both groups share citizenship, cultural heritage, and the plight of poverty. A greater awareness of these commonalities may improve their relationship and enrich each other and the rest of society.

The relationship of the Puerto Ricans with other Hispanics is intimately connected with their common cultural roots. With African Americans they share largely the race and the deep cultural roots that African slavery contributed to the birth of what is today the Puerto Rican people. With the rest of the American people, Puerto Ricans share the ties of citizenship. Perhaps among these relationships the latter is the weakest.

As a rule, Puerto Ricans settle in the ethnic neighborhoods of the large cities of the United States. These neighborhoods had already been developed within a particular ethnic background and had become integrated into what was then known as the "melting pot," with an identity connected in large part to the United States and the English language. Puerto Ricans come into this reality as American citizens but speaking another language, with different traditions and customs, and without anything to begin their new life. There is a mutual lack of knowledge and orientation as to how to integrate these two worlds. Thus a relationship between the Puerto Ricans and the white Anglo community based on common citizenship has not been established. This difficulty may be reflective also of the existing lack of clarity of the political status of Puerto Rico in its relationship with the United States. It is uncertain as to how the rest of the American citizens view the Puerto Rican citizens. In 1992, for the first time, the people of Puerto Rico voted for a government that supports the statehood of Puerto Rico as the definitive relationship with the United States. The future is still uncertain, because this election was also marked by a desire to solve the economic crisis of the country, with statehood presented as the solution. Puerto Ricans will have to decide in the future if they desire to cease as a people and become indeed Caribbean Americans.

By looking at these relationships, it may be possible to somewhat perceive the context of Puerto Ricans in the United States. It is within this context that Puerto Ricans try to survive without becoming assimilated.

Pastoral Experience

Religious Journey

In spite of much syncretism, the religious practices of Puerto Ricans are rooted in the Catholic faith of the conquistadors. To be a Catholic is to belong to a Catholic community. It is a religion based on relationships. Relationships with the saints, with the Blessed Virgin Mary, and with Jesus are carried on in the personal relationships with godparents *(compadres)* and patron saints. It is a religion that develops around life rather than the church building or the official minister (cf. Fitzpatrick, 1971, 116).

The influence of the Spanish colonizers is not the only one in the development of the religious world of the Puerto Ricans. Traces of religious rites of the Taínos and those of the African slaves are mixed in the Catholic popular practices.

The religious world of the Taínos was centered around the communal life of the tribe. There was the god of good, the god of evil, and the mother of all the gods, mother nature, to whom worship was given. These religious practices of the Taínos were more similar to those of the African slaves who came later than to the Christian practices introduced by the Spaniards. The slaves soon married the Indians and both married the Spaniards. This racial and cultural heritage is also part of the religious world of the Puerto Ricans. The African influence is manifested primarily in the music, the language, and the practice of spiritism that influences popular religiosity.

Religion became the basic means of continuity for the values of the African slaves. Some of the practices became part of the syncretism of the *criollo,* but others, like spiritism, remained separate from Christian practices (Hanns, 1972, 4).

Some elements of the religion of the slaves continue to be part of the cultural religion of the Puerto Ricans. Some examples are (1) the direct relationship between the natural and the supernatural and between the sacred and the secular (the Supreme is known by instinct); (2) the importance of the relationship with the supernatural world through the spirits; (3) the meaning of music in evoking and inviting the supernatural; (4) the bonds between the world of the living and that of the dead (this latter being the definition of the limits of the community and of the family); and (5) the importance of participation in communal celebrations. All are participants; there are no observers.

All of these were part of the religious world, since there was no separation of the two worlds. Spiritism in itself is not necessarily directly descended from the African slaves, but their religious practices seem to have offered the proper setting for its development. So deeply is spiritism part of the people that despite the strong opposition of the Catholic Church these practices continue today among the people.

As early as 1875 a spiritist society was established in Mayagüéz. Spiritism is practiced on different levels. There are those for whom it has become their religion. Others have recourse to it in times of material or spiritual need. But for the majority the influence seems almost unconscious; never doubting the power of the spirits, they are therefore cautious.

The Catholic Church has been concerned over the years about the practice of spiritism in Puerto Rico. But there has not been any intensive research into the African influences in the present popular religiosity of the Puerto Ricans and how this could be understood and integrated into a true evangelization. There are some popular beliefs with African roots that have an intimate relationship with popular religiosity: bad luck—the belief that one could do harm to another through the spiritist; evil eye—the belief that the exterior physical energy could influence a person, even kill the person; reincarnation—the belief of having previously seen and been in another place through the power of the spirits.

There are certain practices based on belief in the power of the spirits that are part of the religious world of the Puerto Ricans and found among other peoples as well. Some of these are that having a horseshoe by the door brings good luck; opening an umbrella in the house may cause the death of a relative; placing the broom upside down allows the visitors to leave; wearing an *azabache* prevents the evil eye. These are part of the African influence in the religious world of the Puerto Ricans.

The practice of spiritism goes beyond a mere expression of religion. Several studies in New York have shown the importance that medical professionals have given to this practice among Puerto Ricans. The process of healing in spiritism has a strong group or community significance. The person can go free because the root or fault of the problem is in the spirits and not in the person.

José Morales-Dorta gives several reasons why he considers spiritism and pentecostalism as mental health alternatives for the Puerto Rican community. Institutionalized religion is too distant, too rigid, and too dogmatic to gain the faith and trust of the poor who need to unburden, to be listened to, and to receive compassion. The small group offers security and a sense of belonging. The leader is from the community and at the same level of academic formation. The small group offers progress based on faith and hard work. Meetings, almost always three times a week, focus on facilitating intimate relationships centered on the sacred. Thus spiritism becomes warm, understanding, unifying. Morales-Dorta considers it the native religion of resistance (despite the censure of the Catholic Church) and a folklore system of psychotherapy (Morales-Dorta, 1976, 7).

He concludes that the greatest influence for the continuation of spiritism has been the transference of the African world of the spirits to Christian concepts. Examples of this are the use of the Bible and Christian prayers in the spiritist centers. Also, the lives of the saints are used as models of spiritists who went through many trials before becoming fully capable of exercising all their powers.

The lack of adequate religious formation prevents the people from seeing any contradictions between spiritism and their Christian or Catholic faith. The religiosity of the people continues to develop in the home and not in the Church. For the majority of the people spiritism is not a substitute for their religion but rather a supplement.

Given the socioeconomic reality of the Puerto Ricans, Fenton's theory (Fenton, 1969) may be of much use in the analysis of their religiosity. Fenton presents the theory that spiritism has a greater impact in communities that undergo a drastic cultural change and are losing their traditional way of life. It becomes a way of releasing the tensions and anguish created in other areas of life. Thus the poor and oppressed are more predisposed to such practices and are easily manipulated by them. From this outlook, spiritism becomes one of the components of the popular religiosity of the Puerto Ricans and has great socioeconomic implications in the process of their liberation. It can be part of that world of religion that is not liberating.

The Taíno and African influences have enabled Christianity to acquire its own characteristics in the island. It is a combination of the Catholicism of the colonial time (1500), the *criollo* syncretism (Indian and African), and the secular influence of the last century. Religion is part of daily life. Expressions of greetings or farewells ("Vaya con Dios," "Que Dios te bendiga") include the religious dimension inseparable from the cultural expressions.

The religious value of relationships is carried out in the choice of *compadres,* who become part of the extended family. The community dimension is also strengthened by the many devotions and celebrations done in community. Death and suffering are accompanied by extensive religious practices that support the family during the grieving time. This home religious practice has not been replaced by the funeral or commemorative Mass in church. Sacramentals (holy pictures, medals, holy water, the rosary, ashes on Ash Wednesday, palms on Palm Sunday, etc.) are more part of the religious practices than are sacraments.

Great feasts are public celebrations over and beyond participation in church. Christmas and Holy Week are extraordinary examples of this. Communal religious celebration is extended to the patron feasts of each city, the whole community takes a week to feast together under the banner of the patron saint. All of these contribute to strengthening the communal bonds and bringing forth an identity and a strong sense of belonging and family in the socioreligious atmosphere of the people.

Pastoral Care of the Catholic Church

Given the importance of religion to Puerto Ricans, who claim to be at least 85 percent Catholic, the Catholic Church has an indispensable role in the future development of this people, as it has had with previous Catholic immigrants. The Catholic Church continues to be the institution closest to a people whose Hispanic identity is integrally related to their identity as Catholic.

The Catholic Church could offer the evangelical vision as the perspective through which the Puerto Ricans can analyze their socioeconomic situation. This pastoral care cannot be blind to the situation of poverty in the Puerto Rican community and its existential relationship with the situation in Puerto Rico itself.

For the majority of Puerto Ricans who came to the United States before the Second Vatican Council, to be Catholic meant primarily to be baptized and to belong to a Catholic people, a cultural religion (Fitzpatrick, 1971, 116). In their experience in the United States, there is a more direct relationship with the life of the Church, more participation, and more active awareness of the Catholic faith. Unfortunately, however, this experience has been true for only a small group. It is still not reaching the great number of Puerto Ricans in the United States.

The participation of the Catholic Church in the development of immigrants is nothing new. From the beginning religion has been an integral part of the development of the American people. Religion became part of being a good citizen.

This past history of the Catholic Church in the United States has been challenged by the Hispanic experience, which insists on its cultural identity and resists being Americanized in order to fully participate in the life of the Church. Archbishop Jean Jadot, addressing the National Conference of Catholic Bishops in 1976, said, "American Catholicism has a certain cultural arrogance towards minorities." "One Lord, one faith, one baptism" (Eph 4:6) is not the same as one culture and one language. The pastoral thrust of the past cannot simply be imitated.

The massive migration of Puerto Ricans to New York in the 1950s awakened the Catholic Church to its pastoral responsibility toward Hispanics. In 1955 and again in 1957 conferences of diocesan directors for Hispanic ministry in twenty-two dioceses were held in Puerto Rico and in New York to create an understanding of Puerto Rican migration and to seek ways of responding to their pastoral needs. This was an urgent necessity, since Puerto Ricans, like other Hispanic groups, did not bring with them native priests and religious. Those caring for the Puerto Ricans were primarily foreign to their culture and their Catholicism and, for many, even their language (Spiritual Care, 1955).

Despite these early attempts, Puerto Ricans have not been part of the national Hispanic Church leadership. It was not until 1985 that the first Puerto Rican bishop in the United States was ordained. By the 1990s only two U. S. Catholic bishops were Puerto Ricans. The lack of participation of Puerto Ricans in the leadership of the Catholic Church reflects that within the larger society. In the early years there were significant local efforts toward the development of Puerto Rican leadership within the Catholic Church. In Chicago, for example, the development and contribution of the Caballeros de San Juan had lasting effects in the community. From them came another strong Catholic organization, Los Hermanos de la Familia de Dios. Many of these became Cursillistas and later deacons. In the late 1960s there was also a strong youth involvement through the Juventud Revolucionaria Católica.

Puerto Rican leadership within the Catholic Church in the 1980s, however, was almost nil. The lack of political self-determination is reflected in their minimal participation in the active life of the Catholic Church. Puerto Rican religious as well as civic leaders come primarily from Protestant denominations, who have given Puerto Ricans the opportunities and possibilities for such development within their communities.

The reality of the Puerto Ricans calls the Church today to be of the poor, of the rejected, of the migrant, of the powerless, of all those who do not count in the dominant society. Help is needed to distinguish between evangelizing elements and oppressive ones in the popular religiosity of Puerto Ricans. The Puerto Rican community offers the Church, and society at large, its youth and its capacity for maturity.

Puerto Ricans are part of the national reality of Hispanics in the United States. The pastoral challenge for the Church in regard to its mission to the Puerto Rican people is, How can the good news of Jesus Christ be presented as hope and meaning in the human struggle?

Conclusion

The Puerto Rican experience in the United States is rooted in the cultural heritage (Taíno, African, and Spaniard), the unresolved political status of the island, the ongoing economic crisis, and the religious history, all of which are part of the Puerto Rican identity as a people. Their presence in the United States brings cultural, racial, economic, political, and religious challenges to the dominant culture. The 1990s can be seen as a determining period in the life of the Puerto Rican people. The political status must be determined, the economic crisis resolved, the flow of migration faced, and self-identity recognized.

The pastoral perspective depends on the presence of the Church and the style of this presence among a religious people. Puerto Ricans seek to respond to the challenges of life from a faith that has been part of their history and their identity as a people. Christ brought good news to the poor and liberation to the oppressed: "When I was hungry, naked, in prison, a stranger . . . you fed, clothed, visited, took me in" (Matt 25:31-46). The Church fails in its mission when it does not offer this message to today's poor and oppressed. Puerto Ricans in the United States, like the poor and oppressed of Jesus' day, call the Church to this fidelity.

Bibliography

Alvarez, Nazario Manuel. *El Elemento Afronegroide en el Español de Puerto Rico, Contribución al Estudio del Negro en América.* San Juan: Instituto de Cultura Puertorriqueña, 1974.

Babin, María Teresa. *La Cultura de Puerto Rico.* San Juan: Instituto de Cultura Puertorriqueña, 1970.

Beardsley, Clarence. "Boricuas emigran a Nueva York tienen alto nivel educativo pero saben poco inglés." *El Mundo.* San Juan: March 3, 1983.

Commonwealth of Puerto Rico. "Puerto Ricans in the United States." New York: Migration Division/Dept. of Labor. *8th Day Report,* 1975/1983.

8th Day Report. Vol. 15, no. 1. Chicago: 8th Day Center for Justice, 1990.

Fenton, Gerry. "Understanding the Religious Background of the Puerto Rican." *Sondeos* 52 Mexico: CIDOC, 1969.

Figueroa, Loida. *Breve Historia de Puerto Rico.* Rio Piedras, Puerto Rico: Edil, 1979.

Fitzpatrick, Joseph P. *Puerto Rican Americans: The Meaning of Migration to the Mainland.* Englewoods Cliffs, N.J.: Prentice Hall, 1971.

__________. *One Church, Many Cultures: The Challenge of Diversity.* Kansas City: Sheed & Ward, 1987.

Friedman, Robert. "Future Bleak for Migrants to New York." New York: *The Daily News,* 1983.

Hanns, Albert Steger. "El Transfondo Revolucionario del Sincretismo Criollo." *Sondeos* 86 Mexico: CIDOC, 1972.

Heyer, Robert. "La Iglesia Hispana." *New Catholic World*. New York: Paulist, July/August 1980.

Morales-Dorta, José. *Puerto Rican Espiritismo: Religion and Psychotherapy*. New York: Vantage, 1976.

Noriega, David. "Emigración y desempleo." *El Nuevo Día*. February 3, 1984.

The Rican, A Journal of Contemporary Puerto Rican Thought. Chicago: Spring 1973.

Rodríguez, Clara. *Puerto Ricans Born in the U.S.A.* New York: Unwin-Hyman, 1989.

Rodríguez Otero, Eladio. "La Personalidad Cultural de Puerto Rico y el Status Político." Position paper, Comisión de EE. UU. y P.R. San Juan, 1965.

Schmidt, Randolph E. "Latinization of U.S.? Hispanics Becoming Big Force in American Life." *South Bend Tribune*, March 18, 1990.

Silén, Juan Angel. *Historia de la Nación Puertorriqueña*. Rio Piedras, Puerto Rico: Editorial Edil, 1973.

"Spiritual Care of Puerto Rican Migrants: Report on a Conference." New York: Archdiocese of New York, 1955.

U.S. Bureau of the Census. "Census of Population and Housing, 1980." Washington: Government Printing Office. "Persons of Spanish Origin by State: 1980."

Vice Acosta, Cynthia. "A las Puertorriqueñas pobres, Nueva York les ofrece el mundo . . . en una fábrica." *El Diario-La Prensa*. San Juan: March 3, 1983.

__________. "Y volver, volver, volver . . . el sueño de cada Puertorriqueño." *El Diario-La Prensa*. San Juan: March 4, 1983.

Wagenheim, Kal. "Puerto Rico: A Profile." *The Puerto Rican Experience, A Sociological Sourcebook*. Ed. Cordasco, Francesco, and Eugene Bucchioni. New Jersey: Littlefield, Adams & Co., 1975.

__________. *Survey of Puerto Ricans on the U.S. Mainland in the 1970s*. New York: Praeger, 1975.

__________. "Higher Education Levels of Migrants Noted by Survey." *Caribbean Business*. San Juan: December 8, 1982.

__________. "Current Fiscal Year Looks Like Major Migration Period." *Caribbean Business*. San Juan: December 22, 1982.

4

The Cuban Presence in the United States: A Pastoral Perspective

Guillermo Fernández-Toledo

Cubans make up the third largest group of Hispanics living in the United States. According to the Bureau of the Census figures, there were 1,043,932 Cubans dispersed throughout the country in 1990. The great majority of them can be found in the Miami–Dade County area in Florida, although there are other important Cuban enclaves such as those in the Union City–West New York area of New Jersey, in New York City, and in Los Angeles.

In this article, I intend to explore the religious idiosyncracy of the Cuban immigrant population in this country, specifically as evidenced in their predominant faith, Roman Catholicism. As a group, Cubans consider themselves Catholic. However, experience has shown that the great majority do not practice their faith according to the prescriptions of the Roman Catholic Church. Rather, on their own, they participate in religious practices and beliefs mostly associated with popular religiosity. I will explore this religious experience, taking into consideration the history of the evangelization process both in Cuba and in the United States, and then offer some thoughts on the pastoral challenges that must be confronted in order to carry out a successful evangelization among them, both now and in the future. And I do so mostly from a personal perspective due to the very limited scope of bibliographic material available. As anyone interested in this subject will discover, most of the research studies done on Cubans tends to concentrate in all areas except religion. Not even the American Church has kept accurate records of the impact Cubans have made in the United States, as is the case, just to mention one, with the Archdiocese of Miami, which counts 52 percent of its faithful as Cuban.[1]

Some Facts About Cuban Americans

Cuban Americans share many characteristics with other Hispanic groups in the nation, in particular, language, culture, and religion. However, there is one characteristic that sets them apart from the others. While other Hispanic groups have immigrated mainly, although not exclusively, in search of greater economic opportunity, the majority of Cubans are here because of the political oppression that has existed on their native island since the establishment of a communist regime in 1959. It is only fair to say, however, that prior to that year there was a considerable number of Cubans who resided in the United States, mostly for economic reasons. The Cuban presence in this country, which dates back to the nineteenth century, was the result of both economic and political conditions. Political instability on the island brought as a result the transference of Cuban businesses and capital to American soil, as was the case with the tobacco industry that flourished in Key West in 1868, and later on, in Ybor City, present-day Tampa. In turn, the economic opportunities and the demand for Cuban labor in this industry, along with the beginning of the Cuban wars of independence and the need for political asylum, made it possible in many cases for thousands of Cubans to leave the island and settle in the United States. Later on these same Cubans would finance with their own economic resources the last war of independence, led by Cuban patriot José Martí.

Economically, Cuban Americans have done fairly well, as reflected by the census figures. They have the highest income among Hispanic groups in the nation, although lower than for the average American, and in that same group they are the least unemployed. The reasons for this economic success are varied.

First, education has made it possible for Cubans to have the highest number of high school graduates as well as the highest number of people with a university degree of four years or more; this is why they rank second in the labor force compared with other Hispanics.

Second, the family has played a tremendous role in this economic achievement, since it is organized in such a way as to encourage and promote success. Census figures show Cubans have the highest number of married couples, the smallest family units, the lowest percentage of families that live under the poverty level, and the fewest households headed by a female. Moreover, other studies show a high percentage of women in the work force and an extended family system where everyone who is able contributes to a common pot (even the older members of the family, although they may be retired or living on welfare); a high level of economic adaptability that is somehow connected to the political instability they have experienced; and a "middle-class ethics" that has placed them on a par with their American hosts.[2]

Third, due to the series of historical events and experiences that have shaped their social character and nature, Cubans generally have exhibited a combination of entrepreneurship, competitiveness, and hard work, which has contributed greatly to their economic success as immigrants. One factor that should not be overlooked when considering some of the strategies used for enterprise is the importance placed on the "ethnic enclave" as a means of progress. Some examples of such enclaves are the Southwest 8th Street area (or Little Havana) in Miami and Bergenline Avenue in the Union City–West New York area of New Jersey where, in a twenty-year period (from 1965 to 1985), Cuban-owned and managed business establishments developed and prospered. Further into the 1980s, these same businesses set up branches in other locations to serve the needs of both the growing Cuban (or rather Cuban American) population and the new migrations of Cubans to the United States as these settled in other areas. Notably, several of these businesses have been able to cross ethnic boundaries and now serve a much larger non-Cuban segment.

The Cuban "Soul"

There are three main components of the Cuban "soul," or national identity: the Indian, the Spanish, and the African.[3]

The Indian influence in Cuba is not as strong as the other two. However, its presence is still manifest in the character of Cuban *guajiros,* or peasants; in their dwelling places *(bohíos* and *caneyes)*; in an endless array of words and names that were incorporated into the Spanish language *(batey, guateque, Cuba, Habana)*; and in edibles of the Cuban diet such as cassava, *boniato, malanga,* and corn. There were three main indigenous groups on the island prior to the coming of the Spaniards, and none of them were nearly as civilized as the Aztecs, Mayans, or Incas: (1) *Taínos,* who lived in settled agricultural and fishing communities in the eastern part of the country; (2) *Ciboneyes,* hunters and foodgatherers, who lived on the coastal areas and at times were subdued and had to coexist with the Taínos; and (3) *Guanahatebeyes,* the most primitive of the three groups, who lived on the western part of the island.[4] Most of them were extinguished in the Spanish colonization.

The Spanish influence began in 1492 when Cuba was discovered during Columbus' first voyage. It was not until twenty years later that the island began to be colonized, but even then most of the settlers would leave for other countries because the Cuban subsoil was lacking in precious metals. However, with time Cuba became the strategic center for Spanish economic interests in the New World, as Spanish *flotas* (ships) used Havana as a way station on their voyage back to the "mother country." Spain brought its language, its culture, and its religion, and gradually the Spanish settlers began the process of *aplatanamiento* (accultura-tion). By the nineteenth century the children of Spanish settlers gave birth to a new class, the *criollos*, who identified themselves as Cubans and who became the pioneers of a new national identity. Cuba, along with Puerto Rico, was the last bastion of the Spanish colonial system in the Americas. After independence there were still strong ties with Spain, mostly through Spanish citizens who stayed and intermarried with Cubans.

The African influence on the island is the direct result of the cruel slavery system of the colonial period. Blacks were brought to replace the Indian work force as it began to diminish. The enormous amount of suffer-ing caused by this oppression brought them closer to their ancestral reli-gious beliefs, although by law they had to be instructed and baptized in the Catholic faith. A syncretism was born, now known as *santería*, which is manifest to this very day and which has greatly influenced the popular religiosity of Cubans. Africans have also contributed significantly in lan-guage (words such as *chévere, fuácata, aché, bilongo*); literature (mostly through the works of Cuban ethnologist Lydia Cabrera); politics (several important Cuban patriots, such as Antonio Maceo and Juan Gualberto Gómez, were black); music (rhythms such as *rumba, mambo, cha-cha-cha*); and other legacies.

How do Cubans see themselves? They see themselves as emotionally expressive, family and group–oriented (i.e., an extended family system is prevalent where *compadres* and old-time neighbors are considered family members), *gente alegre* (happy people), *comelones* (gluttons or good-eaters), generous and welcoming; they claim to have *chispa* and to be *la candela* (a rough mixture of intelligence and shrewdness), to be hardworking, crea-tive, and enterprising; on the negative side, they are *machistas* (proud, exaggerated) and *alardosos* (show-offs). And finally, in the religious sphere, they see themselves as very devout, not in an institutional sense but in a popular religious one. There is a strong devotion to some Catholic saints such as Our Lady of Charity, San Lázaro, and Santa Bárbara, who also have deity counterparts in *santería*. A typical Cuban expression *católico a mi manera* (I am a Catholic according to my own rules) illustrates the syncretic mentality so prevalent among Cuban Americans.

How are Cubans seen by other Hispanics? In a negative light, they are seen as *bulliciosos* (noisy), proud, arrogant, and as classicists with a strong Spanish influence. In a positive light, they are seen as industrious, ambitious *(con espíritu de superación)*; always ready to offer a helping hand, hospitable; they have a good sense of humor, are *fiesteros* (the partying type); and they have a healthy nationalism. In religious terms they are seen as devout: again, in the popular syncretistic context where Catholicism, *santería*, spiritism, and *brujería* (witchcraft) coexist.[5]

Catholicism in Cuba: The Evangelization Process

Catholicism was brought to Cuba in 1492 with the arrival of the Spanish to the "most beautiful land human eyes have seen," as described by Columbus in his diary. But it was not until twenty years later, with the colonization, that Christianity was established. Franciscan and Dominican priests were the first to arrive, the most famous being Fr. Bartolomé de las Casas. From the very beginning the Spanish Crown was boastfully concerned with the evangelization of the Indians, and thousands of them were baptized. Of course, evangelization in those days had a different meaning than it has today. It was a basic religious "instruction" that had to be memorized in order to receive the sacraments and their graces and thus a guaranteed participation in eternal life; this was sufficient since "real" life was something beyond "this veil of tears." Church and Crown were two aspects of a single reality, since both served God albeit in different ways. The Church, aside from its evangelical duties, took over the two most fundamental tasks that every society must undertake in order to ensure a certain degree of well-being for its citizens: education and health care.[6]

In the sixteenth century, Cuba became an even more desolate place. Most of the people on the island left for other parts of the hemisphere, looking for gold and riches. Life was harsh and the scarce inhabitants were poor and uneducated. The first bishop was appointed in 1517 to the city of Baracoa, the first episcopal See of Cuba. Five years later, at the request of Bishop Juan de Witte Hoose, the See was transferred to Santiago de Cuba. By the end of the century, seven bishops had governed the diocese, along with the Florida territory, which had been placed under Cuban jurisdiction.[7]

By the seventeenth century all the inhabitants of the island had been Hispanicized and Christianized. The first bishop of this century, Juan de las Cabezas y Altamirano, was by all means a pastoral prelate, very much loved and respected by his flock. By that time, native vocations were being ordained to the priesthood, and in 1622 a secular priest from Havana, Fr. Dionisio Resino, became the first Cuban-born bishop. It was around 1608–12 that three Cuban men, known as *los tres Juanes,* found a statue of the Virgin Mary resting on a tablet that read "I am the Virgin of Charity," floating on the waters of Nipe Bay. This is considered the most important religious event in the history of Cuba, since all Cubans, no matter their social background, have found a common unifying element in this Marian devotion. It was also in this century that the sugar and tobacco industries began to flourish, bringing a certain amount of stability to the incipient Cuban economy and, as a result, a slight increase in population.

Bishops were now less concerned with being appointed to "better" episcopal Sees in other parts of the hemisphere, and the Church increased its influence over all segments of the society.

In the eighteenth century the Church of Cuba improved greatly with the appointment of ecclesiastical figures such as Bishops Jerónimo Nosti Valdés and Pedro Agustín Morell de Santa Cruz. This was a time of tremendous growth for the Church, with the creation of hospitals, hospices, schools for poor children, nurseries, and the like. The spirituality of the people was strengthened, as can be seen in Bishop Morell's letters. By the end of the century and under the leadership of Cuban bishop Santiago José Echevarría, the island was divided into two episcopal Sees: the central-eastern one, under the jurisdiction of the bishop of Santiago de Cuba, and the central-western one, under the jurisdiction of the bishop of Havana, who also had under his jurisdiction the Churches in Louisiana and Florida. By the end of the century the Church in Cuba gained more prestige as it became the center of ecclesiastical authority throughout the Caribbean. In 1795, Santo Domingo, the primatial See in the Americas, was handed over to the French, and Santiago de Cuba was chosen as metropolitan See because of its geographical location between Havana and San Juan, Puerto Rico. In that same year the diocese of Louisiana was created (the second diocese in the United States after Baltimore in 1789), under whose jurisdiction the territory of Florida was placed: the first bishop was the Cuban-born vicar general of Havana, Fr. Luis Ignacio Peñalver y Cárdenas.[8]

The nineteenth century began with one of the greatest prelates in colonial times, Bishop Juan José Díaz de Espada y Fernández de Landa, who introduced in Cuba many ecclesiastical and societal reforms and who came to be recognized as one of the most enlightened minds of that period. It was Bishop Espada who appointed the newly ordained priest Fr. Felix Varela to teach constitutional law at the Seminario San Carlos in Havana. Father Varela became the teacher of a whole new Cuban-born generation and inspired in them a love for freedom and human rights. He was later called by one of his disciples, José de la Luz y Caballero, "the first who taught us how to think." Eventually, Varela was expelled from Spanish territories and became perhaps the first Cuban political exile. He settled in New York where he performed tremendously well among Irish immigrants, became vicar general for the diocese, and obtained a theological doctorate from St. Mary's Seminary in Baltimore, the first Hispanic to be awarded such a degree in the United States.[9]

By the second half of the century Cuban Catholicism had greatly deteriorated. A letter written by Bishop Ramón Fernández Piérola in 1880 explained the state of affairs of his Havana diocese: large territories, few parishes, and few priests who had to serve many different communities, most of whom lacked apostolic zeal. Most people had no religious instruction at all, did not follow the Church's precepts, and lived happily without the faith and the sacraments, except for baptism. There was total indifference toward the Church. In one of his letters, Bishop Piérola said that "everyone takes care to participate in the soul of business but no one in the business of the soul."[10] Out of 200,000 people in the entire population of the city, only 3,000 attended Mass. He blamed fifty Masonic lodges hostile to the Church that existed in Havana at the time, but he also blamed the Spanish priests, being himself one, for not properly evangelizing the native population. He proposed the creation of religious institutes for teaching the faith and carrying out missions throughout the countryside. He believed the task to be easy, and he pointed out that people were docile and very welcoming to religious personnel. He even suggested that some Spanish religious orders be forced to go to Cuba to evangelize the population.[11] This poor spiritual situation got worse when the Spanish Crown used the Church as a political tool at a time when Cubans were involved in the wars for freedom. The Church was "decubanized" with the appointment of Spanish bishops loyal to Madrid and opposed to political independence.[12] As a consequence, the Church was seen as the natural ally of the Spanish Crown and so lost much of its influence among the Cuban patriots and the people in general. This is perhaps one of the causes for the current reservations and aloofness expressed by Cubans toward the Church.

With the coming of the twentieth century the Church saw the creation of several new dioceses; nevertheless, it still played a limited role in people's lives. Most Cubans failed to practice their Catholic faith and were as a whole religiously uneducated. Strong sentiments of anticlericalism also prevailed among the educated classes. It was in 1925 that the Church began to gain some ground with the creation of new apostolic movements, all of them related to Catholic Action, which brought new religious vigor to students, workers, and other segments of the population. There was a tremendous growth in the Church: pastoral, social services, personnel, and so forth. The coming of the Cuban Revolution in 1959 was initially welcomed by the Church although later opposed by it as the new regime began to turn communist and atheist. Thus began a process of open confrontation with the government, and as a result Catholic schools and institutions began to be closed and priests and religious personnel began to leave or were expelled from the island. The Church in Cuba was terribly weakened as the majority of its leaders and practicing people left the country. For those who remained, the conditions were less than ideal: all religious activities had to take place inside the churches, proselytism was banned, and Catholics had no access to education or to mass media. Those who practiced religion, whether Catholic or any other, were discriminated against and ostracized and were denied the opportunities otherwise en-

joyed by citizens in a free and open society. A period of gloom and silence
for the Cuban Church had begun, as had been experienced in previous
decades by other Churches in Eastern Europe.

The Cuban Presence in the American Church

The Cubans who began arriving on American shores in 1868 were a
representative sample of the Cuban population in their attitudes toward
the Church. As Michael J. McNally points out in *Catholicism in South
Florida: 1868–1968*, the majority of Cubans who lived in Key West did
not attend Church regularly, did not know their faith, were superstitious
in many areas, and although they were insulted if considered anything else
but Catholic, their Catholicism was limited to the reception of baptism
and extreme unction. There were many attempts on the part of the Church
to serve the spiritual needs of the Cuban population. It was very difficult
for those efforts to succeed, however, given not only the Cubans' own indifference toward the Church but also the attitudes of priests, who, coming from a totally different cultural background, were unable to understand
this "new" type of Catholicism. In 1898, 44 percent of the population in
Key West was Cuban, yet despite this fact, most remained unevangelized.

The Cubans who began arriving in 1959 came from a different reality
than those mentioned above. With this I do not intend to say that the
Church had successfully evangelized the entire Cuban population by this
time, but it had begun to evangelize on several fronts, mainly students
and workers, and this had proved to be considerably effective. The Diocese of Miami, which had been created in 1958 under the leadership of
Bishop Coleman F. Carroll, opened its arms and welcomed the Cubans,
helping them in whatever ways it could, mostly through social aid and later
by sponsoring a program to take care of unaccompanied Cuban children.
As the Cuban political situation stabilized with Castro's firm grip on power,
the Church began to realize that Cubans were here to stay, and a policy
of integration and assimilation was begun by Bishop Carroll, later to be
archbishop of Miami.

This policy, in practice, never worked because most Cubans would
not participate in Church life: they didn't understand enough English and
felt totally out of place in the social and cultural settings of their new parishes. Most Cubans who attended Mass went to San Juan Bosco Church,
an old garage turned into a sort of mission church, which, although not
considered a national Church, functioned as one. Later, a shrine was built
in honor of Our Lady of Charity, and it soon became a pilgrimage center
for Cubans, not only for those in Miami but for those who lived in other
states and countries as well.

Catholics who had been evangelized through Catholic Action back in
Cuba, together with Cuban and Spanish priests, began the creation of

several lay movements for Spanish-speaking people in Miami. The first Cursillo was celebrated in 1961, later to be followed by, among others, *Movimiento Familiar Cristiano, Caballeros de Colón,* and *Agrupación Católica Universitaria.* These organizations served as the ideal means of reaching the unchurched while keeping the faith alive among those who were already churched. Some pastors, however, were hesitant to allow Cuban parishes to organize a separate Spanish-speaking apostolate. In time, these lay organizations came into conflict with the hierarchical Church and, as a result, were never recognized as part of the Diocese of Miami during Carroll's episcopacy.[13]

With the appointment of Archbishop Edward A. McCarthy the situation changed for the better as lay organizations in Spanish were incorporated into the official Church structure. Archbishop McCarthy brought with him a new apostolic zeal and a new approach to lay ministry. Apostolic movements have flourished and developed tremendously under his leadership. Almost all areas of ministry, both diocesan and parochial, have a Spanish-speaking counterpart, and there is, in general, good communication between Hispanics and Americans. However, there is still debate as to whether Cubans are fairly represented in the power structures of the archdiocese, since they make up the largest percentage of Catholics in the archdiocese but are not proportionally represented.[14]

Pastoral Challenges

The commemoration of the 500th anniversary of the arrival of the Spanish in the New World and with it the first proclamations of the gospel message to the indigenous population has provided an opportune occasion to reflect on the meaning of the evangelization process and the new challenges to this process that continue to emerge. First, however, we must face up to the past with honesty in order to be better able to interpret the present and gain the insights and perspectives we need for the future, so that we might respond effectively to the pastoral needs of the people.

A review of the history of the evangelization process of the Cuban people reveals many failings that cannot be ignored. Nonetheless, we gain nothing by attempting to justify past mistakes. The past is over; our work must begin anew with the present and with the conditions available to us today. Cuban Americans, the subject of our focus, must be viewed not only within the context of their social milieu (and reality) in this country but also within the context of their religious experience, be it within or outside the Church, since most of them identify with the Catholic community of faith.

Evangelization to Cuban Americans must be carefully planned and geared to two different groups: (1) those who are already in the Church, who participate and take religion seriously and who have experienced a certain degree of "conversion"; and (2) those who are waiting to be evangelized, who seldom go to or participate in Church, but who are somehow open and willing to receive the message of Christ.

For Those Who Are Already in the Church

The proclamation of the good news is an invitation to participate in the community of faith, the Church. But it frequently happens that our faith communities are lacking in many areas. For good evangelization we need vibrant and live communities where everyone feels a sense of participation and ownership. It is only in this way that we experience the living Christ who lives within us, with us, among us, in his community. We must first experience the living Christ, so that we can later learn about that Christ; it is never the other way around.

The parish needs to be the center of our life as a Church. As such, the parish has to provide a sense of solidarity and sacramentality within the context of cultural pluralism, where everyone may be different but where everyone can feel spiritually related to the other because they share the same faith. We need a revival in our parishes. We need to revive our parish groups, our outlook, and our sense of community within a larger community. Are our parishes ministerial? Are they involved in different ministries that respond to the needs of their members? Are they involved in the continuing education of laypeople? Are they places where people feel they are growing not only as human beings but also as baptized members of the Church? Parishes with schools must reflect on the meaning of Catholic education. Do we have schools because we offer a better education or because we believe education is a means by which to evangelize? Do our schools offer good opportunities for the spiritual renewal of our children and their parents?

Apostolic movements, which have done an excellent job in the evangelization of the Cuban people, must also evaluate their work in the same context. Are they keeping up with the constant changes of society, or are they trying to safeguard practices that worked well in the past but are no longer effective? Are they sensitive to the needs of Cuban American children and young adults who are not and cannot be 100 percent Cuban but who are also entitled to participate fully in our faith communities? These are just a few of the questions we need to ask ourselves and reflect upon in order to help our people grow in their faith response to God.

For Those Who Are Waiting for Our Call

It is in this second group that the real challenge lies and where the task will be much harder to accomplish. I am sure that at one time or another the Church has knocked on these people's doors with no positive result. At other times people have turned their backs on the Church because of its own sinfulness and shortcomings. We must acknowledge our limitations and reinforce our process of conversion by living as witnesses of Christ, taking very seriously (1) our prophetic mission *(martyria)*; (2) our experiential fraternity *(koinonia)*; (3) our sacramental life *(liturgia)*; and (4) our commitment as a liberating force *(diakonia)*. It is only through this conversion from within our own faith communities that we will be able to impact and attract others.

A model of Church as a faith community that lives in accordance with the four points listed above has a strong appeal to those who are open to receive the message of Christ and especially to those who, because of a specific cultural background, feel comfortable in such a model. Cubans, for various sociohistorical reasons, have mistrusted institutions. The Catholic Church throughout its history in Cuba has lived a model of Church that has been mostly, and is still to a large extent, an institutional model. The Church needs to be presented in a different light: a Church that although necessarily institutional, is also charismatic and open to the signs of the times.

Three of the components listed above are already manifest in certain characteristics of Cuban culture as well as Hispanic culture in general: *koinonia* is evident in the importance placed on the family, the group, the helping hand owed to one another on the basis of belonging to the same community *(ad intra)*; *liturgia* is in line with the Cuban sense of celebration and festivity, the reverence for the sacred that is so apparent in popular religiosity, and the outlook of life as *lo real maravilloso*, as it has been called in literary circles; *diakonia* is reflected in the spirit of generosity and hospitality *(ad extra)* so prevalent in the Cuban people, with its perennial hope for a better tomorrow and a free Cuba, and which, from a theological perspective, could be interpreted as that immanent human longing for the kingdom of God, already begun but not yet fully completed. These three ecclesial components are already present in the Cuban culture; they just need to be brought out, perfected, Christianized, evangelized, as is the case with other cultural antivalues that need to be transformed according to Gospel principles.

It is only then that the fourth component, the prophetic mission, or *martyria*, will be achieved. No one is able to give of what he or she lacks. Cuban history has proved that when properly evangelized, the Cuban people have responded positively and generously, as can be seen through thousands of Catholic Action members who have served their Church and their country at the worst of times. I am reminded of those Catholic students and workers who fought against the Batista regime and for a better social order in the 1950s and who, later on, opposed the atheistic principles of Castro, many of whom were martyred while shouting *"Viva Cristo*

Rey"; of the suffering and the silence of the Church in Cuba during these last thirty-four years, a Church that has been a witness of Christ despite all the difficulties; and finally, of those pastors who have decided to stay with the people and the lay brothers and sisters who have been discriminated against because they have not given up on their faith.

We must look into the future with a sense of pride and obligation. The seeds of faith in our Lord Jesus Christ have been implanted in the hearts of our people; it is time now for the patient task of nurturing. Cubans, and especially Cuban Americans, have also been called to share in the good news of our Lord Jesus Christ. Their presence in the American Church is a reality that cannot be denied and will prevail, even when political changes do occur in Cuba and some Cuban Americans choose to return. And it is precisely the American Church, their Church also, that must evangelize them, along with other groups, with the same urgency with which the disciples set out to proclaim the good news entrusted to them.

Notes

1. María Cristiana Herrera, "The Cuban Ecclesial Enclave in Miami: A Critical Profile," *The Catholic Historian* 9, nos. 1 and 2 (Winter/Spring 1990) 209–21.

2. Lisandro Pérez, "Adaptación económica del inmigrante y organización familiar: revisión del éxito cubano," *Hispanos en los Estados Unidos,* ed. Rodolfo J. Cortina and Alberto Moncada (Madrid: Ediciones de Cultura Hispánica, 1988) 307–20.

3. Florinda Alzaga, "Raíces del alma cubana," *Concurso Literario Jorge Mañach* (n.p., 1976) 16.

4. Leví Marrero, *Cuba: economía y sociedad,* vol. 1 (Puerto Rico; Editorial San Juan, 1972) 53.

5. Mario Vizcaíno, "Cubans," a pastoral handout (Miami: Southeast Pastoral Institute, 1991).

6. Orignal documents of Encuentro Nacional Eclesial Cubano.

7. Reinerio G. Lebroc, *Cuba, Iglesia y Sociedad: 1830–1860* (Madrid: n.p., 1976) 5–15.

8. Michael V. Gannon, *The Cross in the Sand* (Gainesville: University Presses of Florida, 1983) 110.

9. Joseph McCadden and Helen M. McCadden, *Felix Varela: Torch Bearer from Cuba* (San Juan, Puerto Rico, n.p., 1984) 113.

10. Manuel Maza Miguel, *El alma del negocio y el negocio del alma: testimonios sobre la Iglesia en Cuba, 1878–1894* (Santiago, Dominican Republic, n.p., 1990) 12.

11. Ibid., 9–16.

12. *Encuentro Nacional Eclesial Cubano,* documento final e instrucción pastoral de los obispos de Cuba (Conferencia Episcopal Cubana, 1988) 37–38.

13. Michael J. McNally, *Catholicism in South Florida: 1868–1968* (Gainesville: University Presses of Florida, 1982) 164.

14. Herrera, *The Cuban Ecclesial Enclave in Miami,* 219.

Hispanic Realities and Theology

5

Biblical Exegesis from a Hispanic Perspective[1]

Barbara E. Reid, O.P.

The Importance of the Bible

A group of Latin American women, beginning a process of initial reflection on the Bible, were asked, "What is the significance of the Bible in your life?" Typical responses were: "I haven't read it, nor has it interested me." "It is the Word of God given only for a few select, like the priests." "It is the Holy Book, revealed by God, not accessible to all." "It is the book that says everything one should and should not do." "It is a book of the past." "It is a Holy Book that a woman should not know."[2] Likewise Ada María Isasi-Díaz and Yolanda Tarango, two U.S. Hispanic theologians, state that the Bible does not play a prominent role in the lives of Hispanic women:

> They do not read the Bible and know only popularized versions of biblical stories—versions Hispanic women create to make a point but that often distort or imaginatively interpret the original versions. Their Christianity is informed by Christian tradition and practice rather than by the Bible. . . . Biblical revelation and truth are not negated, but they are not given much attention, simply because they are not part of the daily experience of Hispanic women.[3]

The reasons for the limited role of the Bible in the lives of Hispanic women are historically and culturally rooted.[4] First, the type of Christianity that was brought to the Americas by the Spanish *conquistadores* was not a biblically based Christianity. Rather, it was one in which doctrines, commandments, and Church practices were emphasized. A second factor is the centrality of the saints in Hispanic devotional piety. The saints are more readily seen as intercessors and models to be emulated than is the Jesus of the Gospels. Women, in particular, find that Mary understands their lot and offers consolation much more readily than could her male son. A third reason for the marginal role of the Bible is that it is perceived to be difficult to understand and its interpretation belongs to the domain of the official Church. Devotions to the saints, by contrast, allow for a greater degree of control and creativity on the part of the faithful.

This attitude toward the Bible is not peculiar to Latin Americans nor to U.S. Hispanics,[5] the majority of whom are Catholics. In the experience of most pre–Vatican II Catholics, the Bible, if it had a place at all, was a family heirloom that collected dust on the coffee table or on some obscure shelf. On rare occasions it might be opened to record the latest family birth, marriage, or death. But it was not something that would be read regularly, or even once in a while. Everyone had their own rosary to pray with, but personal copies of the Bible were rare. Devotions, novenas, and First Friday observances were the more common mode of pietistic expression.

This has changed significantly since the Vatican II document on revelation advocated that Catholics read and study the Bible, and that preaching be from the Scriptures. The surge of interest in the Bible for Hispanics and non-Hispanics alike is evident in its popular use in parish RENEW groups, the charismatic movement, *comunidades de base*, and Bible study groups. Many have discovered the Bible as "guide and light for our lives," "source of power and enablement," "liberating Word for all," "the book that interprets my life."[6]

Liberation Theology and Biblical Exegesis

When Vatican II first began to encourage biblical study for all the faithful, the reigning method of biblical interpretation was a historical-critical one, with its tools of form criticism, source and redaction criticism, and word studies in Greek and Hebrew. The basic goal of the method is to determine as well as possible what the text said and meant in its original context before applying it to the present day.

A distinct new way of entering into biblical interpretation has emerged from the work of liberation theologians of the last three decades. Although its birthplace is Latin America and not the United States, its underlying principles have been taken up by pastoral ministers, scholars, and the faithful in Hispanic Catholic communities throughout the United States. In what follows we will first describe the fundamental dynamics of biblical exegesis from a liberation perspective. Then we will make some observations about the new juncture in which liberation theology finds itself. Finally, we will remark on the use of the method by U.S. Hispanics.

First of all, as Carlos Mesters has stated, the principal objective of reading the Bible is not to interpret the Bible but to interpret life with the help of the Bible.[7] The method employed is threefold: *ver, juzgar, actuar* (see, judge, act). The first movement is to *see,* that is, to see from the perspective of the real-life experience of grass-roots believers. For the majority in Latin America, this is the experience of poverty and oppression. The second step is to *judge,* to analyze the social and political reasons for the poverty and oppression. In the process, a correlation is sought with the biblical stories of deliverance and liberation. The final step is to *act* on what one sees and understands.

Who Interprets the Bible

This first crucial component of the method is that it relies on the faithful reflection of ordinary people of faith, not solely or even primarily on that of biblical scholars. What is required to engage in the process is a willingness to reflect on experience in light of faith and the biblical tradition in solidarity with other believers. One need not have a degree in theology or be trained in biblical exegesis to do this. Telling one's own story, the joint story of the community, and relating that to the biblical story is essential. Narrative mode is particularly important: parables and stories of lived experience are the stuff of both real life and the biblical text.

Experience of the Poor

Crucial to the method is the experience of the majority: the poor and oppressed. Liberation theology does not claim to be neutral. The deliberate bias is for the poor. Clodovis Boff and Jorge Pixley,[8] for example, demonstrate how in every section of the Bible, God's concern is for the poor. In the Exodus, God is revealed as a liberator of the oppressed (Deut 7:7-8). In the Law, the poor receive special privilege (Exod 22:20, 21-23, 24; 24:14-15). The prophets continually speak out against oppression of the poor (Amos 8:5-6; Isa 10:1-4; Jer 22:13-19). In the Psalms, the poor turn to Yahweh as their defender (Pss 6; 10:8-14; 37:14-16; 94:3-7). Wisdom literature also recognizes that God favors the poor (Prov 14:31; 15:25; 22:22-23).

So too, in the New Testament: Christ is the incarnation of God who sides with the poor. Paul's letters speak of Christ's solidarity with an intrinsically poor humanity (Phil 2:3-11; 1 Cor 1:27-28; 2 Cor 8:9). In the Gospel of John (1:11-12, 14; 4:1-42) Jesus' poverty is seen in his rejection by his own and his acceptance by outcasts. Luke traces Jesus' whole life as lived in solidarity with the poor (Luke 4:18; 6:20, 24; 18:18-23; 9:46-48; 22:24-26). Patterned on the example of the poor Christ, the first believers held all things in common (Acts 2:42-47; 4:32-37) and took up collections for the needy (Rom 14:26; 2 Cor 8:8-9). Few of these early followers were of high estate (1 Cor 1:26-31).

Based on this reading of the Bible, Boff and Pixley articulate a vision of discipleship that entails solidarity with the poor, service to the needs of the humblest, and readiness to suffer the persecution that follows from these actions. They show that not only Jesus but Moses, Elijah, Jeremiah, and the Servant of Deutero-Isaiah embody this same ethos, as also the poor Mary and Paul the manual laborer. Finally, they demonstrate that the poor have always been the first recipients of the biblical message: from the slaves in Egypt to the exiles in Babylon to the first Christians. Thus when liberation theology today takes the stance of option for the poor, it is in continuity with the whole biblical tradition. Although Christians have always concerned themselves with love for the poor, liberation theology insists that that be expressed not as charity but as justice in the social and political arenas.

A Communal Endeavor

A third component of biblical exegesis from a liberation perspective is its communitarian nature. Biblical interpretation is not a solitary endeavor, a gleaning of spiritual nuggets for one's personal advancement in holiness. Rather, a liberation method relies on groups of believers sharing their experience, reflecting together on the Word of God, and acting to embody that Word in the present.

The Word of God in the Present

Liberation theology regards the Bible not as a deposit of timeless truths formulated in a bygone day that can be mined and applied equally in every time and place. Nor is biblical interpretation an attempt to arrive at "the correct meaning" of the text. Rather, it is a way of understanding the living Word by which God speaks in our midst today, revealing new possibilities of meaning.

Clodovis Boff, a Brazilian theologian, has made an important contribution to the understanding of how the Bible is actualized in the present.[9] He distinguishes between an exegetical approach based on "correspondence of relationships" and one based on "correspondence of terms." The latter reproduces a gospel story in a contemporary context with twentieth-century figures replacing the biblical ones. Boff's mathematical illustration of correspondence of terms is:

$$\frac{\text{Jesus}}{\text{His Political Context}} = \frac{\text{Christian Community}}{\text{Its Political Context}}$$

An example of such is found in *The Gospel in Solentiname,* commentaries on the Sunday Gospels by Nicaraguan peasants, collected by Ernesto

Cardenal.[10] In their reflections on Matthew 2:12-23,[11] The Slaughter of the Innocents, those massacred in the biblical story were equated with slain union leaders and local farmers; the families fleeing to Egypt were seen as equivalent to the *campesino* families having to leave their homes in many parts of Nicaragua; Herod and his soldiers are equated with Somoza and his National Guard.

Although *The Gospel in Solentiname* makes an important contribution toward seeing the gospel texts enfleshed in the present, Boff raises certain questions about the model it uses:

> Have the historical, cultural, political, ideological, and especially religious conditions (for example, the influence of apocalypticism) influencing Jesus been respected? Has due consideration been accorded the extreme complexity of our society, and the degree of development of political awareness to which we have attained, on the level of analysis and on the level of ideology, during the twenty centuries which separate us from the gospel events? Can our political contexts be so closely identified, thematically, with the political context of the Bible that resembles them, that we should read "oppression" for "Egypt," "liberation" for "exodus," and "political assassination" for "cross"?[12]

For Boff, making parallels too facilely between first-century Palestine and a twentieth-century situation underestimates the task of hermeneutics. It borders on a naively uncritical approach to the text. Furthermore, it presupposes that history simply repeats itself: ever has it been and ever shall it be.

Instead, Boff offers a model of "correspondence of relationships" illustrated thus:

$$\frac{\text{Scripture}}{\text{Its Context}} = \frac{\text{Ourselves (a theology of the political)}}{\text{Our Context}}$$

In this model, the task is to "re-effectuate the biblical act, the act that gave birth to the Bible itself as a text."[13] To do this, Boff advocates the use of all the critical tools of modern exegesis to understand as best we can the process of "creative fidelity" used by the early Christian communities to interpret and transmit the words and deeds of Jesus. By entering into the same kind of process of creative fidelity to the text, the aim today is the same as that of the first evangelists: to evoke a commitment of faith from the recipients of the biblical texts.

With this model, Boff asserts, two pitfalls in interpretation are avoided. The first is "semantic or textual positivism," which claims that the original intention of the biblical author and the meaning of a text can be determined and fixed for all time and applied in all situations. The second is "hermeneutic improvisation," an approach that takes from Scripture only what serves to prove one's preestablished theological positions. This approach often wrenches from the text meaning that is very much removed from its original significance. In Boff's estimation, what these two approaches have in common is an underlying desire to manipulate and control the text rather than to enter into the dialogical process between text and reader.

The Reign of God in This World

One of the most controversial aspects of biblical interpretation from a liberation perspective is its call for radical change in this-worldly social, political, economic, and relational structures. This stands in direct contrast to a spirituality derived from such texts as John 18:36, "My kingdom is not of this world," that advocate patient endurance, "offering it up," bearing one's cross, looking for a promised future reward as compensation for the sufferings of the present. Liberation theologians ask why, if Jesus intended the reign of God only for the next world, did he embark on a path that brought him into direct confrontation with the rulers of his day, one that he knew would result in his own death? Why, too, did he teach his disciples to pray for the coming of God's reign "on earth as it is in heaven" (Matt 6:10)? Liberation theologians see in the Gospels a Jesus who meant for the reign of God to be incarnated to some degree in this world. Consequently, liberation is not only liberation from personal, individual sin; but is, rather, liberation from unjust, sinful structures. This understanding of liberation entails not only personal conversion but action that aims at dismantling oppressive structures.[14]

New Junctures for Liberation Theology

The use of social analysis by liberation theologians and their insistence on the need for radical change in present sociopolitical systems was often perceived as a condemnation of capitalism and an embracing of Marxism. With the disintegration of communism in Eastern Europe and the former Soviet Union, some are sounding the death knell of liberation theology. Although many liberation theologians have explicitly espoused socialism as the sociopolitical avenue for implementing their theological vision, it is not accurate simply to equate liberation theology with Marxism.[15] The recent monumental shifts in the shape of the globe do, indeed, affect the direction of liberation theology. However, these do not signal its demise, but rather, a rethinking of its role and program. Pablo Richard[16] observes that the basic structure of liberation theology, as critical reflection on God's self-revelation in the experience of the poor and praxis for liberation, has not changed. Indeed, it is more necessary than ever. But there are changes in the present situation that demand new responses from liberation theology.

One shift noted by Peter Burns[17] is that while liberation theologians remain basically sympathetic to socialist values over capitalist, they are less inclined to advocate a specific socialist political and economic program. There is a risk that liberation theologians could retreat to the realm of speculation without continuing to engage in social analysis and political action in the concrete, resulting in a taming of liberation theology's most challenging aspect. Pablo Richard advises that in the new historical situation it is critical that liberation theologians take up anew critical and creative dialogue with the social sciences, especially economics, ecology, and anthropology, so as to continue to construct an alternative vision.

Another change is that the contrast between development (the political stance of capitalism toward poor nations) and liberation has now shifted to one of life versus death. The struggle is no longer for liberation rather than dependence but a battle for existence itself. With the triumph of capitalism and the First World now at peace, the Third World simply does not matter.[18] The latter is valued for its raw materials, but its population is considered "surplus." In the face of a capitalist system that sacrifices the life of many for the life of a few, theology of liberation must become theology of life—life for all and for the entire cosmos. It must aim to recover full human dignity and value for all the living.

Another shift is that the concept of "the poor" is being extended to include not only the economically poor but also those who are oppressed because of race, culture, or gender. Thus liberation theology is now expanding into new ecumenical and universal horizons that focus on the realities of women, African Americans, indigenous peoples, and youth.

Liberation Perspectives for U.S. Hispanics

Latin American liberation theology has provided the basic optic for pastoral practice and theological scholarship for U.S. Hispanics. When employed in the United States, liberation methods not only challenge situations of oppression in this country but also confront First World countries with their role in creating oppressive situations in the Third World.[19]

The Importance of the Bible

Ada María Isasi-Díaz articulates four reasons for the urgent need to recognize the central role of the Bible in the everyday lives of Hispanic women.[20] First, the Bible already plays an indirect role in their lives. Although the biblical stories are modified and embellished, they are the primary source of the symbolism and imagery of Hispanic devotional piety. The foundation for biblical study is thus already laid.[21]

Second, with the changes since Vatican II—for example, the liturgical Scripture readings in the vernacular, the ready availability of new translations of the Bible, and the rise of groups that use the Bible (RENEW, Bible study groups, charismatic prayer groups)—it is essential that attention be given to training people to interpret the Bible. The new enthusiasm for using the Bible has not been matched by adequate education in methods of interpretation. The result is that the Bible is often used in fundamentalist and pietistic ways.[22]

A third aspect is that Hispanics in the United States find themselves confronted with a culture in which the Bible plays a prominent role. One frequently encounters mainline Protestants, televangelists, and political groups on the religious Right invoking biblical authority on many societal issues.

Finally, the Bible could be an ally for Hispanics in the daily struggle for survival and dignity. Informed reading of the Scriptures gives authority to the struggle for liberation and undermines attempts at using the Bible to reinforce oppressive situations.

Who Interprets the Bible

Just as Latin American liberation theologians have insisted on interpreting the Bible from the perspective of the poor, Hispanic theologians are calling for new readings of Scripture that proceed from the particular experience of U.S. Hispanics.[23] It is necessary for Hispanics to articulate for themselves their own experience in dialogue with the text.

The need for Hispanic biblical scholars is critical.[24] It must be realized, however, that the simple fact that one is Hispanic does not necessarily mean that she or he will do biblical exegesis differently than anyone else. If trained in traditional American or European universities, Hispanics could adopt the consciousness and methodology of the dominant culture.

A further caution is that scholars should not underestimate the capacity of the faithful to engage in critical theological reflection. Access to the ability to interpret the biblical text carries with it a power that must not be restricted to a select few. As Olga Pavisich-Ryan, a Bolivian lay leader, remarked, "Don't withhold knowledge. It's a power. People are very capable. They need you to help open the knowledge of the Scriptures up to them. Otherwise you keep them perpetual children."[25]

Experience of the Poor

Since poverty is also the experience of the majority of Hispanics in the United States, this aspect of liberation theology remains pertinent. There are, however, Hispanics who are upwardly mobile and whose experience is no longer one of poverty. Liberation methods demand that Hispanics who "make it" use their resources to dismantle the systems that keep their sisters and brothers in poverty. Also, poverty is understood not only as material but also as oppression based on racial, cultural, and gender biases.

A Communal Endeavor

The importance of the communal aspect of theological reflection is evidenced in the prevailing model of pastoral practice in U.S. Hispanic circles: *pastoral de conjunto.*[26] Hispanic scholars, too, prize this dimension. In his presidential address to the 1990 annual meeting of the Academy of Catholic Hispanic Theologians of the United States (ACHTUS), Roberto Goizueta urged his colleagues to "challenge the prevailing view of scholarship as a fundamentally individual activity, undertaken in isolation from the community. Our theology," he said, "is grounded in the praxis of accompaniment or solidarity."[27] Some Hispanics are also calling for a sense of community that extends more broadly across racial and ethnic lines.[28]

The Word of God in the Present

One Spanish word that most Anglos know is *mañana*. As Justo González describes, it is used by people in the dominant culture who wish to deride Hispanics as lazy folk who always put off doing anything until "tomorrow."[29] However, *mañana* is more often the discouraged response of oppressed people, who have learned that no matter what efforts they make, the status quo rarely changes. There is also an eschatological dimension to *mañana*: it pronounces judgment on today and looks to a tomorrow that is radically different. The future holds the promise that God is creating a new order of justice and peace.

Two opposite responses come from such an eschatological perspective: one may simply do nothing, waiting and enduring until the *mañana* that God will bring. Another may hear it as a clarion call to action that effects change in the present social and political order, a working with God toward incarnating the eschatological reign in the here and now.[30] Elsa Támez's definition of patience captures the difference between these two approaches.[31] The former waits patiently for *mañana* with passive resignation; the latter with "militant patience" that watches for the propitious moment to act. It is the latter attitude that is espoused by Hispanics working from a liberation perspective.

The Reign of God in This World

The attention of liberation theology to understanding the biblical message in the present day and to embodying the reign of God in this world offers to many a hopeful vision. It provides a biblical basis to believe that things can be different, not only in the next world but in the here and now as well. Evangelical churches have been good at understanding this dynamic. They offer *pan y café y la Biblia,* food for the body along with food for the soul, and have drawn many Hispanic Catholics into their ranks.

Alternatively and perhaps surprisingly, this same dimension of embodying the reign of God in this world does not appeal to all U.S. Hispanics. Some who have turned to Churches with a fundamentalist bent are looking for a religion that will reinforce the old-time values. Hispanics looking for stability and moderation in their lives often find the fundamentalist sects providing sure doctrines, simple morality, and literal, authoritative truth of the Bible.[32] A process of biblical interpretation that involves social and textual analysis and structural change is perceived by some as too complex and confusing. Some also claim that with its stress on social justice, the Catholic Church is more issue-oriented than Christ-centered.[33]

Some Hispanics cannot really accept a this-worldly Catholicism,[34] nor the image of a liberator Christ. Traditionally Hispanic spirituality has centered on identification with the suffering Christ. Faith in Jesus is not experienced as posing a challenge to unjust social structures, or even as inviting personal transformation. Rather, identification with the Suffering Christ serves as a kind of catharsis, giving solace in the knowledge that one's pain and suffering is known and experienced by one's Lord.[35]

In the 1990 annual meeting of ACHTUS, Hispanic scholars shared their experiences of devotion to the cross:

> The cross is part of our human existence, a symbol of suffering, something ordained by God with which we have to put up: *"Carga tu cruz, aguanta."* Accepting the cross entails accepting the mystery of suffering and dealing with it as best as we can. We confront suffering and accept it with resignation. This leads to a sense of dignity in suffering. The cross represents suffering in the context of the story of Job, who never got an explanation or an understanding of it.[36]

It is not surprising, then, that the biggest day of the year in a Hispanic community such as Pilsen, in Chicago, is Good Friday, when the Way of the Cross reenacts Christ's suffering and crucifixion. María Hernández, one of the organizers of the Pilsen area's first passion play in April 1977 explains: "The *Vía Crucis* is something we live in the barrio. The Virgin Mary cried for her son and now the mothers cry for their sons who use drugs and are in gangs. It's real."[37]

Pentecostal Churches offer another response to the reality of suffering that many Hispanics find attractive. Rather than work to change the structures that cause it or to find comfort in identification with the crucified Christ, they help their members escape consciousness of surrounding pain and sorrow.[38] In the robust singing, enthusiastic praying in tongues, and giving oneself to the power of the Spirit, one can shed the burden for awhile of the pain and hopelessness of one's circumstances.[39]

The challenge for U.S. Hispanics is to articulate a biblically based Christology that is liberating but does not ignore the suffering Christ. Thus, working for a greater incarnation of the reign of God in the present, one would at the same time not lose sight of the fact that the fullness of God's reign is "not yet." Faith in the resurrected Christ brings hope and joy and the conviction that reality can change, but without the pain and suffering of the crucified Christ joy is reduced to a shallow illusion.

Hispanic Women

A crucial component of U.S. Hispanic theology is the contribution of Hispanic women, both at the grass-roots level and in the scholarly world. In very many instances it is women who lead *comunidades de base*, Bible study gatherings, parish renewal groups, and the like; it is their voices that are increasingly heard. Hispanic women are naming the double oppression they face: not only a cultural suppression but also the subjugation that stems from sexism and patriarchalism. Hispanic women scholars employ both the tools of liberation theology and those of feminist theologians. The use of the Bible is an integral part of their endeavor. They recognize that in the majority of cases the Bible has been used to reinforce and legitimate the subjugation and inferiority of women. Thus they call for a new reading of Scripture that leads to fullness of life for all, women and men alike. They see in the egalitarian praxis of Jesus no room for justifying any exclusion of women. These discoveries by Hispanic women about the significance of the Bible, shared in the community, recover the true, liberating character of divine revelation.[40]

Conclusion

The contributions of the community of U.S. Hispanic believers, pastoral ministers, and scholars are gifts of utmost importance not only for the Hispanic Catholic community but for the whole Church. The whole Church is poorer without their prophetic vision. Moreover, if there are poor, oppressed, suppressed, or voiceless members of the Church, the whole Church suffers. True liberation results in freedom for the whole body, not just for an individual member. As St. Paul states, "If one part suffers, all the parts suffer with it; if one part is honored, all the parts share its joy" (1 Cor 12:26).

Notes

1. I am indebted to Dr. María Pilar Aquino, Assistant Professor of Theology at the University of San Diego, for her time and gracious hospitality in sharing with me her theological reflections and resources as this work was in preparation. I am grateful, as well, to my colleagues from the faculty of Catholic Theological

Union, to Sr. Dominga Zapata, executive director of the Midwest Hispanic Catholic Commission for NCCB Regions 6 and 7, and to Dr. Fernando F. Segovia, from the Divinity School of Vanderbilt University, for their insightful comments and critique.

2. From interviews shared with me by María Pilar Aquino.

3. Ada María Isasi-Díaz and Yolanda Targango, *Hispanic Women: Prophetic Voice in the Church* (San Francisco: Harper & Row, 1988) 66.

4. Ada María Isasi-Díaz, "The Bible and *Mujerista* Theology," *Lift Every Voice: Constructing Christian Theologies from the Underside,* ed. Susan Brooks Thistlethwaite and Mary Potter Engel (San Francisco: Harper, 1990) 262–65. The remarks of Isasi-Díaz refer to the experience of Hispanic women. A study of the perspectives of Hispanic men would be valuable.

5. The use of the term "Hispanic" is notoriously problematic. Generally, "Hispanic" or "Latino" are umbrella terms used by Anglos to refer to persons from a variety of Spanish-speaking cultural backgrounds: Mexican American, Puerto Rican, Cuban American. Each group has its distinct historical and cultural heritage, while at the same time sharing many similarities. See further Fernando F. Segovia, "Hispanic American Theology and the Bible: Effective Weapon and Faithful Ally," Roberto Goizueta (ed.), *We Are a People! Initiatives in Hispanic American Theology* (Minneapolis: Fortress, 1992) 21–50.

6. Responses from the same group of women cited at the opening of this essay after having shared in a series of sessions of reflection on the Bible and their life together.

7. Carlos Mesters, "Como se faz Teologia hoje no Brasil?" *Estudos Biblicos* 1 (1985) 10.

8. Clodovis Boff and Jorge Pixley, *The Bible, the Church, and the Poor,* Theology and Liberation Series (Maryknoll, N.Y.: Orbis, 1989).

9. Clodovis Boff, *Theology and Praxis: Epistemological Foundations* (Maryknoll, N.Y.: Orbis, 1987).

10. Ernesto Cardenal, ed., *The Gospel in Solentiname,* 4 vols., trans. Donald D. Walsh (Maryknoll, N.Y.: Orbis, 1976–82, 1976, 1977, 1978).

11. Ibid., vol. 1, pp. 70–86.

12. Boff, *Theology and Praxis,* 145–46.

13. Ibid., 269.

14. A number of exegetes have engaged in a rereading of New Testament texts that is specifically political. See, for example, Fernando Belo, *A Materialist Reading of the Gospel of Mark* (Maryknoll, N.Y.: Orbis, 1981); Ched Myers, *Binding the Strong Man: A Political Reading of Mark's Story of Jesus* (Maryknoll, N.Y.: Orbis, 1988); Herman C. Waetjen, *A Reordering of Power: A Socio-Political Reading of Mark's Gospel* (Minneapolis: Fortress, 1989); Adela Yarbro Collins, "The Political Perspective of the Revelation to John," *JBL* 96 (1977) 241–56.

15. See Peter Burns, "The Problem of Socialism in Liberation Theology," *Theological Studies* 53 (1992) 493–516.

16. Pablo Richard, "La teología de la liberación en la nueva coyunctura. Temas y desafíos nuevos para la década de los noventa," *Pasos* 34 (March–April 1991) 2–8.

17. Burns, "The Problem of Socialism in Liberation Theology," 503.

18. Franz J. Hinkelanmert, "Crisis of Socialism and the North-South Fight," *Blueprint for Social Justice* 45 (December 1991) 2–7.

19. See Christopher Rowland and Mark Corner, "Liberation Theology in a First World Context," *Liberating Exegesis: The Challenge of Liberation Theology in Biblical Studies* (Louisville: Westminster/John Knox, 1989) 156–90.

20. Isasi-Díaz, "The Bible and *Mujerista* Theology," 265–67. Although Isasi-Díaz's remarks are directed to Hispanic women, I believe much of the same could apply to Hispanic men.

21. Gilbert Romero has made an important contribution with *Hispanic Devotional Piety: Tracing the Biblical Roots* (Maryknoll, N.Y.: Orbis, 1992). He studies the biblical analogues for four devotions: Ash Wednesday, the *Quinceañera*, the home altar, and the *Penitentes*, using methods of historical criticism, structuralism, reader-response criticism, and insights from cultural anthropology and language theory.

22. In the 1987 *National Pastoral Plan for Hispanic Ministry*, the U.S. bishops recognize the need to "invite centers of Bible studies and materials production to produce programs and materials to assist Hispanics in the use and understanding of the Bible" (no. 82).

23. See especially the work of Fernando F. Segovia.

24. One of Fernando Segovia's consistent comments in his recent review ("A New Manifest Destiny: The Emerging Theological Voice of Hispanic Americans," *Religious Studies Review* 17 [April 1991] 101–9) of six works of Hispanic theologians is the need for a more critical reading of the Scriptures.

25. Personal interview at Catholic Theological Union, Fall 1990.

26. See the definition by Ana María Pineda in chapter 9 of this volume.

27. Roberto Goizueta, "Presidential Address," *ACHTUS Newsletter* 2 (Winter 1990) 4–6.

28. See, for example, Ada María Isasi-Díaz, "A Hispanic Garden in a Foreign Land," *Inheriting Our Mothers' Gardens: Feminist Theology in Third World Perspective* (Louisville: Westminster, 1988) 100.

29. Justo L. González, *Mañana: Christian Theology from a Hispanic Perspective* (Nashville: Abingdon, 1990) 165.

30. Isasi-Díaz speaks of "relishing the struggle" that is life ("Hispanic Garden," 99).

31. Elsa Támez, *The Scandalous Message of James* (New York: Crossroad, 1990) 52–56.

32. Allan F. Deck, "Fundamentalism and the Hispanic Catholic," *America* 152 (1985) 64–66.

33. John Catoir, "Fundamentalists on the Move," *America* (September 17, 1986) 142–44.

34. Deck, "Fundamentalism," 65.

35. See Antonie Wessels, "The Scourged Christ," *Images of Jesus: How Jesus Is Perceived and Portrayed in Non-European Cultures* (Grand Rapids: Eerdmans, 1986) 57–80.

36. *ACHTUS Newsletter* 2 (Winter 1990) 2.

37. Constanza Montaña, "Passion Play Unites Pilsen," *Chicago Tribune* (March 26, 1991) sec. 1 pp. 1, 14.

38. One should not be left with the impression that evangelicals are not politically oriented. Many evangelical groups do combine faith and politics. But they do it in quite the opposite direction of liberation theologians. Evangelicals are

usually engaged in right-wing politics "to fight the communist devil." Hundreds of millions of dollars of fundamentalists go toward supporting the large U.S. nuclear defense budget, U.S. troops in El Salvador, the CIA's work with the *contras* in Nicaragua, and the like. See D. Nathan, "Indigence and Bliss: Can Pentecostal Hispanics Escape from Escapism?" *Neighborhood News, The Reader* 13/32 (May 11, 1984) 3, 44–45.

39. Piri Thomas ("The Pentecostals," *Prophets Denied Honor: An Anthology on the Hispanic Church in the United States,* ed. A. M. Stevens Arroyo [Maryknoll, N.Y.: Orbis, 1980] 151–52) gives a poetic description, which follows in part: "The most beautiful thing about the Pentecostals was their ability to pour themselves into the power of the Holy Spirit. They could blend—like nobody's business— into the words of the Holy Scriptures and do their best to uphold their conception of Christianity. It was a miracle how they could shut out the hot and cold running cockroaches and king-size rats and all the added horrors of decaying rotten tenement houses and garbage-littered streets, with drugs running through the veins of our ghetto kids. It was a miracle that they could endure the indignities poured upon our Barrios."

40. María Pilar Aquino, "Comentario al Plan Pastoral Nacional para el Ministerio Hispano," forthcoming in a collection of essays edited by Rosa María Icaza.

6

Exploring a Praxis-Oriented Methodology in Theological Formation

Gary Riebe-Estrella, S.V.D.

Introduction

This article proposes to explore a praxis-oriented methodology in theological formation. An introductory comment on five of the aspects of this stated purpose may be helpful. First, these reflections originate from a concern to prepare more adequately both Hispanics and non-Hispanics for pastoral ministry in the U.S. Hispanic Catholic community. To distinguish these two foci is to reject the temptation that culturally responsible theology is really only skill enhancement, that is, teach a couple of "how-to's" wrapped in folklore fiesta style and the question has been addressed. It may be interesting to note that the cultural perspective is not specifically mentioned in the title of this article at all. This fact mirrors a growing sense that problems in theological method and pedagogy, though occasioned by the pastoral needs of one or the other cultural group in the U.S. Catholic community, have carry-over applications to other cultural communities, minority and majority. The question to be addressed is not simply theology for minorities but the theological enterprise itself.

Second, this article is exploratory. Though in the past four or five years more theology from a U.S. Hispanic perspective is being written (e.g., by Allan Deck, Orlando Espín, Roberto Goizueta), this theological corpus remains relatively small. Also, most of these works have seen themselves as essays into a relatively unexplored field. The present article should be seen within this same context of exploratory theology.

Third, the first major section of the article focuses on methodology. Methodology is here understood as the systematic approach used by professional theologians in their work of understanding the faith of a community. The attempt here will not be to spell out exhaustively all the steps

89

of a theological method but to focus on those that appear most relevant for the cultural focus of this article.

Fourth, the methodology to be explored is called "praxis-oriented." This terminology would seem to imply that there is a theological methodology that is nonpraxical, an implication worthy of challenge! The clarity of the role of praxis in theology and the strictness of the definition of praxis *in se* are questionable; however, all theology is praxis based.

Finally, the purpose of this article is to explore methodology in theological formation. This setting implies the question of pedagogy, a matter substantially distinguishable from, though related to, methodology, since it focuses on the "how" of sharing with others the results achieved by the methodology employed by the professional theologian. Though I am not degreed in education, I will attempt some reflections on a pedagogical approach in theological formation in the second section of this article.

Methodology

Praxis and Theological Method

As mentioned above, the title of this article, "Exploring a Praxis-Oriented Methodology"[1] seems to imply that there exists some theological method that is apraxical, that has no relation to praxis. If, however, theology is "faith seeking understanding," and if faith is not to be understood as some disembodied mental act detached from life but rather as a conscious posture taken toward life and its meaning, both theology and faith contain in their own definitions the elements that make up praxis: action and reflection and their mutual interrelatedness.

Theoria, as often opposed to praxis, is defined by Thomas Groome as "the quest for truth by contemplative/reflective/nonengaged process."[2] However, any theology, no matter how contemplative or nonengaged, is a reflection back onto a faith rooted somewhere in the life experience, the action, of someone. Actually, to speak of praxis theology is not to posit a nonpraxical theology but to opt for action as the first moment in theological method and to acknowledge the social nature of both action (first moment) and reflection (second moment) in a theological method.[3] It is to choose an inductive approach in doing theology, rather than a deductive one, and to see the *materia prima* out of which the induction is performed as the faith life of a community or a people as they deal with the world in which they live.[4] This method for theologizing locates not only the style (inductive) and the source material (social, the engaged life of a community) but also demands the conscious locating of the theologian, since the reflection of theology is always done (1) out of action that is located in a concrete, historical situation of a community (2) by one whose way of understanding arises out of a concrete historical situation and its history. In other words, the theologian acts in service to the lived faith experience of a community, which community is always circumscribed by its historical reality. There is no theologizing on ("seeking to understand") an unincarnated ("pure") faith posture. In addition, no matter what the action that stirs the reflection, the reflector is always one who is rooted in a concrete faith-life situation (and history) whose parameters form, in a sense, the lens through which the reflector reads every situation.[5]

In dealing with one's own faith tradition, the tendency is to focus primarily on the parts (the particular text, ecclesial action, historical event) without seeing the whole (the system of thought and values), within which the parts are viewed and according to which they are analyzed and judged. Even the "sources," for example, Scripture, magisterium, liturgy, are read through this same lens (not to mention that they have their own historical location, which often remains unexamined).

In dealing with faith traditions not one's own, the temptation in theological methodology (as in most areas of human living) is to so focus on the different as to leave unexamined the lens used for focusing, for detailing the differences, that is, that mental schema running in the background that holds *my* experience, understanding, and judgment to be *the* set of criteria that identifies the different as different. The great problem caused by this lack of self-implication and self-location in doing theology across traditions' lines is that the *different* faith experience/reflection is always being judged in terms of a faith experience/reflection just as historically situated, and therefore limited, but that has become the touchstone of judgment primarily because it is mine/ours. A theological method that would take seriously the praxical basis of all theology would have to see one's own theological tradition as one among many (each responding to certain historical coordinates) and would have to move from seeing what is not mine/ours as *different* from seeing it as *other*. The *other* faith experience/reflection may look the same as mine, may have the same contours and interpretation, or it may be unlike mine; in either case it is still *other* because its source is a distinct historically situated faith experience/reflection.[6] It is not *different* as if an apriori value judgment could be made on it because it is not mine/ours, but it is *other* because its source is distinct, with no implication of its value being judged within the frame of reference of my/our faith experience/reflection.[7] In fact, one might say that the reality of the other within my world is a result of the other's initiative, not mine; that is, the other impinges on my world and the other's existence demands that I revitalize the totality I have imagined my world to be, whether that world be the world of my social class, my political ideology, my culture, or my theological method,[8] and in so doing, to acknowledge the other as other. The other calls me to respond. It may well be that one cannot discover the relativity and, therefore, the uniqueness of one's own theological world without the other. In this sense, the theological method we are exploring might be termed "culturally *responsible* theology," *responsible* to oneself as well as to the other.

Culture and Theological Method

Within the world of Catholic theology, moving from "differentness" to "otherness" has extraordinary implications for dealing with culturally distinct faith traditions within the Catholic communion.[9] If we understand "culture" in its most basic sense as the social expressions of the understanding a people have of themselves and of their world, to speak of culturally distinct faith traditions within the Catholic communion is precisely to speak of the reflections (systematic or otherwise) on the posture toward life and its meaning that are done in and by communities and that reflect those communities' understanding of their own peculiar historical situation.

Culturally distinct faith traditions are *other*, one from another; yet none can claim to be *the* tradition. The encounter of one tradition with another (for example, North Atlantic with Hispanic) must be seen as the juxtapositioning of two *others,* the recognition of a true theological polycentrism. In a genuine theological polycentrism there is not *a* theological center, with other theologies on the margin,[10] that is, *a* theology, with variations on a theme. There is no "one tradition" that takes form in different cultural settings in such a way that it can be unmasked in its *pure form* by removing the cultural constraints from the "one tradition" as one would remove the husk from a kernel.[11] However, does this not leave us with a certain relativism? Following the thought of Enrique Dussel, Goizueta would answer in the negative "if by that word [relativism] is meant, not that human beings are finite . . . , but that human beings are incapable of discovering truth. Truth is indeed absolute . . . *for everyone situated in a given horizon of comprehension.*"[12]

Rather, the encounter of culturally distinct faith traditions calls for a dialogue in which each cultural community is called upon to retrieve its own past and to "re-member" the journey that has given birth to its present faith expressions, be those in the form of popular religiosity, theological statements, narratives, songs, or some other.[13] In such a mutually respectful dialogue each community listens to the re-membering of the other and in that history sees those points that are held in common.

The identification of points held in common is not a variation on the theory of correlation: there are not some truth statements that can be gleaned from each community's history and that begin to form a "deposit which acts as the source of union in the faith of the communities."[14] Rather, the listening community resonates with the rhythms of the faith life of the other in such a way as to be able to say that had it lived through the same experiences, its faith would probably have taken a similar shape, focus, emphasis. There is a sense of seeing oneself reflected back, though in a new guise formed by a distinct constellation of historical circumstances.[15] Access to such unity of faith in the midst of otherness demands that each culturally distinct faith tradition analyze itself in mutual dialogue with other traditions (without such dialogue, the relativizing of one's own totality becomes a near impossibility) in terms of its history, folklore, sociopolitical-economic development, process of being evangelized, philosophical framework, and so on—all of which is to say, its "culture."[16]

For the discussion of theological method, a primary component of cultural analysis must be a cultures epistemological underpinnings (i.e., its foundational approach to the *viewing* of reality). Not only do these assumptions affect the form theology takes—narrative, wisdom, praxis, "sure knowledge"[17]—within a given culture but they also serve to determine the resonating images that form the starting point and the context for the development of the content of a cultural community's theology. For example, the image of Jesus as "personal savior" found at the heart of much U.S. evangelical theology flows easily out of the rank individualism of Western (read "North Atlantic") post-Enlightenment philosophical and psychological centeredness on the "I," or ego, versus the image of Jesus as "liberator," which in Latin American theology always contains a primary communitarian dimension. The tendency in North Atlantic theological circles would be to see these two images as complementary, that is, "liberator" is the social dimension of the "personal savior" (which latter image usually claims priority). In Latin American or U.S. Hispanic circles the communitarian "liberator" is not seen as complemented by another, equally valid image. Rather, the image of "liberator" is seen as primary and that of "personal savior" as secondary and derivative. The primacy of "liberator" even determines the means for the achievement of "personal salvation," that is, through a praxis that affects the destiny of the *community* and especially its poor.[18]

Obviously the place and shape of ecclesiology, ministry, sacraments, would also be significantly different in these two schemata.[19] And the origin of the difference is epistemological and anthropological, or "cultural." In this sense, the theological method we have been exploring might be termed *"culturally* respons*ible* theology," that is, one that is *able* to respond to a *culture* that is other. As well, the recognition of the location of the theologian and of the theologian's community (usually accomplishable only in mutual dialogue with the other) allows one's theology to be *culturally* respons*ible,* even within one's own cultural tradition.

Pedagogy

A culturally responsible theology demands a culturally responsible pedagogy. A theological method that envisions itself as communicating *the* tradition while allowing, without self-implication, for adaptations or variations for the accommodation of this tradition to various cultural groups, would easily employ a pedagogy centered on the transfer of clear and concise information in order to "in-form" students (who would generally be considered as consumers). This pedagogy is commonly referred to as the banking method.[20] A theological method that envisions itself as a mutual listening by culturally distinct faith traditions would employ a pedagogy of collaboration in order to "e-ducate" students (who would be seen as embodiments of those faith traditions being explored).[21] In both cases the pedagogy enacts the methodology, but in the second case the context is that of *sharing* the theological enterprise.

The Students

The role of students in a collaborative theological pedagogy is not "to receive," but to actively engage in a partnership one with the other and with the professional theologian. In a sense *most* of the work is theirs, since, as each is the embodiment (though always partial) of the faith tradition that has developed in his or her cultural group, it is they who hold the source of the theological reflection. As partial embodiments, even a group of students from a single cultural group have reason for partnership, since their mutual re-membering creates a fuller understanding of their common faith tradition. A mix of students who are culturally distinct one from the other directs partnership toward the discovery of self through identification of the other.

The quality of theology done by a group of students will depend on their knowledge of their own tradition, their ability to analyze or name its determining factors, their capacity for listening nondefensively to the other, their ability to sense the commonality among traditions and to re-member their own tradition after its conscious engagement with another tradition. However, the actualization and perfecting of these capacities depend in great measure on the educator.

The Educator

It is the attitude of the professional theologian as educator that determines the role students play in the learning setting. Is knowledge to be considered first and foremost as "power to dominate and control,"[22] or is teaching a way of leading people out to their future possibilities?[23] Though the pedagogy employed by a professional theologian is affected by that theologian's training, classroom experience as a student, and willingness to risk taking a different approach,[24] in reality the pedagogy adopted by a theologian depends in great measure on that individual's self-understanding as a theologian, which is itself embodied in the theological method used for his or her own research.

The use of a theological methodology that results in a culturally responsible theology such as the one explored above would seem to call for a self-understanding on the part of the theologian with at least these two characteristics: (1) self-implication/location and (2) openness to the other.

In a culturally responsible pedagogy, theologians not only acknowledge their location within a specific tradition with its attendant limitations but also locate themselves in relation to the community out of whose tradition they come: "The role of the whole community is often one of raising the questions, of providing the experience of having lived with those questions and struggled with different answers, and of recognizing which solutions are indeed genuine, authentic, and commensurate with their experience. The poet, the prophet, the teacher, those experienced with other communities may be among those who give leadership to the actual shaping into words of the response in faith."[25] As a result, the active connectedness of educator's with their communities is central for their ability to locate the theology they are doing.

The conscious acknowledgment of this twofold locatedness (i.e., *within* a specific tradition and *to* a specific cultural community) is achieved by the educator's openness to the other. Even if the students are of the same cultural faith tradition as the educating theologian, the necessity of recognizing the other in order to identify oneself would seem to call for the exploration of a faith datum *always* from at least two cultural perspectives. Theology done only within a single cultural perspective risks conceiving itself as universal and losing sight of the uniqueness it has because of its historical and cultural location. In those situations in which the students are of culturally distinct faith traditions (Hispanic, African–American, Asian) it is of even greater significance that the pedagogy be one of collaboration.

The Process

A collaborative pedagogy is essentially one of mutual dialogue. In considering any theological topic each participant is called upon to re-member the culturally distinct faith tradition out of which he or she comes. This re-membering demands an analysis of those factors (history, folklore, sociopolitical-economic development, process of being evangelized, philosophical framework) that have impacted the topic or theme under discussion.[26] The re-membering is shared and respectfully listened to by the others with the objective of each one's better re-membering his or her own tradition (or in the case of a single tradition, with the objective of each one's better re-membering his or her own partial embodiment of that tradition). In this first moment of dialogue, the precision of the educators own re-membering serves as a model for how to do the re-membering and for making more precise the results of the students' analyses. The second moment of dialogue is the attempt to sense the mutual resonance of the stories, that is, the basis of faith communion, and to enunciate the lines of mutual resonance. The third moment is that of sensing the resonance of each story and of these together, with the acknowledged sources of the faith communion (for the Catholic communion these would particularly be Scripture, the magisterium, including the *sensus fidelium,* and the Liturgy). In practice, this would seem to mean sitting in front of the biblical and magisterial texts, noting areas of resonance and dissonance (or agreement and challenge). In this third moment the professional theologian plays an extremely critical role as the expert in the sources of the communion of faith, both in terms of their content and of the skills needed to access them. The fourth moment of the dialogue is that of *mutually* exploring the reasons for the resonance and dissonance of each tradition (or partial embodiments of a single tradition) in terms of the sources of the faith communion and, finally, to articulate the conclusions reached and the questions yet to be answered.

These four moments of dialogue, however, would not exhaust a culturally responsible pedagogy. Founded as this pedagogy is on praxis, the reflection, which originally arose from action, must issue in new action in which the accuracy and veracity of the reflection is proven and new questions for reflection are born. In Catholic programs of theological formation, this third step would seem to be found most clearly in the ministerial activities of the students. Obviously, the actualization of this step demands a clear and close integration of academic and pastoral formation. In addition, it would also seem to indicate that academic theological formation must *always* be accompanied by ministerial involvement.

At this point the pedagogy repeats itself as the new ministerial action is submitted to the three-step process of re-membering, dialogue, and action.

Obviously, this type of collaborative pedagogy is far more time consuming in dealing with a specific theological theme than is the lecture method. The happenings in each classroom session are also far less under the control of the educator. This is due primarily to the difference of objective. While the lecture method is generally directed to the communication of information, this suggested collaborative pedagogy is directed to the communication of a method, that is, not teaching the student theology but teaching the student how to do theology. This difference of objective would seem to call for significant changes in the time allotted for each theological theme as well as in strategies for testing.

Conclusion

As in any attempt as ambitious as this article, some areas have received less attention than they might deserve, some may have been overemphasized, and others perhaps overlooked. Nevertheless, it is hoped that the general directions of this exploration are clear. A culturally responsible theological method demands an acknowledgment of the historical and cultural location of the theologian, the sources, and each culturally distinct faith tradition. The acknowledgment of location allows for the emergence of the different as other and the resulting relativization of each faith tradition. The emergence of the other calls for a respectful mutual dialogue among the traditions as each is re-membered and for a common search for the resonances that found a communion of faith. The pedagogy that flows out of such a culturally responsible theology is a collaborative one in which the educator and students are seen as partners in a process of re-membering, dialogue, and new ecclesial action.

Notes

1. The word "oriented" is not understood here as directional (meaning "leading to" praxis), but rather as relational, i.e., a methodology *related to* praxis.

2. Thomas H. Groome, *Christian Religious Education: Sharing Our Story and Vision* (San Francisco: Harper & Row, 1980) 153.

3. Mark Kline Taylor, *Remembering Esperanza: A Cultural-Political Theology for North American Praxis* (Maryknoll, N.Y.: Orbis, 1990) 19.

4. One can place further determinants on the word "praxis" to indicate the slant on experience or the direction of the reflection. For example, see Robert Schreiter's discussion of the transformative nature of praxis in his *Constructing Local Theologies* (Maryknoll, N.Y.: Orbis, 1985) 91. It is much more in this narrower sense that liberation theology would generally use the term.

5. For a thorough discussion of the role of self-location in the works of contemporary U.S. Hispanic theologians, see Arturo Bañuelas, "U.S. Hispanic Theology," *Missiology* 20:2 (April 1992) 275–300; also see Fernando F. Segovia, "A New Manifest Destiny," *Religious Studies Review* 17:2 (April 1991) 101–9.

6. And ultimately because the subject of this reflection/experience is ontologically distinct from and independent of me.

7. Robert Goizueta sees this distinction between "different" and "other" in this way: "The primary evil is the objectification of the Other (el otro) by denying his or her exteriority and making him or her into simply one more thing (lo otro) within my world." See his *Liberation, Method, and Dialogue: Enrique Dussel and North American Theological Discourse* (Atlanta, Ga.: Scholars Press, 1988) 72.

8. See Roberto Goizueta's discussion of "the Totality" in *Liberation, Method, and Dialogue,* 64.

9. There are also attendant implications for the question of ecumenism; however, those are not the subject of this article.

10. Robert S. Goizueta, "United States Hispanic Theology and the Challenge of Pluralism," *Frontiers of Hispanic Theology in the United States,* ed. Allan Figueroa Deck (Maryknoll, N.Y.: Orbis, 1992) 13–14.

11. Schreiter, *Constructing Local Theologies,* 7.

12. Goizueta, *Liberation, Method, and Dialogue*, 56.

13. Groome emphasizes that such "re-membering" cannot be just a calling to mind; rather, it demands first breaking apart the pieces of the community's past in order to reveal how their interconnectedness has produced the present. They are then reassembled or "re-membered." See Groome, *Christian Religious Education*, 186.

14. One can speak of "sources" within the Catholic communion, e.g., Scripture, magisterial statements, Liturgy, but these too must be re-membered from within their own unique historical situations. I will return to this subject briefly in the section on pedagogy.

15. It is little wonder that in the Catholic Church, the test of the communion among Churches is preserved primarily in the communion of persons (bishops) rather than in bare creedal statements. The dialogue among persons representative of Churches allows for the possibility of the identification of common rhythms, even though forms may be distinct. Taylor speaks of the same phenomenon when he talks of truth as "disclosure," as "an event laden with surprise." See Taylor, *Remembering Esperanza*, 54–55.

16. See Schreiter's exposé of semiotics as a method for reading a culture in his *Constructing Local Theologies*, 39–74.

17. Ibid., 80–92.

18. For a discussion of some of the epistemological differences in the underpinnings of North Atlantic and U.S. Hispanic theologies, see Goizueta's "United States Hispanic Theology and the Challenge of Pluralism," 17–18.

19. For example, in an individualistic economy, the Church as institution rises to the fore as the means to pull together and to relate otherwise disparate entities, while, in a communitarian culture, Church is seen foundationally in terms of its "people-ness." This, then, has implications for understanding ecclesial organization, authority, and law.

20. See Stephen Bevans, "Seeing Mission Through Images," *Missiology* 19:1 (January 1991) 48.

21. "E-ducate" is here used in its etymological sense of "to lead out" or "to draw out."

22. Matthew Lamb, "Distorted Theological Receptions of Latin American Theologies in the United States" (photocopy) 8.

23. Groome, *Christian Religious Education*, 137.

24. These are some of the reasons Katarina Schuth gives for the reticence of some theological faculty to depart from a more traditional pedagogy. See her discussion of this in *Reason for the Hope: The Futures of Roman Catholic Theologates* (Wilmington, Del.: Glazier, 1989) 186.

25. Schreiter, *Constructing Local Theologies*, 17.

26. See Groome's insightful analysis of this dialogical process, particularly his insistence that dialogue among participants presumes the participant's initial dialogue with himself or herself. *Christian Religious Education*, 189.

7

Basic Church Communities in the Mexican American and Mexican Community and Their Ecclesiological Significance

John E. Linnan, C.S.V.

Introduction

This study of basic Church communities is limited in its scope and in its purpose. It is based on a very limited experience of basic Church communities as they actually exist in the Diocese of Brownsville, Texas (January 10–17, 1991), and on a brief visit with the director of the Hispanic Pastoral Planning Office of the Archdiocese of Omaha, Nebraska, who is engaged in developing basic Church communities among Hispanics in that archdiocese (January 18–20, 1991).[1] The purpose of the study is to explore, at least in an initial way, the ecclesiological significance of the concrete reality of basic Church communities as they actually exist in the context of North American Catholicism.

There are four parts to this study. The first part is a brief overview of the regional contexts in which basic Church communities are developing. In the second part I will try to describe briefly how the basic Church communities in Brownsville define themselves and their life of faith and mission. The third part of this study will note by way of comparison some of the questions and problems that surround the development of basic Church communities in a northern urban center. In the fourth and final part of the study, I will try to address some ecclesiological issues raised by the existence of basic Church communities.

My hope is that this study will clarify for non-Hispanics, particularly those who have little or no contact with Hispanic Catholic life, what is distinctive in the development of basic Church communities among Hispanics in North America. Let me be quick to acknowledge, however, that I have only skimmed the surface of what is to be known and understood

99

about basic Church communities. The information I have acquired is limited; the conclusions I have reached are tentative. However, I believe that the Church in the United States has much to learn from the basic Church communities that are developing among our Hispanic brothers and sisters.

Contexts

The "Valley" and the Church of Brownsville

The Lower Rio Grande Valley, or the "Valley," describes the four-county (Starr, Hidalgo, Willacy, and Cameron) area of Texas lying just to the north of the Rio Grande (in Mexico, the Rio Bravo). It is bordered by the Gulf of Mexico to the east, the King Ranch (an 880,000 acre spread, approximately thirteen hundred square miles) to the north, and the Rio Grande itself to the south and west. The Valley was part of Mexico, as was all of Texas until 1836, when settlers from the United States created the Republic of Texas. From 1836 until 1845 the territory lying between the Nueces River to the north and the Rio Grande in the south was jointly claimed by Mexico and the new Republic of Texas without either being able to give real administrative or political effect to its claims. For a very short time (282 days) in 1840 this territory was constituted the independent Republic of the Rio Grande, with its capital at Laredo. Only the victory of the United States in its war against Mexico in 1848 made the region definitively part of the United States. The major cities in the area are Brownsville, Harlingen, and McAllen.

Today, as one might suspect from its history, the population of the region is predominantly (80 to 90 percent) Mexican American and Mexican. The rest of the population belongs to various other ethnic groups but without any significant number of African Americans. Unlike many regions in the United States, the population is young, with 39 percent (1988) under the age of seventeen. The major industry is agriculture: vegetables, citrus fruits, cotton. The soil is rich, the region being an alluvial plain irrigated by the Rio Grande. The growing season averages 360 days a year, allowing in most instances as many as three crops annually. The region also plays a major role in trade between the United States and Mexico. The Foreign Trade Zone in McAllen is the largest in tonnage and dollar volume in the United States, and the *maquilas* (U.S. manufacturing operations in Mexico) operating across the border in Mexico are responsible for significant employment and trading volume in both Mexico and the United States. A third major industry is retailing. The area is replete not only with specialty stores and shops but also with a multiplicity of large shopping malls, which seems excessive for the U.S. population (750,000) of the four-county area until one realizes that these also serve large metropolitan areas on the Mexican side of the Rio Grande: Reynosa (ca. 1,000,000), eight miles from McAllen; Matamoros (ca. 500,000), just opposite Brownsville; and Monterrey (ca. 3,000,000), a major industrial center in Mexico 150 miles southwest of McAllen. Finally, tourism is a major industry in the Valley. "Winter Texans," mostly retired persons from the northern regions of the Midwest, increase the population of the area from December to May by as many as 225,000. Trailer courts, RV parks, motels, and hotels are abundant throughout the area. South Padre Island on the Gulf shore is becoming a major resort for "upscale" Winter Texans, and during the spring break it has become a popular alternative to Florida for many collegians.

At first glance, the area, especially towns like McAllen, Harlingen, and Brownsville, seems to be a prosperous center of economic development. However, this prosperity affects most directly the English-speaking community and only a relatively small percentage of the Mexican American and Mexican communities. The political and economic power of the Mexican American and Mexican communities is far from being realized. Unemployment among Mexican Americans and Mexicans in the area runs between 17 and 35 percent, depending on the season. Large numbers of the Mexican American and Mexican population must go north to find seasonal employment as migrant workers. Nor is it surprising that a large percentage of this population lives in dire poverty in urban *barrios* and in scattered rural settlements, *colonias*, in the unincorporated areas between the cities and towns of the regions that cluster along U.S. Route 83, which is the transportation and economic lifeline of the Valley.

Except in the prosperous school districts of the area, the educational system is poor. The extremes in the levels of funding of Texas school districts has led the courts to require the state to reform its system in order to achieve a more equitable formula for financing education in the state. The Mexican American and Mexican communities in *barrios* and *colonias* are the most evident victims of this egregious inequity. They suffer severe disadvantage in education, which is aggravated by the fact that many children who must migrate with their parents four to six months a year miss at least a couple of months of school. Among the adult population of Mexican Americans and Mexicans, the language of life is Spanish, and among the very poor and the recent immigrants, entirely Spanish. Functional illiteracy in English in these communities is estimated variously between 56 and 80 percent. Thirty-six percent of the adult population has less than a fifth grade education. So many adults have had either no education or so little that it is a major accomplishment to write one's name and identify basic informational signs.

The Diocese of Brownsville is composed of the four counties that constitute the Lower Rio Grande Valley. The See city, Brownsville, the largest city in the area (133,000), is a border town on the banks of the Rio Grande just a few miles to the west of where the river enters the Gulf. The third bishop of Brownsville is Bishop John Fitzpatrick (1971). The diocese has sixty-three parishes and slightly more than that number of mission stations. Some parishes in rural areas and small towns have as many as four or five missions. There are about 170 priests in the diocese, about 70 of whom are members of religious communities. There are about 200 women religious in the diocese, a score of men religious who are not priests, and a large complement of married deacons, who are very active as leaders in the mission stations.

What is most significant for the purposes of this paper is that there are 417 basic Church communities, almost all of which are composed of Mexican Americans and Mexicans, most of whom live in urban *barrios* or in the *colonias* in unincorporated areas. About five hundred people are engaged as leaders of basic Church communities and as parish and diocesan coordinators. The vast majority are laypeople. The communities range in size from as few as eight to as many as thirty adults. The children, who are also members of the community, augment the size of each community considerably. A rough estimate suggests that between seven and eight hundred thousand adults are active in basic Church communities.

Significant also is the large role that women and laity play in the diocese at all levels. Most of the directors of major diocesan offices and programs are women, lay or religious. Several laymen also occupy important positions in diocesan administration, for example, as directors of social services and youth ministry. The chancellor is a woman religious, and the chief financial officer of the diocese is a laywoman. Several of the most innovative and most difficult of the many efforts at evangelization and development in the diocese are led by women, for example, basic Church communities, *Casa Romero,* the Arise literacy program. Many of the pastoral administrators of mission stations are women, either lay or, occasionally, religious.

The diocese is also the home of the Shrine of La Virgen de San Juan del Valle, a beautiful and extraordinarily impressive shrine that draws hundreds of thousands of pilgrims each year from Texas and Mexico. It is under the care of the Oblates of Mary Immaculate.

The City of Omaha and the Archdiocese of Omaha[2]

The Archdiocese of Omaha comprises twenty-three counties in northeast Nebraska. The total population of these counties is approximately 800,000, 26 percent of whom are Catholics, or slightly more than 200,000. The archdiocese has 157 parishes and missions. In recent years there has been a serious decline in the number of priests and women and men religious in the diocese but a significant increase in married deacons and lay pastoral agents.

Significant Mexican immigration to Nebraska and the Omaha area began in 1910, prompted by revolution in Mexico and the availability of work on the railroad in Nebraska. This immigration increased in the period from 1920 to 1933, when the need for seasonal farm labor (harvesting sugar beets) and workers in meat packing plants attracted many more Mexicans. In 1929 there were two thousand Mexicans in Omaha. However, the depression and forced emigration reduced this population to less than a thousand by 1930. The *bracero* program in the 1940s and 1950s once again drew thousands of Mexicans to Nebraska and Omaha, as did the meat-packing industry. Today the Hispanic population of the Omaha metropolitan area numbers close to twenty thousand, 90 percent of whom are Mexican Americans and Mexicans, many of whom are second and third generation Mexican Americans, and many of these are upwardly mobile, being represented in the professions and entrepreneurial segments of the population. The center of ministry to Hispanics in Omaha is the parish of Our Lady of Guadalupe, a nonterritorial parish for Hispanics founded in 1928 and, until 1987, staffed by Augustinian Recollects. In 1987 the archdiocese took full responsibility for ministry to Hispanics and commissioned the director of the Hispanic Pastoral Planning Office with the mandate to implement the *National Pastoral Plan for Hispanic Ministry*. In 1991 there were eight people engaged in full- or part-time ministry with Hispanics: two priests, three women religious, one permanent deacon, and three laypersons, all of whom are bilingual. Seven of these ministers work in Omaha.

There are clearly two distinct Hispanic communities in Omaha: (1) the more assimilated, upwardly mobile second- and third-generation Mexican Americans, many of whom cannot or simply do not speak Spanish; (2) the more recent immigrants, largely Mexican but also including people from other Latin American countries, many of whom come from rural areas, are poor, have little or no education, and lack sufficient English to obtain access to secure employment. The more assimilated Mexican Americans have acquired the values and lifestyles of the dominant culture and hesitate to be identified with a Hispanic Church community that is increasingly "foreign and poor." The more recent immigrants, whose religious values are centered on family and cultural traditions, find the American parish-centered Catholicism cold and unwelcoming. They are beset by language, social, cultural, and economic problems, and they are also the target of aggressive proselytizing by charismatic and Pentecostal Churches.

Further complicating the issue of ministry to Hispanics is that the one nonterritorial parish, Our Lady of Guadalupe, no longer represents an adequate structural approach to this ministry. The Hispanic community is no longer exclusively located in the area of South Omaha where the parish is but is now scattered throughout the city in areas reflecting the socioeconomic level of the assimilated Mexican American families.

One positive element (among many others) in addressing the particular problems in the ministry to the Hispanic community in Omaha, and throughout the archdiocese, is the effort undertaken in collaboration with the Office of Small Christian Communities to establish Hispanic small Christian communities. Significant steps have already been taken in this direction by Our Lady of Guadalupe parish.

Comunidades Eclesiales de Base in the Church of Brownsville

Some Terminological Issues

The issue of how to understand and, consequently, how to translate the expression *comunidades Eclesiales de base* is not without theological significance. It has been variously rendered as "small Christian communities," "base communities of faith," "grass-roots Christian communities," and "basic Church communities."[3] The issue is significant because of the insistence of Boff and others that the *comunidad Eclesial de base* is not a club, an association, a movement, a program, or a subdivision of a parish but a new way of being Church, *una manera nueva de ser Iglesia.* Time and time again, I heard at meetings with groups and individuals the expression *Somos Iglesia,* "We are Church." Nevertheless, there seems to be some ambiguity about how the *comunidad Eclesial de base* should be understood, especially among non-Hispanic Americans. They tend to see it as a means to revitalize or to renew parishes and parochial structures, basically, a program to continue and make permanent various parish renewal programs such as Christ Renews His Parish and RENEW. However, this does not seem to be the understanding current in Latin America and among the Mexican and Mexican American communities I visited. Consequently, I shall try to use consistently the translation, "basic Church communities."

Definition and Description

The basic Church communities in the Diocese of Brownsville define themselves in terms of who their members are, the relationship existing among them, their life of faith and service, their mission as disciples of the Lord, and the characteristics of their common life together. In their description of who and what they are, the basic Church communities place great emphasis on the fact that they are a "community," they are "Church," and they are "basic": foundational, a Church of the *barrio,* a grass-roots Church, a Church of the people.

A basic Church community is a group of Christians who form relationships of friendship, brotherhood and sisterhood, and who are at the service of the neighborhood; who reflect on their daily life in the light of the gospel; and who celebrate their existence in the Eucharist and the sacraments of the Church. It is a community that seeks to recognize and know the Lord in order to establish his rule among men and women who commit themselves to transform the world. It is a community that is a new expression of the Church's preferential love for the poor. It is a new way to be Church.[4]

As "community," it is characterized by a small, mixed membership, global awareness, permanence, participation of all its members, shared leadership, the use of the gifts and talents of its members for the common good, and openness to others.[5]

As "Church," the basic Church community takes up the same mission that Jesus left to his Church: to be prophet by announcing the good news and denouncing injustice; to be priest by celebrating the word, the life, and the brotherhood of Jesus; to be king by serving the community; to be a Church that is a liberating ferment in order to change the world in which we live so that all may be sons and daughters worthy of God.[6]

As "basic," it is the Church in the *barrio* (neighborhood) because the people in the *barrio* are the Church; it is in the *barrio*, where life is lived by families; it is where people recognize one another as friends and know the joys, sorrows, celebrations, and needs of one another; it is the family, the domestic Church, committed to improve the community of the *barrio*.[7]

What is necessary for a basic Church community? Faith in Jesus, communication of that faith, sacraments, mission, ministry of unity, living in community, celebration of faith, prayer, relationship with other levels of the Church.[8]

Community Meetings

A basic Church community is composed of as many members as can establish among themselves real relationships of friendship, brotherhood, and sisterhood. It is usually small, between twenty and thirty-five adults together with their children. The community meets once a week, usually in the evening, for about two hours. The format of the meetings is simple but carefully structured. Central to the structure of the community meeting are the traditional principles derived from Catholic Action movements: "observe, judge, act."

The meeting begins with the *bienvenida*; the welcoming of each member individually as he or she arrives is an essential part of the meeting. Once gathered, the community opens the meeting with *cantos*, a song (or two). After song comes the *oración*, a prayer seeking the presence and guidance of the Holy Spirit.

A period of time is then set aside for the *noticias,* during which each member briefly recounts the news: familial, local, and national events of the past week as these affect their lives.

Ver (observe) then follows. It is a careful consideration of an event or a situation in the reality of daily life, usually presented in the form of a story. After the story a period of silence and reflection is provided, followed by discussion of the questions raised by the story.

Juzgar/Pensar (decide/think) consists of a reading from the Scriptures, usually drawn from the assigned readings for the following Sunday. This, too, is followed by a period of silence and reflection. There follows a community sharing of the Scripture reading in terms of the questions raised by the reading and its bearing on events or situations in the reality of daily life.

Actuar (act) is the community's response to what it has observed in the reality of daily life as understood in the light of the gospel. It always requires a commitment on the part of the community to a concrete action to be undertaken in the light of the gospel.

After the community has made its commitment to act in a specific way, time is set aside for the *memoria,* a brief moment in which a designated member of the community makes a resumé of the discussion and decisions taken by the community. These are later recorded in the minutes.

There follows the *oración,* an extended period of prayer shared by the community, which is concluded by a closing prayer and the Our Father. The meeting closes with another *canto,* and *conviviencia,* a sharing of a little food and drink.

This structure is simple and seems to be uniform in all the basic Church communities in the diocese. Once a month every basic Church community leader receives from the parish or area coordinator of basic Church communities a one-page program for each of the meetings to be held the following month. The program contains (1) a story to be read recounting an event or situation from the reality of daily life, called "A Reading from the Book of Life"; (2) the book, chapter, and verses of Scripture to be read; and (3) questions and ideas to be used to stimulate reflection and discussion of both readings. The program is meant only to be a help to the community. When an event or situation in the life of the community itself is of great importance, the community is urged to make that the "Reading from the Book of Life." In fact, the communities are encouraged to develop their own program for each meeting, using material from their own life experience.

Ministries

Each community has a number of designated ministers who function for agreed-upon periods of time. Service in the ministries is rotated to encourage the community to be a community of ministers. Each ministry is carefully defined not only in terms of its function but also in relation to the other ministries. While there is a leader of the basic Church community, the leader is essentially a coordinator of ministries. He or she does not do everything. Leadership in the basic Church communities is shared leadership.

The *anfitrión* is the minister of welcome, who welcomes each member of the community when he or she arrives for the meeting, regardless of whether the meeting is being held in the home of the *anfitrión* or not. The *coordinador/facilitador/lider* is the leader of the community, who may be compared to a conductor of an orchestra, whose task is to make sure that everyone's gift is used.

The *lider de oración* is the leader of prayer, who makes the opening and concluding prayer, and the *lider de música* is the leader of song. The *secretaria* is in charge of making the resumé, or *memoria,* at each meeting and of keeping a brief record of the meeting. In addition, there is the *animador,* who has the responsibility of calling the community to account for its failures. The *practica* is in charge of leading the community in its discussion of the questions posed by real life and the Scripture reading, taking responsibility for keeping everyone on the subject and, if necessary, cutting off those who monopolize the discussion. The *noticias-reportero* is the person responsible for making sure that in the *noticias* there is a sense of what is going on in the wider world, giving the community a global perspective. Finally, there is the *campañero/cronometrista,* the person charged with making sure that the community completes its meeting on time. Communities are free to establish other internal ministries as needed. The governing principle is that leadership is shared in the community.

There are also external ministers. These are persons designated by the community to serve the wider community in ways that are defined by the community.

The Ministry of Unity Within the Diocesan Network

Central to the organization of the basic Church communities in Brownsville is unity. Fundamentally, the ministry of the leader of the community *(coordinador)* is to facilitate the unity of the basic Church community as well as the unity of his or her community with the other basic Church communities in the parish or area. In addition to the leaders of basic Church communities, there is also a coordinator for all the basic Church communities in the parish or area. Once each month all basic Church community leaders meet with the parish coordinator for formation, encouragement, dealing with problems, and instructions for the meetings of the following month. On the fourth Saturday of each month all the parish coordinators meet with the diocesan coordinator to receive the suggested program for each of the following month's meetings. Each coordinator is encouraged to bring, in rotation, one or several of the leaders of the basic Church communities within the parish or area so that gradually all local community leaders will become acquainted with other community leaders, parish coordinators, and the diocesan coordinator. Once a year there is an *encuentro* of all community leaders and parish coordinators with the diocesan coordinator and the bishop.

In a sense this organization parallels the parish/diocesan organization and also enables basic Church communities to exist in relationship to the diocese, even in those parishes where the pastor is either uninterested in, or as is sometimes the case, opposed to, basic Church communities.

Social Action

What is most impressive about the basic Church communities I visited is their commitment to mission, to transforming the world in which they live, their own neighborhoods. The basic Church communities have committed themselves to improving their *barrios* and *colonias*. I heard many stories to confirm this level of commitment. Major initiatives include voter registration drives; forcing the county to install sewers and pave roads (most of the *colonias* are located on flood plains, and in heavy rains flooding makes it impossible for children to get to the school buses); air conditioning of local public schools; organized demonstrations at the state capitol to demand equitable funding of public schools; closing troublesome bars. In addition, there are less dramatic but equally important projects that have been developed: assisting the elderly and new mothers, providing child care, promoting education, visiting the sick, evangelizing the neighborhood, visiting newcomers, inviting others to become members of the basic Church community, and the like.

Sacramental Life

Though the basic Church community is in theory the locale of the sacramental life of the community, in fact, at least to the degree I was able to observe, such is not the case in the Diocese of Brownsville. Sacramental life is still the prerogative of the parish. It is in the parish (or the mission) that baptism, Eucharist, marriage, and reconciliation take place. This disjunction seems to threaten a separation of "real" Church life, which takes place in the community, from "sacramental celebration" of that life, which takes place only in the parish church or mission. The effect of this dichotomy is yet to be seen clearly, but it is worth serious theological reflection.

Formation

It is impossible to overestimate the role of formation of leaders and communities in the development of basic Church communities. The basic church communities are the products of years of diocesan-wide formation efforts: Christian Family Movement, charismatic prayer groups, lay ministry training programs, Cursillos, adult religious education programs, RCIA, and so on. But one of the characteristics of formation of leaders and other ministers of basic Church communities is the close and staged association of formation with "on-the-job training." Continuing formation at all levels is a key to the successful development and growth of leaders and to the effective implementation of the principle of shared leadership.

Conclusion: An Assessment

I was deeply impressed by every community I visited and by the leaders and coordinators with whom I spoke. The level of dedication is almost overwhelming. In fact, a major problem in the communities is the excessively high expectations that community leaders have of themselves and of their communities, which can lead to discouragement. These communities are Church, and trying to become Church, much as all of us are. The meetings are warm, friendly, confusing, with children from teenagers to toddlers and sleeping babies. The education of most of the members of the communities is very limited. Some can barely read. Yet the reflections of the members are profound and grounded in the reality of their lives. Some of the members are exegetes in the narrative tradition. Their prayers are simple yet all embracing. They express their fears and hopes, their needs and ideals, and their concerns for the Church and the world outside their immediate experience. Most of the *coordinadores*, leaders of basic Church communities, are women. This led me to reflect on the role of women in this "new way to be Church." My conclusion is that women are simply better at leading in a community where personal relationships are central. As one parish coordinator said, "The best formation for a basic Church community leader is being a mother of a family." What I also found striking is the degree to which basic Church communities empower their members and the community itself. In the community the members come to be, they exist, they can act, they become real people, *las hijas y los hijos dignos de Dios.*

Comunidades Eclesiales de Base in the Urban North

The conception of Church in the dominant culture of Catholic Americans is centered on the parish. Consequently, basic Church communities tend to become not a "new way to be Church" but more like a program to establish small or grass-roots Christian communities as parochial sub-structures designed to draw people into the life of the parish and to revitalize participation in the parish. In this vision, the basic Church communities are either a *praeparatio evangelica*, the narthex of the church, leading into the nave and toward the sanctuary, or an extension of the parish into the realm of everyday life. In either case, the real life of the Church is still located in the parish. The parish is the fundamental structure of Church. To be Church is to be part of a parish.[9]

There also seems to be a tendency in some approaches to small Christian communities to neglect *actuar:* commitment to action as a community to transform the world. Action for social justice does not seem to be the priority. Instead, the emphasis seems to be on deepening the faith of the members from a psychological point of view. There seems to be more emphasis on self-affirmation, self-actualization, community formation, bonding among members. In fact, in order to promote bonding, there is a tendency to close the community, to make boundaries clearer and more forbidding to outsiders.

The Archdiocese of Omaha has embarked on a very different approach to the development of small Christian communities. It is encouraging the restructuring of parishes into what it calls "small Church communities."[10] The goal of this restructuring is not simply to establish small basic Christian communities as a program available for interested people in the parish but to establish small Church communities as essential structures of Church life. In this sense, the small Church communities, as envisaged in the Archdiocese of Omaha, would be very similar to the basic Church communities that exist in the Diocese of Brownsville. They would constitute a new way of being Church, yet within the framework of a parish, whose primary function would become the facilitation, support, and encouragement of the small Church communities. The parish and its staff would become the facilitators and coordinators of the small Church communities. These would become the real centers of Christian and ecclesial life. Furthermore, the program to restructure parishes into small Church communities is intended not only for the parishes composed primarily of ethnic minorities but also for parishes composed of Catholics whose members belong to the dominant culture, and in both urban and rural areas.

The restructuring of parishes into small basic Christian communities in Omaha is still in its initial phase. Whether it will succeed is still uncertain. The contrast between a parish restructured into small Church communities and the typical parish Church structure may be disconcerting to many Catholics. It will raise the question of what level of community is needed for a people to be Church. It will also lead some to question to what degree the parish structure has been deformed by the individualistic, self-centered traits of the dominant culture. It seems clear that small base Christian communities, if they are to be more than programs to revitalize the parish, will challenge not only the very nature of the parish but also the character of the Christian life it supports. Small base Christian communities redefine what a parish is and what corporate Catholic life is meant to be.

Even among Hispanic Americans in Omaha the concept of small base Christian communities will not necessarily be attractive. Many upwardly mobile, assimilated Hispanic Americans are profoundly shaped by the dominant culture. Many have lost the language and retain only certain aspects of their culture of origin (e.g., special feasts, cuisine) and a vague solidarity with fellow Hispanics. They are more individualistic and less committed to family and community values as these are traditionally expressed in the Hispanic community. The more assimilated Hispanic Americans are involved socially in many communities from which they derive resources for their personal, family, and professional lives. A Church community is just one among many communities in which they participate. They find the relative anonymity of the parish, with its minimal demands on them personally, more congenial. These Hispanic Americans may find it very difficult to form the kind of face-to-face community characteristic of the small base Christian communities.

Among the poor and the recently arrived Hispanic immigrants, however, the small base Christian community will probably be more attractive and respond better to their need for empowerment. Also, their alienation from the parish structure leaves them in a situation in which they are more ready to accept a "new way to be Church." They may find it easier to say, *"Nosotros, la gente, somos Iglesia."* Those who are engaged in ministry with Hispanic Americans and in developing small base Christian communities in Omaha seem to be well aware of the issues involved in seeking this new way to be Church.

Some Reflections on Ecclesiological Issues

As an outsider who observed the life and activity of basic Church communities in the Mexican and Mexican American community of Brownsville, albeit only briefly, I was struck by significant differences between the ecclesial life of these communities and the ecclesial life of the parishes in which I have participated as a member of the dominant Catholic culture of the United States. On reflection, I found I was able to define for myself what distinguishes the basic Church communities I visited from the parishes I have known in terms of six characteristics, which I am inclined to consider as fundamental: (1) their conception of leadership, (2) their sense of mission, (3) their face-to-face character, (4) the poverty of their members, (5) the role of women in the community, and (6) their sense of being Church in a new way. Perhaps it is appropriate at this point to consider what theological significance, if any, these fundamental differences may have for the future of the Church in the United States.

Leadership

Leadership in basic Church communities must have two fundamental characteristics: (1) it must be leadership within the community, not from above or outside it, and (2) it must be leadership effectively shared by a multiplicity of persons, each functioning as leader in terms of his or her own talent for a specific kind of leadership. The essence of the basic Church community as a form of ecclesial life is that it emerges from the community in which it lives and develops by discovering and energizing the talents and abilities latent in the members of the community itself. The basic Church community may need the services of external agents to call it into existence and to help it discover its own capacities, but it is from the community itself that its leaders must emerge. It is also the basic Church community that must be the principal, though not necessarily the sole, agent in authenticating its own leaders. It is only the community's constant and ongoing authentication that gives its leaders the authority attached to the particular leadership task. Accountability is informal but constant and is achieved in the face-to-face contact of leaders and their communities. The shepherd knows the sheep, and the sheep know the shepherd. The basic Church community can never allow external agents with their abilities and resources to substitute for the members themselves. External agents and resource people need to be very attentive to the danger of inadvertently replacing the community and its leaders. Tutelage destroys the energy and creativity of the community. It undermines the community's already fragile sense of self-worth, which is always threatened by the constant pressure from the dominant culture and by the oppressive social situation in which the community exists.

Not only must leadership be indigenous to the community, it also must be effectively shared within the community. There is no room for the paramount leader. The fact that leadership tasks are defined and effectively parceled out among the members tends both to increase participation and to establish barriers to the tyranny of a sole leader and its milder forms—egotism, manipulation, and the "dictatorship of the expert." However, for leadership to be shared effectively, the community must carefully define the tasks of leadership the community needs. These tasks must also be defined in terms of the real needs of the community. Functions that have no realistic relationship to actually experienced needs create leaders who must constantly scramble to acquire "turf."

It is evident that these ways of understanding leadership do not accord well with the contemporary *praxis Ecclesiae*. In today's Church and for most of its history, leadership of ecclesial communities has been restricted to those who are ordained, and ordination has been the prerogative of other ordained leaders. The leader of an ecclesial community (a parish or a diocese) is appointed by higher authority. Further, only men who promise to live celibate lives are eligible for ordination as Church leaders. It follows, then, that an ordained leader of an ecclesial community is not ordained to shared leadership but is rather seen as the paramount leader, the one responsible for ultimate decision making. Allowance may be made for consultation and even participation, but this is always a participation in the role of the leader, who retains the fullness of leadership in the community. The notion of a leader emerging from the ecclesial community and being authenticated by it is foreign to current ecclesial practice. Yet is such a conception theologically inadmissible? It seems not entirely. In his consideration of the decline in the number of clergy, the need to maintain the vitality of local Churches, and the frequent discrepancy between ordained and charismatic leaders, which often leads to a certain implausibility in leadership, Hervé Legrand suggests a way of resolving these problems, which he considers both possible and desirable:

> This would be to give to the local Church (bishops, priests, and faithful) an effective role in the choice and reception of its ministers, ordained as well as non-ordained, and especially in the determination of their status, not in a way that is self-sufficient, but in communion with the entire Church, and in accord with the needs of the service of the Gospel. It is very probable, in this way, that on the one hand, "charismatic" personalities would be called to the ministry, and on the other hand, differences of status between ordained ministers and the ordinary faithful would be re-introduced. But this double difference, in charism and status, would in these circumstances be plausible, both for the Church and for those involved in ministry.[11]

Legrand also argues convincingly that the very nature of the Church requires that ordination to leadership in the Church, a Church that is essentially a Church of ministers, be of necessity ordination to shared ministry within which are diversified responsibilities.[12] It also seems that even the notion of collegiality as applied at the level of the leadership of both the universal and the diocesan Church calls for a measure of participation in leadership without, however, evacuating what is specific to the role of pope in the universal Church or to the role of bishop in the diocesan Church.[13]

From a theological perspective, it does not seem that conceptions of leadership in basic Church communities are totally incompatible with the fundamental theology of ministry in the Church, even if, in many instances, they run contrary to the Church's current discipline. In many ways the conception of leadership found in basic Church communities echoes conceptions of ministry found in the early Church. However, there are difficulties. Leadership roles, even that of the principal leader, the *coordinador*, are considered temporary in basic Church communities, whereas ordination to ministry in the Church is considered permanent. Likewise, the Church excludes women from any ordained ministry, whereas the majority of basic Church community leaders are women. Finally, the exclusively lay character of the leadership of basic Church communities, necessary though it be in the current situation, may in the long run weaken the nexus between leadership in the Church and the person of Christ, who is *the* Minister and Pastor of his Church, a nexus that is established in the sacrament of ordination and that makes the community's leader a sign and instrument of Christ's own leadership.

Mission

Mission to the world, to the immediate world of its own neighborhood, is a necessary constitutive element in the basic Church community. A community that does not act, that does not achieve perceptible change for the better, no matter how small, will not endure. A basic Church community must be effective. It is not intended to be a shelter, a self-protective support group. Its reading of the gospel demands justice and liberation, and these not just for the individual but for the group and for society as a whole. In achieving justice for itself, the basic Church community believes it is achieving a society that is more just for all its constituents. A better life for me, for my family, for my children, must also mean a better life for everyone, for all families, for all children; otherwise, my justice becomes just another name for the oppression of others.

From my particular point of view this is the power of Christian weakness, something that perhaps only oppressed people can feel intensely. It is also something not infrequently lacking in traditional parish communities: a conception of Church that seeks to implement the perspectives of the gospel, which find expression in the Second Vatican Council's Pastoral Constitution on the Church in the Modern World, *Gaudium et spes*, and which is summarized in the final number of that document:

> Christians can yearn for nothing more ardently than to serve the men of this age with an ever growing generosity and success. Holding loyally to the Gospel, enriched by its resources, and joining forces with all who love and practice justice, they have shouldered a weighty task here on earth and they must render an account of it to him who will judge all men on the last day. Not everyone who says "Lord, Lord," will enter the kingdom of heaven, but those who do the will of the Father, and who

manfully put their hands to the work. It is the Father's will that we should recognize Christ our brother in the persons of all men and love them with an effective love, in word and in deed, thus bearing witness to the truth; and it is his will that we should share with others the mystery of his heavenly love.[14]

Basic Church communities give corporate, ecclesial expression to this mission, which belongs to every Christian.

A Face-to-Face Community

I am convinced that the face-to-face character of the basic Church community is essential to its vitality and its success. The community must be relatively small to allow, indeed, to compel, engagement and participation of all its members in all aspects of the community's existence. It is the active participation and engagement of every member of the community in accord with his or her talents and abilities that is ultimately its strength, the major resource of the community. A basic Church community cannot for long carry freeloaders, that is, passive or inactive members. It is made up of men and women who individually are weak and powerless in the face of a society deemed by them as hostile and oppressive. Only by the full participation of every member of the group, by loving the abilities and talents each has, can the group become strong and effective in the development of the community's life of faith and service.

This form of ecclesial life challenges in a direct way the more individualistic, voluntary approach to modern American parochial life. The average American Catholic parish serves about twenty-three hundred people.[15] The tendency of parishioners is to evaluate the parish in terms of their needs and those of their families, but more frequently than not, they define their needs in individualistic and not communal terms.[16]

Yet as one of those American Catholics very much shaped by the individualism of the dominant culture, I wonder if such intense face-to-face community can be realized by men and women who live their lives at work and at home under intense pressure and stress from the manifold expectations that our society presses upon them. The anonymity of the large parish is at once solace and escape for many of us. It allows for participation but also enables us to limit the degree of our participation. The basic Church community challenges not only our way of living ecclesial life but also the priorities we have established, the often hectic pace at which we live, and the nature of the society that seems to demand so much of our time and energy. If only as a challenge to our conception of life, society, and Church, we very much need the basic Church community.

Poverty

Nothing is so obvious about the basic Church communities I visited as the material poverty of their members. They had little. They lacked much that most Americans take for granted. They were disadvantaged and oppressed, exploited by the society in which they lived. Their basic Church community *is* the Church of the Poor. They see in their life as Christian community not just the Church's preferential option for the poor but, especially, Christ's preferential option for the poor, the suffering, the oppressed. It seems to me that it is their poverty that opens them to the presence of God in their lives, to the reality of Christ as their savior and liberator, and to the reality of the Spirit who guides them in their life of prayer and in their prophetic work for justice. It is their shared poverty that enables them to see one another as brothers and sisters. It is the poverty, oppression, and exploitation from which they suffer that enables them to hear the gospel as truly good news.

Reflection on the role of poverty in the lives of the men and women of basic Church communities leads me to ask whether any group of people can ever be Church unless they recognize their own poverty, regardless of the social or economic level they occupy, and their responsibility as brothers and sisters to others who are poor and afflicted, regardless of the nature of the poverty and the affliction from which they suffer. Material poverty, suffering, oppression, and exploitation can never be "good" things, but perhaps they are the sacraments of the more profound poverty of self-sufficiency and human egoism from which the comfortable and self-satisfied suffer, often unaware of their affliction. The existence of basic Church communities among the poor and disadvantaged segments of our society are forceful prophetic proclamations that to be Church is to be a community of the poor and for the poor.

Women

The role of women in the basic Church communities, particularly in the disadvantaged Hispanic community, deserves attention. The majority of those occupying leadership roles in the communities I observed were women. The insight, intelligence, and outstanding human qualities of the women who were leading basic Church communities and serving as parish, regional, and diocesan coordinators were simply outstanding.

As an outsider, I had a feeling that there is something to the idea expressed by a number of people I talked with, who said that women have a special talent for community leadership. "Being a mother is the best training for leadership," said one regional coordinator. It may be that there are social and cultural factors at work here: (1) the special role of women in a family-oriented culture; (2) the role of women as the protector and transmitter of familial and, therefore, communal values; (3) the need for men to work, often at several jobs, when and where they can be found; (4) the social, political, economic, and educational barriers that restrict immigrant women in the exercise of their abilities and talents to the home, the family, the neighborhood; (5) the capacity of women to network more effectively than men, precisely because men must function in a more competitive arena in order to secure a minimum of financial security for their families; (6) the role of *machismo* in the culture; and (7) the impact of a hostile and dominant culture, most directly experienced by immigrant men in their struggle to wring a livelihood from an unfriendly workplace, where they are seen as interlopers, newcomers, a new threat to the job security of other workers, which may rob them of the self-esteem and the energy needed to demonstrate their leadership abilities.

I hesitate to make any firm judgments in this area because of my limited experience of the communities I visited. Nevertheless, it is clear that women represent a very important resource in developing and leading basic Church communities. Further, a Church without the full participation of women in its life and leadership becomes increasingly unthinkable in the light of my experience of basic Church communities.

The question of admission of women into full participation in the Church's leadership is a question that cannot be ignored. The negative response of the Congregation of the Doctrine of Faith, *Inter insigniores* (1975), to this question only initiated the serious reflection and discussion that continues today, almost twenty years later. As Hervé Legrand has pointed out, the question of whether or not women can be ordained is not a narrow question concerned only with the theology of ministry. It is more profoundly a question of the consistency of the hermeneutical principles by which we understand the person of Jesus Christ, the meaning of human creation, the nature of tradition, the significance of the rootedness of the Church in history, and the capacity of a woman to represent as a believer the fullness of the faith and communion of the Church.[17] A hermeneutic dominated by androcentrism has thus far characterized official Church consideration of the question of the ordination of women. Can the consistent use of such a hermeneutic adequately respond to these other questions?

Yet at the same time, the role of women can be a two-edged sword in the basic Church communities I have observed. For no matter how valuable the leadership of women in these communities, it remains very important to secure the participation of men in the community and its activities. This is clearly recognized by the women who lead communities. They are quick to point out that it is to their advantage and to the advantage of the family unit that men are engaged actively in the life and the leadership of the basic Church community. At the same time, men need to recognize the special talents that women bring to the vitality of family and community life. It is an extraordinarily delicate enterprise, made more difficult by the sexual stereotypes that afflict contemporary society.

A New Way of Being Church

A constant refrain in the description of basic Church communities is that they are "a new way of being Church." It was a phrase I heard in every basic Church comunity I visited. Basic Church communities are profoundly convinced that they are Church, that they have all the elements that entitle them to be called Church. But even to a casual observer it is clear that they lack two of the basic elements considered essential for ecclesial life. They have no ordained ministers leading the community; their leaders are lay. They have no sacramental celebrations; members of basic Church communities must go to the parish church for Eucharist, baptism, marriage, and reconciliation.

Are basic Church communities really "a new way of being Church"? Or are they only a part of a Church? A program? A group within the parish or within the diocese? This is not simply a canonical question, nor is it a theological quibble. To be Church in a particular place means that the wholeness of what it means to be the Church of Christ is present in this community, even though it is not the whole Church of Christ.

Even after Vatican II it is notoriously difficult to define what is or is not a particular Church. Canon 368 of the Code of Canon Law (1983) defines the diocese as a particular Church, as does *Christus Dominus*, no. 11, the Decree on the Pastoral Office of Bishops in the Church. However, these definitions are definitions of a diocese and not definitions of a particular Church. In *Orientalium Ecclesiarum*, the Decree on the Catholic Eastern Churches, individual autonomous ritual Churches composed of numerous dioceses are considered particular Churches. In *Ad gentes*, the Decree on the Church's Missionary Activity, the term "particular Church" describes all the Churches in a given sociocultural context. Only in *Lumen gentium* does the Second Vatican Council come close to defining in theological terms what it means by a "particular Church," that is, a community that in its particularity gives expression to the wholeness of what it means to be the Church of Christ:

> This Church of Christ is really present in all legitimately organized local groups of the faithful, which, in so far as they are united to their pastors, are also quite appropriately called Churches in the New Testament. For these are in fact, in their own localities, the new people called by God, in the power of the Holy Spirit and as the result of full conviction (cf. 1 Thess 1:5). In them the faithful are gathered together through the preaching of the Gospel of Christ, and the mystery of the Lord's Supper

is celebrated "so that, by means of the flesh and blood of the Lord the whole brotherhood of the Body may be welded together." In each altar community, under the sacred ministry of the bishop, a manifest symbol is to be seen of that charity and "unity of the mystical body, without which there can be no salvation." In these communities, though they may often be small and poor, or existing in the diaspora, Christ is present through whose power and influence the One, Holy, Catholic and Apostolic Church is constituted. For "the sharing in the body and blood of Christ has no other effect than to accomplish our transformation into that which we receive."[18]

It is fairly obvious that this definition of the particular Church is broad enough to include a patriarchate, an ethnic Church composed of many dioceses, the Church of a given culture, a diocese, a parish, and even smaller and less-visible groups of the faithful. What constitutes a particular Church is that it be a group of faithful people, lawfully organized, situated in a given place, united to its pastors, responsive in faith to the call of God in the Holy Spirit, gathered by the preaching of the gospel and the mystery of the celebration of the Lord's Supper, through whose Body and Blood they are formed into a community of brothers and sisters. In such communities, no matter how small or poor or scattered they may be, Christ is present, and through him, the one, holy, catholic and apostolic Church is constituted in that people in that place.[19]

Very much in line with this conciliar statement, Leonardo Boff argues that basic Church communities are indeed entitled to be called "particular Churches," a new way of being Church.[20] His conviction is based on four things. First, the Church as one and universal "consists in the mystery of salvation of God, realized by the Son, in the power of the Holy Spirit acting within history and reaching all human beings."[21] Second, "Faith, therefore, constitutes the minimum constitutive reality of the particular church."[22] Faith, mediated by Jesus in history, is given essentially as communion with God through the Son in the Holy Spirit, and as communion with all those who continue to mediate Jesus' presence in history by their own faith, in the mystery of salvation God works through Jesus in the Spirit.[23] It follows, therefore, that "believers, by reason of their faith-and-community [with God and with one another], are already, in themselves, the presence of the universal church."[24]

There remains, however, one difficulty: the absence of sacramental celebration in the basic Church communities. As *Lumen gentium* points out, a particular Church is an "altar community" where "the sharing in the body and blood of Christ has no other effect than to accomplish our transformation into that which we receive."[25] As noted above, the life of the basic Church communities I visited does not include the celebration of the sacraments. However, as Boff insists, this is not the same as saying that they have no sacramental life, for the very existence of a basic Church community is itself a sacrament of God's saving mystery worked out through Jesus in the Spirit. The concrete historical existence of Church itself is the fundamental sacrament. The concrete existence of a community of faith is already sign and instrument of salvation, sacrament. The community engendered by faith is already an expression (sacrament) of the mystery of God's saving plan, but progressively becomes more so as the life of the community brings to consciousness what is latent in God's saving mystery. This expression, or sacrament, says Boff,

> becomes more perceptible when believers gather together in faith, celebrate salvation, and make themselves available for ministering salvation. This visible expression will be still greater when the group of faithful thus gathered together has a leader among them, a symbol of their oneness with one another and with other communities, and when they can celebrate the eucharistic presence of the Lord sacramentally. Finally, this sacramental expression, this visible expression, can grow greater and greater in larger communities, since these have the capacity to render explicit the whole abundance of riches contained in the mystery of salvation, on the social level, the liturgical level, the theological level, the canonical level. All these expressions, different though they be, concretise, each in its own way, one and the same mystery, one and the same universal church.[26]

Thus, for Boff, even if basic Church communities lack explicit expressions of their sacramental reality by the celebration of the sacraments, these communities, in virtue of their faith and community, realize the presence of Christ and are, therefore, by their very existence a sacrament of Christ.

Nevertheless, Boff acknowledges that the *fullness* of the visible manifestation of the sacramental nature of the Church requires institutional explicitation in sacraments of the Church's own sacramental nature, especially through Eucharist. But how can there be the celebration of Eucharist without an ecclesially authenticated ministry? Here, Boff takes up the argument Schillebeeckx[27] and Legrand[28] have already articulated in great detail, namely, that community gives rise to ministry rather than vice versa, and that ecclesial authentication is fundamentally the recognition by other communities of faith that a given community and the ministers it raises up give adequate expression in their life to the mystery of God's salvation worked through Jesus in the Spirit. The recognition of a community's succession in the faith of the apostles is the requisite ecclesial authentication of a community's ministry.[29] It assures a ministry in apostolic succession. This of course is quite different from a "pipeline theory of ordination in apostolic succession," which is based on what Boff refers to as the "ontologization of the priesthood."[30]

Boff goes on to argue that the anomalous situation in which the Church finds itself today, when access to sacramental celebration is strangled by disciplinary limitations on who may be ordained (ecclesially authenticated) for ministry, may indeed justify the constitution of "extraordinary ministers" of the Eucharist. Along this line, he argues that the one who presides as leader in the community is by that fact designated as the one who presides at the community's celebration of the Lord's Supper. The very fact that the community's leader is recognized by the community, by other communities, and by the bishop of the diocesan Church in which the community lives, is sufficient ecclesial authentication to constitute the community's leader in cases of necessity as the "extraordinary minister" of the Eucharist.[31]

Finally, one of the fears most expressed about the development of an ecclesiology of basic Church communities is that the proliferation of these Churches will lead to schism, heresy, and ecclesial disintegration. The response to this objection made by Boff and others is to insist that ministry at all levels of ecclesial existence (community leader, parish pastor, bishop, and pope) is essentially a ministry to unity in the faith of the apostles, which engenders communion with God and within the community.[32] Concretely, this ministry to union in faith in the basic Church community and to union with other communities is maintained by institutionalization of communion among leaders of communities, much as is done in Brownsville. It is also clear that ongoing formation of leaders is an essential constituent of the institutionalization of this communion at all levels of the Church. What is essential at all levels of communion is that the communion adheres to the communal dialogue, sharing in faith, and orientation to mission that characterizes the dynamics of the basic Church community where leadership is shared, a leadership *in* community, not *above* community.

Boff's insistence on distinguishing but not separating the minimal constitutive reality of Church—faith in God's saving mystery worked through Jesus in the Spirit as uniting believers to the triune God and to one another—from the progressive explicitation in visible institutional forms of this mystery and the communion it generates through faith, has become almost a cliché among ecclesiologists. It is no surprise, then, that Boff, along with most theologians concerned with basic Church communities, defines these communities as Churches. Citing a definition given at a seminar in Brazil in 1972, Boff says that a basic Church community "is a group, or complex of groups, of persons in which a primary, personal relationship of brotherly and sisterly communion obtains, and which lives the totality of the life of the church, as expressed in service, celebration, and evangelization."[33]

Conclusion

On May 6, 1990, John J. Fitzpatrick, bishop of Brownsville, addressed the Catholic faithful of the Diocese of Brownsville in a pastoral letter entitled "Base Communities of Faith." I know of no better way to conclude these reflections on my experience of the basic Church communities I came to know in this diocese than by quoting a few passages from the letter, in which he identifies the significance of the emergence of basic Church communities for the life of the Church and commends those communities to the people of Brownsville:

> Every time a person hears the gospel, enters a Christian community, professes faith, begins to follow the way of Christ and is baptized, the church is born. *The church is not to be found in books, rules, marble architecture or sacred art. It is found in people who believe and form themselves into communities.* Church communities have Jesus as their Lord, the Holy Spirit as their guide, the sacraments and scriptural word of God as their nourishment, communion with their bishop and the universal Church as their protection in truth and unity, and they have each other as their daily strength, consolation and support. . . .
>
> Ironically, it is the successful growth of Catholic parishes over time that has eventually made them also impersonal and unable to provide a sense of real community. The church gradually acquired structures through time that were quite hierarchical and juridical. While these provided enormous strength to survive the tumultuous storms of history, they also greatly deprived the church of its original communitarian character. . . .
>
> Once again, though, *the church is being reborn as small grassroots communities.*
>
> Base communities are not a replacement for traditional parishes, nor mere subdivisions of them. Rather, they are a fresh way of being church within the structured parish. . . .
>
> The success of base communities has been a surprise to many. *Their marvelous growth cannot be explained except by the outpouring of the Holy Spirit.* Because the Spirit is doing something undreamt of in our time, we should not attempt to understand base communities or their potential in terms of familiar past experiences. *To be open to what base communities can accomplish for the church, we must adopt the humble learning attitude of those who have not yet seen or heard or known.* The Holy Spirit appears to be leading us to something truly new. We are not being severed from our Tradition, but we are entering a new stage of it. The mysterious divine-human nature of the church is not changing, but is unfolding in an unprecedented way. . . .
>
> It is not enough for people to work together serving a common cause. Much less is it acceptable for them to attempt to follow the way of Christ by living virtuous but isolated lives. *For the church to be church, there must be true community. There must be love, forgiveness, the shared celebra-*

tion of life, prayer in common, the mutual support in renunciation of sin and in discipleship. This is the promise base communities hold. (Emphasis in the original.)

Notes

1. This essay could not have been written without Ninfa Garza, M.J., diocesan director of Basic Church Communities in the Diocese of Brownsville, and Dolorita Martínez, O.P., Director of the Hispanic Pastoral Planning Office of the Archdiocese of Omaha. Both gave generously of their time and effort in helping me to become acquainted with the reality of basic Church communities. I need also to thank Samuel Fernández, M.C.C.J., one of my students, whose unpublished paper "Base Ecclesial Communities: New Life and Light in the Church" (March 1991), assisted me in achieving a better understanding of basic Church communities.

2. The following information is derived in large part from *Encuentro Hispano Pastoral,* a forty-two page report on the results of a meeting held to develop a Hispanic pastoral plan for the Archdiocese of Omaha. It was published in April 1990 by the Hispanic Pastoral Implementation Office of the Archdiocese of Omaha.

3. See Leonardo Boff, *Ecclesiogenesis* (Maryknoll, N.Y.: Orbis, 1986), which uses the English translation, "basic church communities."

4. *Red de Comunidades,* Diocesis de Brownsville. This is an undated, unpaginated handbook developed and distributed by the Diocesan Office for Basic Church Communities in Brownsville. It is part of the instructional materials used in the formation of the leaders of basic Church communities.

5. Ibid.

6. Ibid.

7. Ibid.

8. Ibid.

9. David Byers, ed., *Parish in Transition* (Washington: United States Catholic Conference, 1986) 18–19.

10. This effort is being sponsored by the Adult Community Formation Director within the Office of Religious Education of the Archdiocese of Omaha.

11. Hervé Legrand, *"La Réalisation de l'Église en un lieu," Initiation à la pratique de la théologie,* Tome III, Dogmatique 2, ed. Bernard Lauret and François Refoulé (Paris: Éditions du Cerf, 1986) 271. (The translation is my own.)

12. Ibid., 210–31.

13. Cf. *Lumen gentium,* nos. 22–23; *Presbyterorum ordinis,* no. 7.

14. Austin Flannery, ed., *Vatican Council II: The Conciliar and Post Conciliar Documents* (Northport, N.Y.: Costello, 1975) 1001.

15. Byers, ed., *Parish in Transition,* 15.

16. Ibid., 18–19.

17. Legrand, *"La Réalisation de l'Église en un lieu,"* 260–65.

18. *Lumen gentium,* no. 26, in Flannery, ed., *Vatican Council II,* 381.

19. Cf. Gérard Philips, *L'Église et son Mystère au Deuxième Concile du Vatican* (Paris, Desclée, 1967) 337–43.

20. Boff, *Ecclesiogenesis.*

21. Ibid., 16.

22. Ibid., 17.

23. Ibid.

24. Ibid.

25. *Lumen gentium,* no. 26, in Flannery, ed., *Vatican Council II,* 381.

26. Ibid., nos. 19–20, pp. 370–72.

27. Edward Schillebeeckx, *The Church with a Human Face* (New York: Crossroad, 1985) 254–57, 265–66.

28. Legrand, *"La Réalisation de l'Église en un lieu,"* 268–73.

29. Boff, *Ecclesiogenesis,* 66–67.

30. Ibid., 67.

31. Ibid., 70–73.

32. Ibid., 92–97.

33. Ibid., 20.

8

Ethics and the Narrative of Hispanic Americans: Conquest, Community, and the Fragility of Life[1]

Paul J. Wadell, C.P.

Even minimal contact with the Hispanic community reveals that their understanding of the moral life is different.[2] If the dominant culture of the United States understands ethics primarily as the application of rules and principles to situations so that decisions can be made and problems solved, Hispanic peoples see the moral life as continuing a story handed on to them. The story is told through their feasts. The celebrations of Our Lady of Guadalupe, Christmas, Ash Wednesday, and Good Friday are not only important days in the Hispanic community but key events in light of which they read and interpret their lives. Collectively these feasts comprise the moral adventure of which Hispanic Americans are a part and reveal the distinctive values, traditions, and concerns that identify them as a people.

The heart of the story is a mysterious and wonderful event that occurred twelve years after the Spaniard Hernando Cortez arrived to conquer Mexico. In the hills outside Mexico City, the Virgin Mother appeared to the Indian Juan Diego and spoke to him in "the language of the conquered."[3] She not only assured him of her compassion and love for a struggling, suffering people but indicated that through them, the conquered ones, God's life would break anew. The feast of Our Lady of Guadalupe marks the "collective resurrection of a new people," a liberation day on which "the roses of Tepeyac . . . take the place of the Easter lilies of western Christianity."[4]

Each feast highlights an element of the people's story. The Mexican American Christmas ritual, the *posada*, tells the story of a God who chose to dwell among the rejected ones of the world.[5] On Ash Wednesday Hispanics gather to acknowledge the sufferings of their people but also to proclaim their hope; it is "a day of sorrow and joy."[6] And Good Friday looms large in the narrative of Hispanic peoples, because by identifying with the sufferings of Christ they are able to find strength and hope in dealing with their own.

We enter the moral universe of Hispanic Americans through their feasts, and it is in them that we can learn and come to appreciate their distinctive moral traditions. If they have values and practices that differ from those of the dominant culture, it is because their history has been different as well. And if their sense of reasonableness and propriety occasionally clashes with those accustomed to being in control, it is because their experience has taught them to see and think differently. Anyone wanting to minister in the Hispanic community must first become acquainted with the stories of their lives, because it is through those formative narratives that we glimpse the attitudes, values, and concerns with which they have identified their lives.

In exploring the moral universe of Hispanic peoples we shall also be investigating a distinctive approach to ethics that focuses not on theories of human nature or arguments for a common rationality but on the pivotal narratives by which our lives are read and transformed. Thus in this essay we shall first examine what is distinctive about a narrative approach to ethics and why it enables us to appreciate what is unique to a particular community's sense of the moral life in a way that standard accounts of morality do not. Second, we shall analyze what is distinctive to the moral traditions of Hispanic Americans by focusing on the pivotal experience of conquest and violation, seeing it, along with the feast of Our Lady of Guadalupe, as the starting point for ethical reflection in the Hispanic community and as key to understanding its moral notions and practices. In light of this definitive experience, we shall then explore the importance given community and family and relationships among Hispanic peoples; their keen appreciation for the fragility of life and the practices that have emerged to address it, especially their strong devotion to the saints; and finally, their distinctive approach to law, authority, and Church moral teaching.

Doing Ethics in a Narrative Mode

The starting point for a narrative approach to ethics is the claim that morality is defined by, and best understood through, the particular convictions, beliefs, values, and concerns of a people.[7] There is no such thing as a general, universal morality that is the same for people everywhere because any morality will be rooted in the central convictions of our lives. A community's ethic is a reflection of its loves and cares, its commitments and attachments; these are not peripheral to morality but its rationale. The lifeblood of any morality are the goods, values, and purposes by which a people have identified themselves and to which they want to be faithful. Thus a narrative approach to ethics is wary of claims for a universal morality common to human beings, whether it be based on natural law theories or Kantian accounts of rationality, because it sees every morality qualified by a community's traditions, goals, and practices.[8]

Proponents of a narrative model for ethics push this argument in response to the view that rationality in ethics and, therefore, moral objectivity demands distancing ourselves from the beliefs and values most integral to our lives. Contemporary ethical theory, largely under the influence of Kant, argues that objectivity and truthfulness in ethics can only be secured when moral agents relinquish everything that makes their lives substantive and distinctive; thus they become rational when they forsake the particularity of narratives and traditions for the presumed objectivity of the anonymous "ideal observer," who steps out of the life he or she knows for a "universal point of view." It is hard to know what such a life would look like or why anyone would ever want to live it, but the claim is that truthfulness can be attained in ethics "only by freeing moral judgments from the 'subjective' story of the agent."[9]

Of course there is a bias at work in this model and it is twofold. If, on the one hand, it is biased against the peculiarities of traditions as being arbitrary, subjective, and contingent, it is biased toward modern science as being (allegedly) objective, disinterested, and universal. Science becomes the norm for judging rationality and truthfulness; thus it is concluded that moral judgments can be true only if they are "the result of an impersonal rationality" and "involve no special pleading from the agent's particular history, community identification, or otherwise particular point of view to establish their truthfulness. . . . Ethical rationality assumes it must take the form of science if it is to have any claim to being objective."[10] Obviously, one response to this argument is that science is no more value-free than ethics, for science is shaped by its own set of traditions and narratives; thus to make it the standard by which all rationality is determined is a very ironic move.

But it is also a very odd move because it misconstrues what it means to be reasonable and how claims of reasonableness can be made. The standard account of rationality argues that we are moral when we are able to view our lives anonymously, seeing "our desires, interests, and passions as if they could belong to anyone."[11] But this is outlandish. A life stripped of everything that identifies us and matters to us is no life at all, at least not a life we would recognize or about which we would care. The standard account of rationality demands that we regard our life as a neutral observer would, but that is exactly what we are not. We are people of strong and abiding devotions, people shaped by experiences and memories we want never to forget. A life that looks like anyone's is neither a life we would want nor one we could possibly imagine. Stepping back from the subjective elements of our lives, as the standard account would have us do, does not make morality objective, it makes it disappear. If in order to be rational you have to vacate morality of communities and traditions, histories and experiences—all the things we love and would even die for— then moral truthfulness is gained at the enormous cost of making our lives so abstract there is no way we could claim them as our own. Contrary to the standard account, narrative ethics argues there is no such thing as a universal, impersonal rationality and "no neutral story that insures the truthfulness of our particular stories";[12] rather, both rationality and truthfulness are tested by the sort of persons a story creates.

An example of the difference between the standard account of rationality and narrative ethics can be seen in how each might approach the question of abortion. Since with the standard account "the 'personal' can only be morally significant to the extent that it can be translated into the 'impersonal,' "[13] questions about the morality of abortion and the language in which those questions are posed are highly abstract and formal, focusing not on what one might believe about the place of children in our lives or the role of parenting but on whether the fetus is a person or a woman has rights over her body. Although such questions are important, they overlook the array of convictions we hold about such significant moral matters, forgetting that the moral status of certain behavior is grasped not by sidestepping our convictions but by knowing what those convictions are and why they have authority in our lives.

What can we conclude from this? First, if rationality is narrative-dependent there is no such thing as an impersonal, universal rationality that operates apart from the central traditions and stories of our lives. That we may apprise situations differently and be attentive to some values more than others illustrates that what matters to us is conditioned by the historical and cultural traditions that have shaped us. H. Richard Niebuhr calls this "temporal and spatial relativity,"[14] challenging the Kantian view that there is a "pure reason" untouched by the concreteness of history and culture; in fact, Niebuhr suggests that what often is sanctioned as "universal reason" is little more than the perspective of a majority that enjoys sufficient power not to take seriously the viewpoints of minorities. If we never venture outside the confines of our traditions by practicing hospitality to the traditions of others, we may fail to recognize how we can absolutize the relative and uncritically accept as reasonable, even normative, what guards our interests without ever asking what those interests do to others. As Virgil Elizondo comments, "Might becomes right because power establishes its views as the objective norm to consolidate and justify its own achievements, its own position of privilege."[15]

Second, in order to appreciate what is unique in the moral notions of Hispanic communities, we need to listen to the stories that have formed them, for it is through those stories that we encounter the values, cares, and devotions integral to their understanding of goodness, rationality, and truthfulness. Truly to appreciate those moral notions requires a kind of epistemological humility that leaves us not only open to alternative viewpoints but actively seeking them, acknowledging the limits of our own point of view and the need to be enriched by a tradition we have too long dismissed. Put differently, in order to understand the impact of Hispanic culture on how Hispanics understand morality, we must be willing to enter their story long enough to learn what the world is like to them and what they might teach us.

Conquest: A Starting Point for Ethical Reflection

To understand the Hispanic soul one must reckon with the fact of conquest, for that is woven most deeply in their psyche. It is a sobering starting point but a crucial one, for nearly everything in their outlook on life and their understanding of morality is colored by a memory that history has only sustained. Even the feasts mentioned above are interpreted in light of conquest. For instance, as a feast of new life and liberation, Our Lady of Guadalupe offers hope and deliverance from conquest; the sufferings of Christ commemorated on Good Friday give redemptive meaning to the hardships and afflictions of Hispanic Americans today. As one Mexican American told me, "Violence and being violated occupy such a central part of our history that it is almost archetypal. So much of our behavior and attitudes are impacted by that history of conquest and violence." Or as another said, "We are a people born out of conflict, looking for dignity and a right to exist. You have to go back to those origins to appreciate who we are."[16]

To understand what counts as reasonable and good in the Hispanic community as well as why certain values are primary, one has to confront the conquest in which their story is rooted and the oppression and injustice they have continued to know. Theirs is a history not of domination and victory but of conflict and violation. Though this might be obvious, it cannot be overlooked because it is key for understanding a community's narrative that is very different from one whose main strands are progress, confidence, and prosperity. Here conflict and violence are the dominant threads holding the cultural fabric together, and it is only when one appreciates this that one can begin to understand why what looms large in Hispanic Americans' catalogue of moral notions are survival, life, community and family, cooperation and sharing, as well as tendencies to fatalism, resignation, and defeat. By contrast, a narrative spun from victory is much more likely to focus on prosperity rather than survival, on autonomy rather than community and cooperation, and to judge fatalism more a moral weakness than an attitude seasoned from misfortune.

In his book *Galilean Journey: The Mexican-American Promise* Virgil Elizondo writes that Mexican Americans trace their origins "to two great invasions and conquests: the Spanish and the Anglo-American."[17] The story of this people began on "Good Friday, April 22, 1519, the day when Hernando Cortez arrived in Mexico."[18] That initial conquest lasted more than fifty years, and from the destruction of one people, a new people were born, the Mexican Americans, or *mestizo,* who emerged from the conquest and oppression of the indigenous peoples of Mexico by the Spanish. They were literally born from violence and nurtured in a context of colonization, a fact that has marked them for over four hundred years. As Allan Deck observes, "There is no question but that the mestizo culture of Mexico finds its origins in a cultural, religious conflict of immense proportions. It was born in physical and spiritual violence."[19] And, he insists, anyone wanting to understand and minister to Mexican Americans must take the tragic origins of their history into account:

> The long and neglected colonial period provides many important insights into the cultural and religious reality of the people. The mestizo not only as a racial type but, more importantly, as a form of humanity, as a culture, literally was forged in this colonial context. Whoever would desire to understand in some small way Mexican society, culture, religion, and values is well advised to dwell at some length on the three centuries of Spanish colonial rule. Whoever is concerned with the fuller life, the evangelization and liberation of Mexicans and Hispanics of Mexican origin in the United States, similarly is well advised to study the salient features of the colonial Mexican experience.[20]

The conquest begun by Spain was continued by the United States, which accounts for the ambivalence many Mexican Americans feel toward the United States. In the Mexican-American War, which concluded with the Treaty of Guadalupe Hidalgo in 1848, Mexico lost almost half its land to the United States.[21] In the years following the war the violence and injustice inflicted on Mexicans in the United States was horrifying. "A man was lynched for getting into a fist fight, a woman for killing a miner who broke into her house, a man for refusing to play the fiddle for a group of Anglo Texans."[22] "In west Texas," Sandoval notes, "Judge Roy Bean could find nothing in the law that made killing a Mexican a crime."[23] Denied the right to vote and excluded from all but menial jobs, Mexicans had little means of protecting themselves from injustice. "Squatters who seized their lands were not prosecuted; neither were persons who assaulted them," Sandoval writes. "But if the victims defended themselves, they were punished severely. Real estate taxes were raised until Hispanic owners lost their properties for being delinquent; then the rates were lowered for the new Anglo-American owners."[24]

The fortunes of Mexicans in the United States hardly changed in the first part of the twentieth century. During this time "Hispanics experienced more violence than ever before. It seemed 'as though there were open season' along the border. From 1908 to 1925, as many as 5,000 civilians—the exact number will never be known—died in lawlessness so widespread that a federal official warned the governor of Texas that action would have to be taken to protect the victims."[25] Viewing this sad chronicle of violence, injustice, and abuse, Elizondo writes:

> Since 1848 there has been a nearly unbroken history of direct and indirect, spontaneous and institutionalized, violence throughout the West and Southwest. Leading institutions, both public and private, secular and religious, have adopted prejudicial attitudes and practices in regard to the Mexican-American population. There is an abundance of well documented cases of the most inhuman types of discrimination in schools, churches, work places, social agencies, law-enforcement agencies, even cemeteries. Nor is this just past history; it is still prevalent.[26]

The conquest was not only political and economic, it was also religious. The doctrinal Catholicism of the Spanish conquerors was imposed on the indigenous people of Mexico. Few attempts were made to understand or appreciate a native religion that was seen by the Spanish to be little more than "idolatry, devil worship, or witchcraft."[27] Both in Mexico and what later became the United States, the religion of the native peoples, with its symbols and practices, was ridiculed and destroyed. "Instruments of worship such as masks, prayer sticks, and prayer feathers were confiscated. Indian places of worship, such as the kivas of the Pueblos, were destroyed or closed," Sandoval writes. "Corporal punishment such as flogging and prolonged kneeling was not uncommon. Native religious leaders who persisted in following their beliefs were whipped or executed."[28] As Elizondo argues, the destruction of their religion was the greatest violence suffered by the indigenous peoples because religious symbols are not only the heart and justification of a people's worldview, but also what best identifies them and gives meaning and coherence to their existence.[29] With great poignancy, he explains why the suppression of their religion was a violation of their spirit and their soul:

> Hence the introduction of new religious symbols, especially when they are the symbols of a dominant group, is in effect the ultimate violence. With nonviolent intentions, Catholic missionaries were the agents of a violence more radical than physical violence. They attempted to destroy

> what physical violence could not touch: the soul of the indigenous people. Despite the missionaries' opposition to the cruel and bloody ways of the conquistadores, the introduction of the religious symbols of the Spanish intruders in effect affirmed and justified the way of the powerful and discredited the way of the powerless at the deepest level of their existence.[30]

In the language of narrative ethics, conquest is the core of the Hispanic inner history. A term coined by H. Richard Niebuhr in *The Meaning of Revelation,* "inner history" is history "as it is lived and apprehended from within."[31] We know our inner history when we look at our life and note those events that stay with us, those experiences that continue to direct and shape us even though they may have happened long ago. Inner history captures events that linger and continue to impact our lives. Inner history is not left behind, it is integrated and commemorated. This does not mean people try to duplicate the past, but they know who they are and what they believe in light of experiences and memories that are intimately part of themselves. As Niebuhr says about inner history, "We are not in this time but it is in us."[32]

"Inner history" can refer to an individual's apprehension of her or his life, but it can also be collective; it can designate the bonding force of certain events that draw people together in a common memory. If to be a self is to have an inner history, to be a community is to have one too. "Inner history" refers to those events that become interpretative keys to a people's existence. This means various things for us personally, but it also means something for us communally. Obviously, these memories and the traditions they form are not inert. They bear on a people's psyche as the singular events through which they come to know who they are. For the Hispanic peoples, conquest remains the paradigmatic shaping event of their existence, and as the heart of their inner history it is the hermeneutic for exploring their sense of morality.

How has it marked their life? More than anything, as a result of conquest and oppression Hispanic Americans have suffered cultural, psychological, and spiritual violence. Because the norms for authentic humanity and success are established by the dominant Anglo culture, Hispanic Americans struggle with feelings of inferiority, even self-hatred. What is constantly communicated to them is that they and their culture are lacking: occasionally interesting but largely without value in a society that measures humanity and success and goodness in vastly different ways. "The conquered are told they must abandon their backward ways if they are to advance and become 'humanized,' " Elizondo comments, and thus many Hispanic peoples come to think of themselves as undignified and uncivilized.[33] Knowing themselves to fall short of the standards of Anglo society, they wrestle with low self-esteem and feelings of worthlessness; thus their poverty is both economic and psychological. As Elizondo argues, "But if you hear again and again that you are inferior, good for nothing, incompetent, lazy, you may eventually begin to believe it yourself."[34] All of this contributes to a spirit of resignation, apathy, and defeat among a people convinced they must remain on the margins of American economic and political life.[35]

It also contributes to a painful dualism in their identity and behavior, in which Hispanic peoples "learn to maintain two standards of belief and action: that of the oppressors and their own."[36] They feel compelled to model and conform to the ways of the dominant Anglo culture in order to gain even minimal acceptance, but internally they reject those ways because they are not their own and, more importantly, because they are not convinced the values and customs of the Anglo society really are superior.[37] Nonetheless, the tension elicited between outwardly conforming to values and behavior one inwardly does not accept further weakens one's identity and self-esteem.

Still, the most devastating effect of conquest and oppression on Hispanic peoples is an ongoing violence against their culture that becomes not only violence against themselves but ultimately a denial that they are living, breathing images of God. Starting with the Spanish, the culture of the conqueror was imposed on the conquered, not only devaluing their distinctive customs, beliefs, and way of life but eventually destroying them. "The new worldview disrupts the worldview of the conquered to such an extent that their ways no longer make sense," Elizondo explains. "The ideas, logic, art, customs, language, and religion of the conqueror are forced into the life of the conquered."[38] Too, "their fundamental spirit is ridiculed, stepped on, and crushed," he continues. "Their world order no longer has meaning or cohesiveness, because it is questioned and threatened by a more powerful world order, which imposes itself as superior."[39]

No one can endure such a total denial of self without starting to doubt one's humanity. Since the dominant group in society "imposes the image of itself as the only one legitimately human, beautiful, and dignified,"[40] the poor and marginalized are persuaded that they are not fully human because they are such poor images of the only group who truly reflects God. The basis for all justice and respect, namely that every human being is a veritable image and likeness of God, is taken from them. Robbed of what is godly and beautiful about them, their belief in their own humanity ebbs. As Elizondo asserts,

> I contend that this is the worst type of poverty and oppression, because it so interiorizes the image of the oppressor as superior and exclusively Godlike that the oppressed begin to hate themselves for what they are and admire the image of the oppressor even in the images of the divine. Even if the oppressed become materially wealthy, they will remain spiritually poor because the powerful have robbed them of the greatest treasure

they possess—the God-given spirit that sustains them in their collective life.[41]

Community: The Principal Means to a Primary Value

It is true that Hispanics embrace a relational ethics in which the family is the primary moral community and the context for individual identity and moral decision making; however, to appreciate fully what this means one must see why the priority of community and relationships in Hispanic ethics cannot be understood apart from the overriding value of survival. In a narrative spun from conquest and violation, survival abides as the key principle and overriding concern of morality. Life is the sovereign good, and the status of every other value is relative to whether it enhances or imperils life. For instance, Hispanics may have a deeper sense of the connections that bond people together, but that is because they know that when you lack power there is no way to survive by yourself. As one woman told me, "You can't think just about yourself," but that is because if you do you die. Family and community are the primary context for morality with Hispanics, but this sense of solidarity is rooted in the experience of deprivation and threat.

This communal emphasis is exemplified in a variety of ways. First, community, particularly family, is a condition for personal identity. Contrary to an approach that says identity precedes community, Hispanic ethics argues that it is impossible to have an identity apart from the primary relationships that constitute our lives; for them the "we" precedes and makes possible the "I." This is symbolized and celebrated by Hispanic Americans when they gather to baptize a newborn child. The sacrament represents not only the child's entry into the life of Christ but also his or her incorporation "into the collective identity and life of the family, the group, and the people. Baptism has never been thought of as simply the entry of another individual into the institutional church," Elizondo explains. "In baptism the child is accepted and welcomed . . . into the life and memory of the entire family—parents, siblings, grandparents, relatives, and in-laws. The newly baptized becomes *uno de los nuestros* (one of ours)."[42]

In Hispanic ethics the family is central. One reason is that the family is where Hispanic Americans feel unconditionally welcomed and accepted; if nowhere else in society, there they experience belonging. If elsewhere they feel unappreciated and overlooked, perhaps even disrespected and rejected, in the family they are loved, esteemed, and included not because of what they have done or not done but because of who they are.[43] No matter what others do to them or how society looks at them, emotionally they are never separated from the family because it remains their single most important source of affirmation and life.

But the family is also central for Hispanic Americans because the self and the family are so tightly interconnected; in fact, to be a self is to be family. As Elizondo writes, "La familia is not the house where people reside; it is the bond that unites persons and allows them to experience that innermost and existential sense of belonging. I am never alone; I am part of the familia and the familia is part of me."[44] This is why, for instance, if a person makes a mistake they are never expelled from the community; to be exiled from family and friends would be not to exist. There is no way a person could sustain an identity apart from the family because for Hispanic peoples the self is the work of the central relationships of their lives. The absolute need for others in order to be is captured in the Mexican proverb, "You die three times: first, you die when you breathe your last breath; secondly, you die when you are put in the ground; and third, complete death occurs when you are forgotten." This great appreciation for the formative influence of community and relationships is a healthy corrective for a dominant culture whose individualism, consumerism, and competitiveness have undermined and impoverished friendships. Hispanic Americans have much to teach a society that no longer understands what good friendships are, why they are important to the moral life, or how one should go about them.[45]

But there is something else at work in the strong emphasis Hispanic Americans put on relationships and community that should not be overlooked. They acknowledge the need of others to enable and enhance personal identity not only because they recognize the essential social character of the self, but also because a narrative of conquest and oppression has bred a strong sense of inferiority and unworthiness deep in their bones. They know they cannot live without others, but that may be at least partially because they think so little of themselves. Positively, this sense of unworthiness solidifies their conviction of the need for other people, but there is no guarantee that family or friends can dislodge an inferiority that history and experience have constantly suggested.

An example of how relationships can be detrimental to identity is the role of women in Hispanic society, particularly in marriage. A liability of forging such a strong connection between relationships and identity is that it can become extremely difficult to imagine oneself apart from a relationship, even a destructive one. As one Mexican American told me, "It is not just the case that you always live in relationship, but that you are that relationship. This is why if you ask a married woman, 'Who are you?' she will answer, 'I am this man's wife.' " The example of marriage is instructive. Unlike the dominant Anglo culture, Hispanic Americans do not think of themselves as autonomous, independent people. In marriage, for example, when a woman marries she relinquishes membership in her original family in order to become a member of her husband's father's family. Once she is married she not only belongs to this new family but receives a new identity through them. She no longer is known through her father's family but is identified through her husband, so much so that she belongs to him and is nobody apart from him.[46] Put most strongly, it is because she is this man's wife that she is at all. This is why separation and divorce are unthinkable for her. Even if she is in an abusive relationship and has suffered physically, spiritually, and emotionally, it is extremely difficult for her to consider ending the marriage because she exists not only for her husband but also through her husband; thus, to abandon him would be tantamount to abandoning herself. For the woman in marriage divorce means not only to lose one's place of belonging but also to lose one's self.[47] The same, however, is not true for the husband because he is not identified through the marriage but through his ongoing link to his father's family.

This is a pressing moral problem in the Hispanic community, which is reinforced by cultural understandings of masculinity. For instance, a double standard for sexual fidelity is often accepted. While the woman must remain faithful, the infidelity of the man is often presumed, even excused. Similarly, no matter how intolerable a marriage may become, the role of the woman is to be long-suffering and patient. It is she and not her husband who must remain faithful, and she more than her husband who will be ostracized if they divorce. Regardless of the circumstances, if she ends the marriage she bears the onus of having abandoned her husband. There is no notion of equality in the marital relationship, no sense that marriage is a life-giving partnership; rather, the woman is more the man's property than his spouse. She is his wife, or even his woman, and as such she is responsible for her man's happiness and satisfaction much more than he is responsible for hers.

Marriage is also undermined by the very different roles the man and woman occupy as father and mother. The father's role is to provide the income and financial support of the family, but he is not expected to contribute to the nurturing of the children. That is the role of the mother, but it can distance her from her husband even more. It is not uncommon for the woman to see herself more as the mother of the children than as wife to her husband; in fact, the woman will commonly refer to the children as "my children" but seldom as "our children." Because she may receive little emotional support from her husband, her children become her primary relationship. If she nurtures them psychologically and emotionally, they do the same for her; thus it is her children and not her husband who become the center of her life.

A final way the emphasis on community is exemplified in Hispanic ethics is that the community, primarily the family, is the principle context for moral evaluation and decision making. If an Anglo-European approach might emphasize the primacy of individual conscience, in Hispanic ethics there is no such thing as a decision of conscience made apart from a com-

munity. Since there is no individual separate from relationships, there is
no moral reflection isolated from the communities with which a person
is primarily identified. As one person put it, "If you can't think just about
yourself, neither can you think by yourself." In this respect, the family
or community is a moral agent, not in the sense that they relieve an individual of the responsibility of deciding but that she or he could not con-
ceive what a purely private decision would be. When they decide, they
do so as people formed in a web of relationships, each of which guides
and informs their decisions. Put differently, it would be unthinkable for
Hispanic Americans to make significant moral decisions without consulting the community, particularly their families, because decisions of conscience are not viewed as solitary meditations but as a community's
conversation about what should be done that all might survive.

The Fragility of Life and Devotion to the Saints

It is precisely because survival is precarious that Hispanic peoples have
a rich appreciation for the fragility of life. In contrast to an overly rationalistic conception of morality that suggests an invulnerability to the con-
tingencies of life, Hispanic moral traditions embody the conviction that
much in life, through no fault of our own, is vulnerable to reversal.

A Mexican fable bears this out. It is the story of a matador who enters
the ring as a strong, confident young man. His instincts are right and his
reflexes quick, so he enjoys much success against the bull. But he is wise
enough to know eventually the bull will win out. His attention may wan-
der, perhaps he will misjudge the bull's movements; no matter what, he
will be bloodied.

The fable is not a hymn to fatalism but to the power of chance events
and our limited ability to escape them. In a more Western, technological
model of ethics the importance of luck, fortune, and chance is given little
attention. It is presumed that as long as one has sufficient freedom and
gives adequate reflection to planning one's life, loss and misfortune can
be avoided; in fact, since it is believed that we gain power and control
through freedom and choice, calamity is attributed not to life's fragility
but to muddled choices. By contrast, a Hispanic approach argues that only
so much of life can be rationally calculated and controlled. This does not
mean one should avoid the responsibility of decisions but that one must
respect the power of chance events to disrupt one's plans in ways that
cannot always be foreseen.

Sometimes fortune smiles on us and everything works out well; indeed,
the world can seem turned to our purposes. But other times our experience
is much different. Life not only fails to cooperate but seems actively to
oppose us. Our intentions and purposes can be upended by the unexpected.

Fortune is subject to change. We plan carefully and make the right decisions, but there are powers in life that can dislodge us from good fortune. From a Hispanic perspective, luck is an important moral category that must be taken seriously, because whether our fortunes are for good or for ill makes a difference not only in our outlook but also in how we assess our possibilities and responsibilities. When our luck is good it is easier to live as we ought, but bad luck can maim, making it exceptionally difficult to live as we feel we ought. As Martha Nussbaum comments, "misfortunes of a severe kind, prolonged over a period of time, impair good living itself."[48]

Good people can be ruined through no fault of their own. Their lives shatter not because they are careless but because they suffer things they cannot control. Though this may sound fatalistic, it describes the realism of a people who are in touch with life's brokenness and do not suffer the illusion of thinking they have the power to make everything work out right. In the Hispanic narrative, the texture of life is such that we cannot be in control of everything, nor can we be responsible for everything. In fact, one comes to appreciate the preciousness of life when one is poignantly aware of its fragility. For instance, it is because life is vulnerable to reversal that Hispanic peoples celebrate it in fiesta. "In the fiesta the Mexican-American rises above the quest for the logical meaning of life and celebrates the very contradictions that are of the essence of the mystery of human life."[49]

One of the mysterious facts of life in the narrative of Hispanic peoples is that the spiritual world is not something that hovers beyond the earth, but is intimately and permanently part of the earth. In the Hispanic cosmology, the world is both surrounded by and subject to powerful spiritual forces, some of which are good but many of which are bad. These evil forces must be taken seriously, their power always acknowledged, because not to be alert to their presence is to stand completely unprotected.

An example is given in Rudolfo Anaya's novel *Bless Me, Ultima*, the story of a young boy, Antonio, and his relationship with Ultima, a *curandera*, a woman able to lift curses and to heal because she "knew the herbs and remedies of the ancients" and had special powers.[50] In one scene Antonio speaks of the "dust devils" coming from nowhere across the desert landscape. He describes them as "made by the heat of hell" and carrying "with them the evil spirit of a devil," adding that "it is bad luck to let one of these small whirlwinds strike you." Still, one can protect oneself from the evil because "the power of God is so great. All you have to do is to lift up your right hand and cross your right thumb over your first finger in the form of the cross. No evil can challenge the cross," Antonio says, "and the swirling dust with the devil inside must turn away from you."[51] This is the world of Hispanic cosmology, a world abundant in good and evil spirits, each vying for control. The evil spirits must be respected, but one lives with the reassurance, Ultima tells Antonio, that "good is always stronger than evil," so much so that the "smallest bit of good can stand against all the powers of evil in the world and it will emerge triumphant."[52]

This is vividly shown in another scene from the novel. Antonio's Uncle Lucas is sick because "he had been bewitched, a bruja had put a curse on him. He had been sick all winter and he had not recovered with the coming of spring. Now he was on his deathbed."[53] His illness was punishment for having "seen a group of witches do their evil dance for el Diablo," and the curse was so strong that not only the "great doctor in Las Vegas had been powerless to cure him," but even "the holy priest at El Puerto had been asked to exorcise el encanto, the curse, and he had failed."[54] Only Ultima the *curandera* has power to wrestle with the evil spirits. She heals Uncle Lucas by performing an exorcism to free him from the evil that possesses him:

> His body convulsed with the spasms of a madman, and his face contorted with pain. "Let the evil come out!" Ultima cried in his ear.
>
> "Dios mio!" were his first words, and with those words the evil was wrenched from his interior. Green bile poured from his mouth, and finally he vomited a huge ball of hair. It fell to the floor, hot and steaming and wiggling like live snakes. . . .
>
> "Ay!" Ultima cried triumphantly and with clean linen she swept up the evil, living ball of hair. "This will be burned, by the tree where the witches dance—" she sang and swiftly put the evil load into the sack. She tied the sack securely and then came back to my uncle. He was holding the side of the bed, his thick fingers clutching the wood tightly as if he were afraid to slip back into the evil spell. He was very weak and sweating, but he was well. I could see in his eyes that he knew he was a man again, a man returned from a living hell.[55]

This great appreciation for the powerful spiritual forces inhabiting the world and influencing events is one reason Hispanic peoples have such devotion to the saints.[56] In a fragile world vulnerable to adversity, it is imperative to have a patron representing one before God. In the Hispanic narrative saints are not strangers but members of an extended family. Each member of the family is given the name of a saint to protect them, and the feast day of the saint is celebrated as one would remember the birthday of a family member. It is not only the case, then, that saints are people to imitate; they are also specially designated advocates whose role is to watch over and protect a person. As members of the family who are specially close to God, they can intercede for the person before God and offer help and protection no earthly member of the family can. Though this might seem quaint or even superstitious to someone accustomed to being in control, it is utterly reasonable to people who realize they cannot make it through life bereft of the protection of spirits who will intercede for them. The world is surrounded by spirits who make things happen for good or for ill, and if that is the case one needs to live under the patronage of a saint.

For Hispanic peoples saints are not odd and baffling creatures but one of us, creatures who once walked the earth but now are much closer to God. And far from being indifferent to our welfare, as former citizens of the earth the saints are our friends. Like any good friend, saints want what is best for us. They watch over us, protect us, and represent us before God. Too, if benevolence is part of any good friendship between human beings, it also marks the friendship the saints have for us. As our sponsors and advocates before God, the saints actively work for our good. And as any close friend who loves us, the saints are available at any time, eager to intercede for us and come to our aid.

But sometimes not even the saints can rescue us from misfortune in a threatening world. Suffering befalls us, and our life, at least momentarily, stops. It is at such moments when evil can appear more powerful than good—and death than life—that Hispanic peoples turn to the suffering Christ in an attempt to find courage and hope in face of difficulties they cannot change or even understand. The devotion many Hispanic persons have to the passion of Christ is based on their conviction that someone who experienced rejection, abuse, torment, and suffering must surely be able to understand the afflictions they endure. The focus is not on a Christ who will take away their suffering, or even enable them to make sense of it, but on a Christ who is bound to feel compassion for them because he entered their world and experienced its pain. It is the kinship of Christ in their affliction that gives them hope, his entry into "the world of the voiceless, the sick, the hungry, the oppressed, the public sinners, the emarginated, the suffering,"[57] that encourages them to go on. Too, like so many Christians, Hispanic peoples find strength in knowing that the crosses of their lives are one with the cross of Christ, their sufferings part of his redemptive death.

Hispanic Attitudes Toward Law, Authority, and Church

If for some people God is Law and for others God is Love, for many Hispanics God is Life. It may seem incidental, but it goes to the heart of Hispanic understandings of law. One person put it bluntly: "Law is there, but if it doesn't make sense why follow it?" He was not being flippant but was suggesting that the laws and teachings of the Church need to be adjusted to the demands of real life. Hispanic ethics is not a collection of laws and rules but an ongoing conversation about what real life demands.

This is obviously not as tidy as an ethics of law, but it makes sense in a narrative in which relationships and not laws are the foundation of society. This is not to dismiss laws as unnecessary for life, but it is to say that law is subservient to community, persons, and the needs of existence. The pivotal importance of community mitigates the force of law. Since society is not built on laws but on relationships, the key to figuring the status or authority of a law is to judge whether it serves life and personal relationships, primarily the family, or harms them.

For instance, like many people, Hispanics will weigh the teaching of the Church on artificial means of contraception against the facts of their situation, especially the number of children already present in a family, the family's financial security, and its overall well-being. It is impossible for Hispanics, especially Hispanic women, to say that the teaching of the Church is more important than the well-being of their family; therefore, they feel that if the Church does not allow them to practice birth control for the sake of the family and its overall life, then the Church neither understands them nor truly wants them.

There are other reasons Hispanic peoples tend to relativize ecclesiastical laws. One has to do with their worldview, the other with their sense of what legitimates authority. In respect to the first, Hispanics can agree that law is a good thing and something, all things considered, we ought to heed; nonetheless, since laws represent ideals and generalizations not capable of fitting nicely every situation of life, we should not expect anyone to conform to them perfectly, nor should they even try. The concreteness and immense variety of life is such that the good cannot always be achieved simply by following a law; rather, discerning the good demands taking into account circumstances, the needs and limitations of persons, and what is genuinely possible. Second, the authority of the lawgiver is legitimate and respected only when he or she stands in relationship to the people, respects them, and appreciates their situation. Hispanic people will not listen seriously to the teaching or guidance of anyone, whether individuals or institutions, who does not take time to know their situation and be sensitive to their needs. As one person told me, "You have no authority with me unless you are in relation to me and respect me."

Moreover, the attitudes Hispanic Americans have toward laws, especially the laws of the Church, cannot be appreciated without considering both the distinctive religious ethos of Hispanic people and their history with the institutional Church in the United States. If the religion of the majority of Catholics in the United States was influenced by the European Enlightenment and Jansenism, thus being characterized by order, dogmatism, and rationalism, the Catholicism of Hispanic Americans was less institutionalized and ecclesial. Its center was not the Vatican but the home and the village. It was a religion not of the clergy but of the people, a way of life "inculcated by grandmother and mother and concretized in a whole gamut of popular devotions."[58] As the popularity of Cursillos attests, Hispanic Catholics seek a religion not of laws but one that is personal and relational, that provides a sense of community and family, and that is much more spontaneous and affective than the Catholicism practiced in most parishes.[59]

Finally, that Hispanics respect Church laws but do not focus on them has something to do with the marginal status they have always had within the institutional Church. They have largely been a Church apart, or perhaps a Church within the Church. This is partially because Anglo-American Catholics did not accept them and because Hispanic people had virtually no representation in the Church until recently. As Sandoval writes, "Hispanics, however, remain a people apart. . . . There is 'social distance' between them and the institutional Church."[60] In short, one reason Hispanic Americans might be more discriminating in their approach to Church laws is that they have had so little say in shaping them.

In this essay we have suggested that anyone ministering in Hispanic communities and wanting to understand the Hispanic moral values and practices needs to see the inseparable connection between their sense of morality and their constitutive narrative, which is identified by and told through the community's major feasts, especially Our Lady of Guadalupe. The moral universe of Hispanic Americans is entered through those feasts, and it is in light of them that Hispanic people read and interpret their lives. It is a story of hope and promise rooted in the unforgettable fact of conquest and violation. It is out of this tragic and formative experience that Hispanic people have come to prize the importance of community and relationships, especially the family; have developed a keen appreciation for the fragility of life and the moral importance of luck and misfortune; and have fostered a respect for laws that remembers the well-being of persons all law is meant to serve.

This examination of the narrative shaping the moral world of Hispanic peoples reminds us that there is no such thing as a common, universal morality because any account of the moral life will always be rooted in the central convictions, experiences, and traditions of a people. But there is no reason we cannot be educated and enriched by a tradition very different from our own. Anyone ministering to Hispanic peoples and appreciative of their moral values and customs knows the immeasurable contribution they can make, and indeed have made, to the life of the Church.

Notes

1. I am indebted to several people for the help, guidance, and insights they shared with me while preparing this essay. Special thanks to the members of the executive committee of CORHIM (Conference of Religious for Hispanic Ministry): Clemente Barrón, C.P., Cathy García, R.S.H.M., Verónica Méndez, R.C.D., Ana María Pineda, R.S.M., Gary Riebe-Estrella, S.V.D., and Elisa Rodríguez, S.L. I am also grateful to Juan Huitrado, M.C.C.J., Ricardo García, and Antonio Medina for the time they spent with me and the wisdom they shared with me. Without the help of all these people this essay could not have been written.

2. Although I shall use the terms "Hispanic" and "Hispanic American" throughout the essay, the limitations and inadequacies of these descriptions must be noted. As Allan Deck observes, "the use of the word Hispanic is problematic. It is an umbrella term that simply does not do justice to the heterogeneity of the people in question. There is really no adequate term to cover the various national groups and the several generations that constitute this 'pluriverse' of Latin American origin in the United States." Allan Deck, *The Second Wave: Hispanic Ministry and the Evangelization of Cultures* (New York: Paulist, 1989) 5.

3. Virgil Elizondo, *Galilean Journey: The Mexican-American Promise* (Maryknoll, N.Y.: Orbis, 1983) 11.

4. Ibid., 43–44.

5. Ibid., 38.

6. Ibid., 34.

7. The foundational work in a narrative approach to Christian theology and ethics is H. Richard Niebuhr's *The Meaning of Revelation* (New York: Macmillan, 1941). More recent treatments besides those cited in this chapter include Stanley Hauerwas, *A Community of Character* (Notre Dame: University of Notre Dame Press, 1981); Alasdair MacIntyre, *After Virtue* (Notre Dame: University of Notre Dame Press, 1981); James W. McClendon, Jr., *Ethics* (Nashville: Abingdon, 1986); George A. Lindbeck, *The Nature of Doctrine: Religion and Theology in a Postliberal Age* (Philadelphia: Westminster, 1984); Stanley Hauerwas and L. Gregory Jones, eds., *Why Narrative? Readings in Narrative Theology* (Grand Rapids: Eerdmans, 1989).

8. See Stanley Hauerwas, *The Peaceable Kingdom: A Primer in Christian Ethics* (Notre Dame: University of Notre Dame Press, 1983) 17–34.

9. Stanley Hauerwas and David B. Burrell, "From System to Story: An Alternative Pattern for Rationality in Ethics," *Truthfulness and Tragedy: Further Investigations in Christian Ethics* (Notre Dame: Univerity of Notre Dame Press, 1977) 17.

10. Ibid., 16.

11. Ibid., 23.

12. Ibid.

13. Ibid., 18.

14. Niebuhr, *The Meaning of Revelation*, 5–16.

15. Elizondo, *Galilean Journey*, 17.

16. I am grateful to Clemente Barrón, C.P., and Gary Riebe-Estrella, S.V.D., for these insights.

17. Elizondo, *Galilean Journey*, 5.

18. Ibid., 10,

19. Deck, *The Second Wave*, 34.

20. Ibid.

21. Ibid., 48.

22. Moíses Sandoval, *On the Move: A History of the Hispanic Church in the United States* (Maryknoll, N.Y.: Orbis, 1990) 27.

23. Ibid.

24. Ibid.

25. Ibid., 50.

26. Elizondo, *Galilean Journey*, 16.

27. Sandoval, *On the Move*, 13.

28. Ibid., 14–15.

29. Elizondo, *Galilean Journey*, 10.

30. Ibid., 10–11.

31. Niebuhr, *The Meaning of Revelation*, 44.

32. Ibid., 52.

33. Elizondo, *Galilean Journey*, 17.

34. Ibid., 23.

35. Sandoval, *On the Move*, 28.

36. Deck, *The Second Wave*, 37.

37. I am grateful to Antonio Medina for this insight.

38. Elizondo, *Galilean Journey*, 10.

39. Ibid., 96.

40. Ibid., 97.

41. Ibid.

42. Ibid., 45.

43. Ibid., 111.

44. Ibid.

45. Ibid., 110.

46. I am grateful to Antonio Medina for explaining this to me.

47. Deck, *The Second Wave*, 81.

48. Martha Nussbaum, *The Fragility of Goodness* (New York: Cambridge University Press, 1986) 333.

49. Elizondo, *Galilean Journey*, 43.

50. Rudolfo A. Anaya, *Bless Me, Ultima* (Berkeley: Tonatiuh-Quinto Sol International Publishers, 1972) 4.

51. Ibid., 51–52.

52. Ibid., 91.

53. Ibid., 76.

54. Ibid., 77.

55. Ibid., 95.

56. I am grateful to Ricardo García and Antonio Medina for the insights developed in this section.

57. Elizondo, *Galilean Journey*, 92.

58. Deck, *The Second Wave*, 56.

59. Ibid., 67–68.

60. Sandoval, *On the Move*, 131.

9

Personal and Ministerial Formation in a Hispanic Context

Ana María Pineda, R.S.M.

Within the past two decades numerous efforts have been initiated in the United States aimed at leadership training of Hispanics within the Catholic Church. Members of the Hispanic community seek to be involved in the ministries of the Church, and both young and old are generally interested in these programs. In spite of the heavy time demands experienced by many, priority commitments are made in favor of participating in leadership formation training programs. An example of such a program is offered at the Tepeyac Institute in El Paso, Texas,[1] the "Institute of Lay ministry of the Diocese of El Paso [which] has as its primary goal the formation of lay leaders to enable their ministry within a border cultural context."[2] Here "border cultural context" takes on a physical manifestation. Literally a step away, Juarez, Mexico, is easily within sight; a reminder of the separation that exists is visibly present in the expansive barbed wire fence that stretches along the length of the El Paso–Juarez border. In many ways the fence is a sad commentary on the U.S. government's futile attempts to contain the Hispanic family. For many Hispanics, the fence is more of a nuisance than an effective means of control; it cannot block the greater continuity of everyday Hispanic life. The involvement in daily events, the celebrations of special family occasions—birthdays, baptisms, weddings, graduations, *quinceñeras,* funerals—go on. A fence cannot put a stop to the flow and rhythm of life that Hispanics cherish. The people live a "border reality."

Tepeyac Institute serves as a symbol of the emergence of U.S. Hispanic ministers and ministries situated on this border reality—a reality that straddles concepts of Church and ministry and that can only be understood by reviewing the historical experience of Church that U.S. Hispanics have lived. How has this history shaped the contemporary emergence of ministry for the Hispanic communities? What implications might this have on the formation for ministry?

Hispanics' Historical Experience of Church

It has already been established that for many Hispanics/Latinos "the era of the Spanish *conquista* of the native peoples of Central and South America serves as the watershed in their history."[3] For many, this historical reality obscures the fact that Hispanics faced a *segunda conquista* under the Treaty of Guadalupe Hidalgo in 1848 when Mexico lost its holdings to the United States. As a consequence of these two events of history, Hispanic Catholicism developed first within the parameters of Church set by Spain and, later, in the pioneering struggle of the Roman Catholic minority to create an "American Church." A brief consideration of both will indicate how these experiences of Church have had serious consequences on the development and understanding of ministry among U.S. Hispanics.

Spanish Missionaries

The zeal of Spanish missionaries who labored in the "New World" has been well documented. Robert Ricard's classic, *The Spiritual Conquest of Mexico,* summarizes the various approaches to evangelization practiced by religious communities like the Franciscans and Dominicans. The determination and the creativity exhibited by the Spanish missionaries furthered Christianity throughout Mesoamerica, and by the mid 1700s Spanish Catholicism had extended into the present-day areas of Florida, Louisiana, Texas, New Mexico, Arizona, and California.

In this effort, the mission system proved to be a significant way of institutionalizing a method of evangelization. The development of this mission system was determined in large measure by each local reality. It is impossible to represent adequately, given the limits of space here, the complex range of differences that existed within the mission system throughout the Southwest. In general terms, however, the missions offered some of the native population food and protection from the danger of abuse and exploitation at the hands of stronger native tribes and/or the Spaniards themselves. The missionaries saw the mission system as a workable structure by which religious instruction could be imparted. Ricard's account indicates that in addition to receiving the faith, the Indians were introduced to Spanish folk traditions, agricultural products and methods, and arts and crafts.[4] In some instances "the friars insisted that native supervisors be selected to direct the new communal duties. These leaders were bestowed titles and symbols of authority and occasionally were rewarded with material advantages beyond what others received."[5]

Nevertheless, while the natives gave some direction to the daily life of the community, basic decisions were made by the Spanish missionaries and by government officials. Within this structure the missionaries managed to teach the faith as well as many of their own religious customs and devotions (for example, *pastorelas*[6] and devotions to the Passion and Infancy). At the same time, the native community acquired skills that could more directly benefit Spanish economic enterprises.[7] The often benign but paternalistic approach employed by the missionaries did not foster great numbers of native vocations nor did it encourage self-determination. The mission system gradually declined in the 1800s, weakened by political strife among Spain, France, England, and the United States.[8] Although Spain withdrew its missionaries in the aftermath of the declaration of Mexican independence in 1821, a number of missionaries continued to minister. In addition, the growth of local Churches in the former New Spain made it possible for the Mexican Church to continue providing ministers to those areas.[9] Although it provided pastoral care for several areas of the southwest United States into the late 1800s, the shortage of clergy became an acute reality by the late 1820s, and the declining number of clergy in the Mexican Church affected the ongoing pastoral care of the Hispanic population.[10] In fact, the religious spirit inherent in ancient Mesoamerica and intertwined with Spanish Catholicism would persevere and be preserved in large measure only by the natural religious leaders in the native Hispanic community.[11] This was a religious leadership that may have been nourished in part by the development of local Churches during the Mexican era.[12] In any event, it can be suggested that the *ministerios caseros*[13] played an important role in the ongoing nourishment of the community's faith despite the general lack of attention by the U.S. Church.

This reliance on the ministries of the people encouraged, in later decades, the emergence of Hispanic lay and apostolic movements in the U.S. Church.[14] A Hispanic lay leadership would be exercised in the promotion of Cursillo, a spiritual renewal weekend experience brought to the United States from Spain in 1957. Another opportunity for lay involvement would be promoted by the introduction of Marriage Encounter *(Encuentro Conyugal/Matrimonial)*, founded in Spain and introduced in the United States in 1968. The Christian Family Movement *(Movimiento Familiar Cristiano)*, a movement that relied predominantly on the leadership of Hispanic couples, would provide an avenue for peer ministry with marriages in need of support and guidance. These apostolic movements and others would be the means through which lay Hispanic ministries would largely be encouraged and realized.

The U.S. Catholic Church as an American Institution

Historically, Henry VIII's repudiation of the papacy and his subsequent demand that he be named the supreme head of the Church in England established an enmity toward the Catholic Church that prejudiced the existence of Spanish and colonial Catholics. Spain had become intimately identified with Catholicism and, thereby, the object of English propaganda that had long considered any advances made against the Spaniards as successful offenses against the papacy.[15] This hostile attitude toward Spanish Catholics was further cultivated by Richard Hakluyt's influential treatise, *Discourse of Western Planting* (1584),[16] which "laid great stress on the need to combat the Spaniards in order to counteract the spread of their superstitious worship in America."[17] Therefore, when the pursuit of religious and political freedom gave birth to the formation of thirteen English colonies in America, and when these colonies gained independence from England in 1783, a new threat was posed for New Spain and for Spanish Catholicism. It was inevitable that the Catholic culture firmly set in place by Spain—and the Catholic colonial minority—would run up against the Protestant culture of the English colonies. The colonial Catholic minority[18] not only experienced hostility in English North American settlements but also found themselves excluded from many aspects of public life. From the establishment of the first permanent English colony in Virginia (1607) until the early nineteenth century, colonial Catholics experienced the consequences of the penal age.[19]

The episcopal consecration of John Carroll on August 15, 1790, as the first bishop of America marked the official beginning of the U.S. Church as an institution.[20] It was an event of monumental significance for the Catholic population in the colonies, which had labored long without an ecclesial leader. Bishop Carroll was fully aware of both the honor and the challenge that his consecration implied for the structuring of the American Catholic Church. In attempting to structure an American Church, Carroll faced the inherent tensions of how to reconcile a religious minority needing to gain respectability while the rapidly growing tide of European immigrants continued to give it a more "foreign" character. European Catholic migration between 1790 and 1850 grew to a total of 1,071,000.[21] This reality forced Carroll and his episcopal successors to attend to the immediate pastoral needs of the Catholic immigrants at a pace that did not permit a slower organization of the American Church. While the Church turned its attention to the incoming peoples of Europe, Hispanics experienced a growing pastoral neglect. This situation would carry well into the mid 1900s.

In spite of Bishop Carroll's attempts to draw on American religious leadership, the fact remained that he drew largely from European religious ranks for the challenging labor of evangelization. American nationalism grew along with westward expansion, and the Church continued to forge its American identity, an identity that would be closely aligned with that of being American. The number of European immigrants continued to grow dramatically, raising the question of how immigrants would become part of the American reality. United States society grappled with theories such as that of Anglo conformity, the melting pot, and cultural pluralism.[22]

The Catholic Church was influenced by these theories in its pastoral approach with the growing European immigrant population. Catholic leadership tended to support a spectrum of approaches, ranging mostly from that of cultural pluralism to that of the melting pot.[23] The religious practices of the native *mestizo* population with its blend of Mesoamerican spirituality and Spanish Catholicism compounded the challenge facing American Church leaders and appeared to be unlikely contributors in the shaping of this Church. The Church focused most of its energy in other sectors of the expanding American Church. The Hispanic population once again found itself occupying a "border" existence. The Hispanic Catholic population in great measure relied on the evangelization received primarily in the earlier period of the Spanish and Mexican Church and on the system of *ministerios caseros,* which the community had developed over the years. As previously mentioned, these *ministerios caseros* would later find a noninstitutional vehicle for exercising native leadership in lay apostolic groups such as Christian Family Movement, Marriage Encounter, and Cursillos.

U.S. Hispanic Catholicism

After the signing of the Treaty of Guadalupe Hidalgo in 1848, the bishops assigned to the newly created dioceses in the Southwest were principally French, although some were Irish and Spanish. In time, the U.S. Church acquired a greater Irish Catholic identity and leadership. Across the country, some attention was gradually given to the Hispanic people but in a sporadic and uneven measure.

The first significant movement toward establishing Church structures for the Hispanics occurred in the 1920s. "In 1923, an immigration office was established by the U.S. Catholic Bishops in El Paso. But the most significant developments came in the waning days of World War II. In 1944, Archbishop Robert E. Lucey of San Antonio sponsored a seminar for the Spanish-speaking."[24] The seminar convened fifty delegates from the western and southwestern regions of the United States to discuss the pastoral attention given by the Church to Hispanics. Archbishop Lucey's initiative motivated other dioceses to follow suit. In 1945, Archbishop Lucey established the first office for Hispanic concerns on a regional level. In 1968, the office would assume national dimensions when it was moved to Washington, D.C., as part of the National Conference of Catholic

Bishops. The leadership for the position of director resided in the hands of non-Hispanics until 1967, when a layman, Antonio Tinajero, was hired. Nevertheless, the office was primarily directed toward the social and material needs of the Hispanic community.

In 1971 Pablo Sedillo, Jr., was appointed director, and under his leadership the office finally assumed a more pastoral role with the responsibility of urging the Church to respond concretely to the pastoral needs of Hispanics. Other significant movements began to occur, marked by the consecration of the first Hispanic U.S. bishop, Patricio Flores, in 1969. In 1972 the first National Hispanic Pastoral Encounter *(Encuentro Nacional Hispano de Pastoral)* was celebrated, initiating a grass-roots process by which the Hispanic community, for the first time in its history, began a search to identify its pastoral needs and its relationship to the U.S. Church. A succession of *Encuentros* would follow, in 1977 and 1985. This process resulted in the formulation of the National Pastoral Plan for Hispanic Ministry, approved by the NCCB in 1987. The net result was a growing consciousness on the part of the Hispanic people of their identity as Church and their role within that Church. For many Hispanics it brought about a greater cultural awareness and with it self-confidence. Hispanics would no longer conform to being a passive presence in the U.S. Church, nor would they readily accept a position of nonleadership.

The Significance of Ministry Formation in the *Encuentros*

The overall significance of the *Encuentro* process (1972–1985) cannot be emphasized enough. Prior to this movement, U.S. Hispanics had virtually no say within the Church structures of either Spanish or American Catholicism. The *Encuentros* represented a first step across the border of pastoral indifference and neglect. For the first time, Hispanics found themselves exploring the question of Church and their place in it. The *Encuentros* offered a major opportunity for communal reflection and decision making for Hispanics on matters of faith and religious values. One of the richest areas of exploration was that of ministry. Some of the insights gleaned over the past two decades clearly indicate fundamental elements the Hispanic community deemed essential for ministry.

I Encuentro Nacional Hispano de Pastoral (1972)

During the *I Encuentro* keynote addresses were given by Bishop Zambrano of Colombia and Reverend Virgilio Elizondo. Both touched upon several aspects of ministry that would later be recognized as important elements for the entire Church: (1) the identity of Church; (2) the place of Church in the modern world; (3) the incarnational reality in which the

Church is rooted; (4) pastoral activity as the proper exercise of the salvific mission of the Church; and (5) the implicit understanding that the response of love expressed through pastoral activity inherently belongs to *all* baptized women and men.[25]

Specific mention was made of the critical need to establish centers and programs for leadership training of bishops, priests, religious, and laity (Hispanic and non-Hispanic). Recommendations were made for non-Hispanic clergy and religious preparing to work in Hispanic ministry:

> The style of ministry of foreign (non-Hispanic) clergy and religious who work in Spanish-speaking communities in the U.S. must be, in the best sense of the word, missionary. That is to say that there must exist, on their part, familiarity, adaptation, and acceptance of the language, culture, and style of Catholicism of the Spanish speaking people. They must have, as their principal goal, the development of native Christian and ecclesiastical leadership, such as, bishops, priests, deacons, religious, and lay leaders.[26]

Recommendations were made for the preparation of Hispanic priests that stressed the importance of cultural identity, bilingual and bicultural formation, strong identification with the Hispanic community, and teamwork as the preferred style of ministry.

II Encuentro Nacional Hispano de Pastoral (1977)

Five years later the Hispanic community deepened its understanding of the concept of ministry. During the process of *II Encuentro* the significance of ministry emerged as one belonging to all Christians through their baptism. The articulation of the emerging concept of ministry was based on the fact that the Hispanic people identified themselves as *Somos pueblo* (We are a people) and *Somos Iglesia* (We are Church). The model of Church favored is that of community. Within this context, ministry is understood as the mission of all the members of the Church without distinction or exception. The gifts and talents of the community are given by the Holy Spirit for the good of the whole. Finally, service is seen as a concrete expression of faith and a way of living the two great commandments.[27]

The task of Hispanics was therefore not to investigate who should be involved in ministry but how best to facilitate the participation of all. It was a participation that sought to stress the equal access to ministry and minimized the distinctions evoked by the terms "ordained" and "non-ordained." In the history of Hispanic communities, such distinctions had given them little or marginal access to ministries within the institutional Church. Within the context of the Hispanic experience, ministry became an essential and concrete part of being a Christian. It was an awareness that did not seem to be the approach to ministry within the institutional Church.

During the process of the *II Encuentro* another consideration for ministry emerged. Aligned with the concept of ministry as belonging to all the baptized was the fact that it was vital to know the context within which ministry was exercised. The three essential elements of culture, historical reality, and serving the actual needs of the community were the indispensable context for ministry. These three elements became both a lens for discerning which ministries were needed and a means for assessing which members of the community possessed these gifts. It followed that the type of ministerial formation provided also needed to take into consideration the foundational elements of culture, historical reality, and actual needs. The theological framework was that of the Incarnation. Formation programs for ministers required the integration of practice and theory in seeking to provide a formation process holistic in method and content. The *II Encuentro* proceedings insisted that in all these pursuits the concept of equality in ministry remain fundamental.

III Encuentro Nacional Hispano de Pastoral (1985)

The *III Encuentro* was not an isolated event in the history of the pastoral ministry of the Hispanic people in the United States. It was rather one more step in a process of ecclesial participation that began with the establishment of Church offices for the care of Hispanics in the first half of this century, for example, in Philadelphia in 1915 and in San Antonio in 1945.[28]

In light of this, the conclusions of the *III Encuentro* were more concisely defined. What clearly emerged was that for those of the Hispanic community who had been involved in the process of the *Encuentros,* the earlier question that plagued Hispanics regarding who could participate in ministry was no longer an issue.[29] The issue now was the fact that goodwill alone was not sufficient for ministry. It was necessary to avail oneself of leadership training programs that would enable the Hispanic people to become skilled contributors in the ministries of the Church. Time had proven that given the complexity of U.S. society and of the existing structures of the institutionalized Church, Hispanic ministers needed adequate programs of formation in order to participate actively in the ministries of the Church. While this was a fact that challenged Hispanics desiring to be effective ministers, it was also noted that even when an effort was made to prepare oneself to serve, the Church did not always recognize and accept Hispanics.[30] In addition, the proceedings raised questions regarding institutional ministry and whether or not it would permit Hispanics to exercise the diversity of gifts they possessed.

Implications of History for U.S. Hispanics' Personal and Ministerial Formation

Paul Wadell suggests in the previous essay that "for the Hispanic peoples, conquest remains the paradigmatic shaping event of their existence, and as the heart of their inner history it is the hermeneutic for exploring their sense of morality."[31] Borrowing Wadell's fine insight, the same could be said regarding the emerging concept of ministry in the Hispanic community and the critical role of culture within it. The conquest by Spain essentially eliminated the cultural and religious identity of a people. Nowhere else is this reality as stark as in the exchange between the Twelve and the remaining wisemen of the Mesoamerican world. Following the doctrinal instruction of the friars, the spokesperson of those assembled responded in part with these words:

> Perhaps we are to be taken to our ruin, to our destruction.
> But where are we to go now?
> We are ordinary people,
> we are subject to death and destruction, we are mortals;
> allow us then to die,
> let us perish now,
> since our gods are already dead.
> It is not enough that we have already lost,
> that our way of life has been taken away,
> has been annihilated.[32]

From this painful clash between two worlds a new race was produced. Elizondo describes this process with the term *mestizaje*: "the process through which two totally different peoples mix biologically and culturally so that a new people begins to emerge, e.g., Europeans and Asians gave birth to Euroasians: Iberians and Indians gave birth to the Mexican and Latin American people."[33] The violence that accompanied such a *mestizaje* made this type of union less than ideal, contrary to what sometimes is suggested. The offspring of this union would be forced to live between worlds, on the border of each but never fully in either one. The *mestizo* culture would never be able to realistically claim their root identity within one culture. On either side of the border they would be considered "different."

The struggle of the *mestizo* for self-definition would be historically reminiscent of the ongoing philosophical and anthropological debate carried on by Spain over whether the natives were humans[34]—a debate that would continue to permeate the political, economic, and religious decisions of both Crown and Cross. It would provoke the sermon delivered by the Dominican Antonio Montesinos in Santo Domingo in 1511 protesting the abuse visited upon the inhabitants of that land through the system of the *encomiendas*.[35] It was the reason used in 1555 in forbidding the ordinations of *mestizos,* Indians, and blacks[36]—a debate that would have consequences not only in the ongoing disregard for the humanity and equality of the inhabitants of the lands appropriated by Spain but also in the denial of their integration into the vital dimensions of decision making in Church and society for centuries to come.

The *segunda conquista,* marked by the westward expansion, and most significantly in 1848 by the Treaty of Guadalupe Hidalgo, eliminated cultural and religious identity in its refusal to acknowledge and credit a *"mestizo* Catholicism" as valid. The concept of mainstreaming and the image of the melting pot reflected an inability to accept difference and diversity as compatible with orthodoxy and unity. In both instances of conquest, the U.S. Hispanic had been robbed of identity. Consequently, one of the critical issues for ministry remains the integration of cultural-religious identity in preparing for personal and ministerial formation. The *Encuentros* are filled with recommendations that stress the need for evangelization to

> begin with the human person; every person is incarnated in a particular culture, time, and place. . . . An evangelization incarnated in a given culture is essential for all peoples, but it is especially important for the Hispanic people in this country. The temptation to cultural assimilation is constantly present, and in many cases it ceases to be only a temptation and becomes a reality. This is not only contrary to the rights of the person, but also an affront to the Gospel itself. Evangelization is true to itself and reaches down to the deepest roots of the person when it is incarnated in a culture.[37]

In this appropriation of identity, it is necessary to affirm the value of language and of cultural and religious values as integral to evangelization. It is a challenge both Church and society must embrace if evangelization is to be truly realized. Otherwise, a significant percent of the U.S. Hispanic population will continue to see participation in the Church as a series of border crossings that offers no definite place of residence.

The issue of race is directly related to the question of inculturation. In fact, cultural identity for Hispanics is a theological issue. "If religion is essentially dealing with the mysteriousness of life that the ultimate questions of our origin, death, and destiny reveal,"[38] or as Paul Tillich understood religion as the inmost source of culture, its core significance,[39] then cultural identity for Hispanics cannot be separated from the enterprise of theology. It is as important for Hispanics to know about their cultural identity as it is to know about God; an understanding of the divine that emerges from within that world.

The intimate links between faith and culture set Hispanics on a quest for self-definition in their search for God. In this quest for cultural identity Hispanics seek not only self-definition but also a right to express their unique relationship to God within that context. This enterprise carries serious implications for Church life on many levels. It calls into question current parish practices (liturgical worship, sacramental celebrations, catechetical programs, preaching of the Word). Hispanics have been defined by a series of historical events, a reality that has determined in large measure how Hispanics have experienced and worshiped God in the U.S. context. The U.S. Hispanic experience will change only when current ministerial formation takes the issue of culture seriously.

The *Encuentro* proceedings leave no doubt in their collective assessment of U.S. Hispanics that culture is fundamental in the task of evangelization. At the root of pastoral neglect of Hispanics is the general unfamiliarity of pastoral agents with the cultural and religious tenets of Hispanics and with their failure to respect its validity. The number of priests and religious possessing an understanding of the language and culture are minuscule given the Hispanic population. The *Encuentro* proposed that what was at stake was the survival of Hispanics in the Catholic Church, given the minimal pastoral attention they were receiving.[40]

In the five-year lapse between the *II* and *III Encuentros* it became evident that Catholic Hispanics were seeking out other Churches to satisfy their hunger for God. The alarming number of Hispanics joining other sects and denominations was increasing at such a rate that it would defy the often-cited belief that by the year 2000 half the Catholic Church would be Hispanic. Culture is a priority in the creation and nourishing of small ecclesial communities.[41] It is an essential element in the development of diocesan pastoral plans as well as in the promotion of a style of ministry that is coherent with cultural values.[42] Culture is the basis for informing pastoral agents on the "how" and "what" of Hispanic ministry. Culture is the tool that facilitates personal awareness and conscientizes pastoral leaders.[43] It is the point both of departure and of return in providing and maintaining Hispanics with their identity as human beings as well as with their religious identity. Its all-permeating importance underscores the central position culture occupies in the faith life of Hispanic peoples and, consequently, in the personal and ministerial formation of Hispanics as well as non-Hispanics interested in Hispanic ministry.

The Present Historical Reality

The popular belief among many is that devotion to the cross, to the Suffering Jesus, is paramount for Hispanics. While this is true, it is surprising that the two images that emerge forcefully from the *Encuentros* are those of the Lord of history and of the incarnation, or humanity, of Jesus. This fact does not negate the former, but it does accentuate the undeniable presence of God in Hispanic history. In pastoral theological reflection language, it is expressed thus:

> At this moment of grace (kairos) that was the process and event of the III Encuentro, in seeking to recapture and value their culture and identity, the Hispanic people have discovered Jesus incarnated in their own history, which confirms them in their dignity as the family of God.[44]

It is within the realm of human history that the reign of God is inaugurated. It is incumbent for Hispanics to become increasingly aware of the social, economic, and political situation in which they live.[45] It is in the marketplace of the world that the matter for ministry is discovered, and it is that reality that elicits a gospel response.

What are the present signs of the times asking for in light of the gospel? Being more attentive to present historical reality assists Hispanics in the living out of their faith as a matter of daily living. In fact, it is the inalienable right of each human being to receive the quality of education that integrates them as active agents of their own history.[46] At the same time, this education must promote a maturity of faith and a sense of responsibility beyond the confines of one's own community.[47] In order to reach this historical awareness, it is important that the method of education employed take this dimension into consideration. This historical consideration enables the minister to respond more appropriately to the current needs of society. This response is shaped by faith, and it is that essential element that differentiates it from mere social analysis. It is through this kind of theological reflection that it is possible to identify more clearly those who are the marginalized in society and to determine the gospel response that is required. Furthermore, it is the needs *in themselves* that determine what kind of ministries are necessary for the mission of the Church.

Finally, this Hispanic reflection on ministry has led to an affirmation that "as baptized Christians and members of the Catholic Church, that to serve is the mission of all the members of the Church. . . . Each one of us is called to serve our neighbors according to the diversity of gifts and talents given to us by the Holy Spirit (1 Cor 12:4-11). By so expressing our faith in a variety of services, we will be able to carry out the great commandment: love of God and love of neighbor (Matt 22:37)."[48]

The process of reflection has led Hispanics to an understanding that in ministry there is a distinction of services but not a distinction in terms of equality (one ministry among many). This understanding places emphasis on the Church primarily as a Church of the people of God and perceives ministry as a service rendered by each member for the good of all. Ministry is not understood as part of a hierarchical construct. That is why the term "professional minister," as often used by schools of theology, communicates the message that some ministries are considered superior. This serves only to create another border that separates Hispanics from attaining an achievable inclusion in the ministerial life of the Church.

Conclusion

For historical reasons Hispanics have not had an opportunity to create a model of Church and ministry of their own. The process of the *Encuentros* has provided U.S. Hispanics the historical moment for such exploration.[49] What emerges from this community-rooted process of reflection is the fundamental role of culture in evangelization and in being Church. It shapes the concept of ministry appropriated by Hispanics, which demands a distinct pastoral approach. It is this pastoral approach that identifies the community as the locus for ministry. It is through the human praxis of solidarity and *acompañamiento*[50] with the community that ministry is most appropriately understood, identified, and actualized.

Fundamentally, ministry in the Hispanic context is a communal activity built on a collaborative style of ministry—*pastoral de conjunto*.[51] It is a historicized ministry that responds holistically to living men and women; it challenges any dichotomy between life and faith, praxis and theory. This model of ministry makes a preferential option for the poor and the marginalized; it is primarily concerned with the needs of persons[52] and less concerned with bureaucratic constraints and guidelines. Historically, the need for a distinct pastoral approach has placed Hispanics in tension with the institutionalized ministries of the Church. This reality brings the emerging Hispanic concept of ministry into conflict with that of the American Church. It questions the distinctions often made by terms such as "ordained" and "nonordained" ministers. It raises issues regarding approaches to ministerial formation employed across the country, not only in seminaries and schools of theology but also in the increasing number of programs created for the formation of laity. For seminaries and schools of theology, it raises crucial issues of how Hispanic candidates are being formed. Is it a formation that alienates Hispanic candidates from their own ethnic communities by deculturizing individuals or by providing them with ministerial tools that prove to be ineffective in the Hispanic context?[53]

Recent efforts[54] to explore this issue indicate that, in general, Roman Catholic schools of theology have yet to find an adequate response to the challenge of ministry in the Hispanic context. Hispanic faculty in these institutions are few, and those present are often burdened with the task of facing the challenge alone in the name of the institution. This is compounded by the small number of existing Hispanic theologians and by the additional factor that often their educational experience has not differed from the traditional training received in seminaries and schools of theology. Regarding the presence of Hispanic courses of study in the curriculum of such institutions, they are for the most part elective and thus do not significantly impact the overall curriculum. In addition, the classical lecture style is often the usual teaching method. This raises questions of whether this is effective pedagogy for Hispanic and non-Hispanic students wishing to prepare themselves to minister in the Hispanic communities.

For programs created for the formation of laity, there is the question of whether the Church has met the challenge of creating ministerial formation programs that are not only appropriate for laity but sensitive to and conscious of the valid role of culture in the design of such programs. While there are a growing number of such programs on the diocesan level, it remains to be seen whether, ultimately, they are designed to prepare Hispanic participants for graduate level degrees and to equip them to participate in decision making arenas of Church life. For both lay and religious programs, there is the question of how the values and experience of Hispanic cultures permeate the formation process for ministry, and if the formation process is capable of accepting a different understanding of ministry.

It is important to acknowledge that tension will continue to be part of the relationship between the Hispanic reality and the U.S. Church's understanding of ministry and Church. It is a consequence of inculturation. The challenge for both will be the pursuit of a dialogue that is based on mutual equality and respect. How does one find an adequate "border" language that will facilitate communication between two realities?[55] How does one address a personal and ministerial formation in a Hispanic context? These are the challenges.

Notes

1. I am indebted to Msgr. Arturo Bañuelas, director and founder of the Tepeyac Institute in El Paso, Texas, for the time spent in visiting this new venture in lay leadership formation. This opportunity provided me with the experience necessary in reaching some of my own insights and appreciation of the subject.

2. Taken from the Statement of Purpose formulated for the Tepeyac Institute.

3. Cf. Mark Francis, "Popular Piety and Liturgical Reform in a Hispanic Context," in the following chapter.

4. See Robert Ricard, *The Spiritual Conquest of Mexico* (Berkeley: University of California Press, 1966) 31.

5. Gilberto M. Hinojosa, "Friars and Indians: Towards a Perspective of Cultural Interaction in the San Antonio Missions," *U.S. Catholic Historian* (Winter/Spring 1990) 6.

6. *Pastorela* is a mystery play of Spanish origin. It is a popular interpretation of the shepherds' reaction to the announcement of the birth of Jesus.

7. Hinojosa, "Friars and Indians," 21.

8. See Robert E. Wright, *Popular and Official Religiosity: A Theoretical Analysis and a Case Study of Laredo-Nuevo Laredo, 1755–1857* (Ph.d. diss., Graduate Theological Union, Berkeley, 1992). Wright examines the dominant historiography of Hispanic Catholics in what is now the southwest United States and concludes that almost exclusive attention to the annals of the Hispanic missions has led to a neglect of the historical emergence of local Churches of Hispanic Catholics on the northern frontier of New Spain, later independent Mexico.

9. Robert E. Wright, "Local Church Emergence and Mission Decline: The Historiography of the Catholic Church in the Southwest During the Spanish and Mexican Periods," *U.S. Catholic Historian* (Winter/Spring 1990) 29.

10. See Robert E. Wright, "Local Church Emergence and Mission Decline: The Historiography of the Catholic Church in the Southwest During the Spanish and Mexican Periods," *U.S. Catholic Historian,* Christopher J. Kauffman, ed. (Pennsylvania: The Sheridan Press, 1989) 27–48.

11. See David J. Weber, *Myth and the History of the Hispanic Southwest* (Albuquerque: University of New Mexico Press, 1988) 89–104. Weber explores the unbalanced, ethnocentric, and incomplete historiography that has been produced of the Mexican era. He suggests that the history has been primarily written by United States historians and has predominantly focused on the theme of American expansion. In light of this, I would suggest that much historical examination must be undertaken in order to ascertain the extent of Hispanic involvement in many areas of life, including that of active Church ministries.

12. This theory is explored by Robert E. Wright in the works already cited. Also, an idea suggested by Juan Romero, "Charism and Power," *U.S. Catholic Historian* (Winter/Spring 1990) 148, is that while the American Catholic Church was developing new structures and institutions, the same Catholic Church under very different leadership had already, for more than two centuries, been developing a culturally adapted and indigenous Church from the soil and people of New Mexico.

13. The term is used to mean ministries or services that were provided by members of the community without institutional Church recognition or assistance, for example, prayer leader, transmitter of the faith, preserver of morality, care of the sick.

14. See Dominga M. Zapata, S.H., "Ministries Among Hispanics in the United States: Development and Challenges," *New Theology Review* (November 1990) 62–71.

15. Cf. John Tracy Ellis, *Catholics in Colonial America* (Maryland: Helicon, 1965) 316.

16. Richard Hakluyt was an Anglican chaplain to the English ambassador in Paris. He presented his treatise to Queen Elizabeth I in 1584. His persuasive argument in favor of the English colonization in the New World, along with his enmity toward Spaniards and Portuguese, was influential.

17. Ellis, *Catholics in Colonial America,* 318.

18. Ibid., 330–31; 344–46. Even Maryland, which held a unique position as a haven for Catholics, did not completely escape from religious prejudices. Missionaries desiring to enter Maryland were subject to the conditions placed by the

land proprietors. Beginning in 1688 a series of penal codes were anacted that discriminated against Catholics.

19. Ibid., 318–19.

20. See Dolores Liptak, *Immigrants and Their Church* (New York: Macmillan, 1989) 3–4.

21. Cf. John Tracy Ellis, *American Catholicism* (Chicago: University of Chicago Press, 1956) 49.

22. Cf. Richard M. Linkh, *American Catholicism and European Immigrants* (New York: The Center for Migration Studies of New York, 1975) 20.

23. Ibid., 21–31.

24. Moíses Sandoval, *On the Move: A History of the Hispanic Church in the United States* (New York: Orbis, 1989) 47.

25. Office of Hispanic Affairs, *Proceedings of the I Encuentro Hispano de Pastoral,* 1972. Printed in binder form for the participants of I Encuentro.

26. Ibid., no. 41.

27. United States Catholic Conference, *Proceedings of the II Encuentro Nacional Hispano de Pastoral* (Washington: United States Catholic Conference Creative Service Office, 1978) 31.

28. United States Catholic Conference, *Prophetic Voices: The Document on the Process of the III Encuentro Nacional Hispano de Pastoral* (Washington: United States Catholic Conference, 1986) 31.

29. The proceedings of the *III Encuentro* reaffirm the earlier intuitions of the *II Encuentro* and extend its reflection on ministry to include this statement: "Fulfillment of the Church's mission depends greatly on an active commitment of the baptized," *III Encuentro* (1986) 13.

30. See *III Encuentro Proceedings* (1986) 14.

31. See Paul Wadell, "Ethics and the Narrative of Hispanic-Americans: Conquest, Community, and the Fragility of Life," in the previous chapter.

32. Virgilio P. Elizondo, *La Morenita: Evangelizer of the Americas* (San Antonio: Mexican American Cultural Center, 1980) 50, 53.

33. Ibid., 17.

34. See Lewis Hanke, *Aristotle and the American Indians* (Bloomington, Ind.: University Press, 1959); Marina Herrera and Jaime Vidal, "Evangelization: Then and Now (?)," *New Theology Review* (November 1990) 17.

35. Montesinos' sermon denounces the abusive treatment of the natives saying: "Are they not men? Do they not have rational souls? Are you not bound to love them as you love yourselves?" Sermon is quoted in H. McKennie Goodpasture, *Cross and Sword: An Eyewitness History of Christianity in Latin America* (Maryknoll, N.Y.: Orbis, 1989) 11–12. See Justo L. Gonzalez, "Voices of Compassion," *Missiology* (April 1992) 163–76.

36. Ricard, *The Spiritual Conquest of Mexico,* 230.

37. *III Encuentro,* 7.

38. Denise Lardner Carmody and John Carmody, *Religion: The Great Questions* (New York: Seabury, 1983) 1.

39. Paul Tillich, *Systematic Theology* (Chicago: University of Chicago Press, 1963) 158.

40. See *III Encuentro Proceedings.*

41. Ibid., 8.

42. The importance of the community is an example of a cultural value that is an essential ingredient in the exercise of ministry from the Hispanic perspective. There are other cultural values that must be part of the weave.

43. *III Encuentro Proceedings* 9, no. 19.

44. Ibid., 9.

45. Ibid., 19–20.

46. Ibid., 8.

47. Ibid.

48. *II Encuentro,* 70.

49. It is important to note that while a significant number of Catholic Hispanics were involved in the process of the *Encuentros,* there were greater numbers of Hispanics who were not even aware of this process. Nevertheless, as a national process it is noteworthy in the lives of Catholic Hispanics, given the historical absence of any ethnic gathering that mobilized for the purpose of voicing its pastoral needs and giving direction to those needs.

50. In Spanish, the term *acompañamiento* means "to accompany." It is a term that is active in nature and that encompasses the human experience of the person with whom one not only journeys but with whom one enters into solidarity.

51. In Spanish, the term *pastoral de conjunto* is understood as the harmonious coordination of all the elements of the pastoral ministry with the actions of the pastoral ministers and the structures in view of a common goal: the kingdom of God.

52. See, in this volume, the section in Paul Wadell's essay "Hispanic Attitudes toward Law, Authority, and Church."

53. A forum on Hispanic vocation and formation was held in Denver in June 1988 under the leadership of Gary Riebe-Estrella, S.V.D., project director of Project 13 of the United States Catholic Conference. It investigated the question of formation of Hispanics for ordained ministry. The results were distributed to seminaries and schools of theology, but whether or not the findings shed light on the current training remains to be determined.

54. In 1989 and 1990, Catholic Theological Union in Chicago engaged in visiting seven sites in the country to gather existing information on how seminaries and schools of theology were attempting to answer the question of how best to prepare ordained ministers for Hispanic communities. The visits, while not exhaustive, gave some indication of the formation approaches that are being employed.

55. The fact is that Hispanics often live in multilevel realities in any given society. The two realities singled out here for the purpose of focusing the discussion are those of the U.S. Church and of U.S. Catholic Hispanics.

10

Popular Piety and Liturgical Reform in a Hispanic Context

Mark R. Francis, C.S.V.

The 1990 conference of the *Instituto de Liturgia Hispana* held in Phoenix focused on the theme "Popular Religiosity of the Hispanics: Myths, Symbols, and Creativity." Over three hundred people were in attendance. Most were Hispanics involved in pastoral ministry on either the diocesan or parish level. Many came with a keen desire to wrestle with the daily challenges that Hispanic popular religiosity poses to evangelization and parochial worship.

The purpose of this article, however, is not to report on or evaluate this meeting. Rather, it is simply to share some reflections from my point of view as an Anglo[1] liturgist who has had some experience in Hispanic ministry both in Latin America and in the United States. I would also like to raise some questions that were sparked by the major addresses and by the small group discussions that were an integral part of this conference.

Hispanic Popular Religiosity and Preconciliar Devotionalism

The first question posed to the small groups was emblematic of the "problem" often perceived by *Anglo* Catholics whose spirituality and liturgical life have been profoundly transformed by the particular way the reforms of the Second Vatican Council were implemented in the United States. I will quote the question in Spanish because it loses something in translation: *"Cuál es el Cristo, la Virgencita y el santo favorito en tu familia y en tu país?"* (Which is the Christ, the Virgin [Mary] and the favorite saint in your family and in your country?) I would suspect that such a question would not excite much discussion in an Anglo parish or among non-Hispanic members of theological faculties in most of the country. Nevertheless, this query elicited a warm response among the participants at the

162

conference, who—in loving detail—shared their family's history of devotion to Christ as the *Varón de los Dolores* (the Man of Sorrows) or the *Santo Niño Jesus de Antocha* (the Holy Child Jesus of Antocha), the *Señor de los Milagros* (the Lord of Miracles); and to the *Virgencita* as *Nuestra Señora de Guadalupe, de la Caridad del Cobre, de Chiquinquirá,* et al.

To enter into the dialogue in some fashion, I had to think back to the period of my childhood when my maternal grandmother used to light candles to the Infant of Prague, or my mother attended a novena to Saint Joseph to pray for a happy death for my critically ill grandfather. I thought back to my time in grade school when we had May crownings of the Blessed Virgin (who I think was Our Lady of Grace, but I'm not really sure). In order to contribute a little more to the discussion, I mentioned that the United States was consecrated to the Immaculate Conception. The response of my fellow participants to this recital was very interesting. Several said that while *Nuestra Señora de Guadalupe* was their favorite *Virgencita,* they also liked the Immaculate Conception, implying that our sharing in admiration for this *Virgencita* was the basis for a relationship of mutual understanding.

While I had to think of the now long-abandoned religious practices of my childhood in order to add something to the conversation, devotion to Christ and Mary under their various titles as well as prayers directed to patron saints is still a vibrant expression of Latin American popular piety; a fact noted time and again in official Church statements made at Medellín (1967), Puebla (1979), in the U.S. bishops' letter *The Hispanic Presence* (1984), and in *The National Pastoral Plan for Hispanic Ministry* (1987). I suspect, however, that while there are points of convergence between the devotionalism of *Anglos* prior to the council and Hispanic popular religiosity today, non-Hispanics who minister in a Hispanic context or those who teach Hispanic students make a basic error by unconsciously equating the devotionalism of their youth with expressions of Hispanic popular religiosity. I would suggest that there are fundamental differences between the two and that these differences need to be appreciated and respected in the process of preparing the Liturgy in a Hispanic community. These differences are due to the historical and cultural background of Hispanics, which *Anglo* Catholics do not share; they demand a distinct pastoral approach to both evangelization and liturgical reform in a Hispanic context, and they also help to explain why the liturgical reform initiated by Vatican II has been relatively low on the list of pastoral priorities among Hispanics in this country and in Latin America.

In order to examine these differences, it is helpful to sketch briefly the origin and development of Hispanic Catholicism, which helps to explain the complicated relationship between Hispanic popular religion and the official Liturgy of the Church.

A Glance at the History of Hispanic Popular Religion

Because the Hispanic presence today in the United States is perceived by many as a new phenomenon, it is often surprising to non-Hispanics that the roots of Hispanic culture in this country go back almost five hundred years. Whatever interpretation is given to this event, the Spanish and Portuguese *conquista* of the native peoples of the "New World" and their settlement of Central and South America is unarguably a watershed in world history. This event continues to be regarded with ambivalence today by many Latin Americans. On the one hand, the Spaniards and Portuguese brought their Iberian form of Catholic Christianity, for which most are grateful. On the other hand, "evangelization" was often done at the point of a sword and was coupled with the destruction of the social, religious, and political institutions of pre-Columbian America and the oppression of native peoples (and later slaves from Africa), who were regarded by their conquerors as "inferiors." During the colonial period a *mestizaje* of peoples took place—native Americans, Spaniards, and Africans—who today are identified as "Hispanic" or "Latino." This *mestizaje*, it must always be remembered, was born of a terrible suffering—the repercussions of which linger on into the twentieth century.

During the early colonial period, the Church, subordinate to the interests of the Spanish Crown under the *Patronado Real,* sent missionaries throughout the "new" continent to evangelize and catechize. Apart from courageous Church leaders such as Bartolomé de las Cásas, Antonio de Montesinos, and Pedro de Córdoba, all of whom spoke for the humanity of the indigenous people and against the rapacity and savagery of the *conquistadores*,[2] the official Church was largely perceived by the native peoples as an alien institution forced on them by the victors. Spaniards and their descendants *(peninsulares y criollos)* not only controlled the civil institutions of the colonial government but, for centuries, were generally the only people admitted to positions of Church leadership as priests and bishops.[3]

This has much to do with the development of Latino popular religion, which, while generally respectful of "orthodox" Catholicism, merged the basic worldview of the native cultures with the Iberian Catholicism imported by the Spaniards. This new synthesis was fertile ground for popular religious expression, which has often been described as *religión casera*—or "domestic religion." While the official rites of the Church were squarely in the hands of Spanish or Creole clerics, the devotion to the Suffering Christ, veneration of Mary (especially under the titles of her many apparitions), and prayers to the saints for their intercession became the affective focus of much of Hispanic religiosity. Interestingly (and understandably), "religious persons" in this context even today are not limited to the clergy but also include the parents and *ancianos* (older members of the extended family, especially women), to whom the care of religion in the home has been confided. It is they who pray in the home at the *altarcito,* which is decorated with candles and statues of Christ, Mary, and the saints; who impart blessings on members of the family when they leave the house or embark on a new venture; who are asked to pray for the intercession of the saints in times of sickness and tragedy; and who function as spiritual guides and mediators between the transcendent Source of life and the family.

The forms that popular religion have taken in Latin America often reflect a cultural resistance of the native peoples to the trauma of the *conquista.* One only need read the *Nican Mapohua* (the account of the apparition of Our Lady of Guadalupe to the Aztec Juan Diego) and see her image, which bears the likeness of a *mestizo* maiden surrounded by elements reflective of the native religion, to appreciate that there is a qualitative difference between this *Virgencita* and Our Lady of Lourdes, who proclaims the doctrine of her immaculate conception, or Our Lady of Fátima, who warns against Bolshevism. Guadalupe represents the very icon of the *raza* for Mexicans and other Latin Americans: the fact that God did not abandon the *pueblo* in the face of Spanish oppression and slavery.[4]

This resistance also took other forms in different regions of New Spain. Interestingly, this resistance was not always Marian in expression. The Sanctuary of Monserrat in Colombia, built by the Spaniards on a mountain overlooking the city of Bogotá, was first dedicated to Our Lady of Monserrat, whose shrine is located in a Benedictine abbey outside of Barcelona in Cataluña. Soon after its construction, the native peoples changed the focus of the sanctuary to a statue of the Suffering Jesus. Thus this place of pilgrimage is to the *Varón de los Dolores,* rather than to an imported Catalán Madonna. These are only two examples of the countless ways in which the indigenous people, while converted to Christianity, maintained a degree of independence and cultural identity even during Spain's political and cultural hegemony in the Americas. The official Church, while long in control of the hierarchy and the celebration of the sacraments—the official worship of the Church—could not control popular religion and the direction it took. Thus much of popular piety strikes a political, social, and cultural as well as religious chord among many Hispanics.

Another often overlooked factor that helped shape Hispanic popular religiosity is its relationship to an official Church that was essentially medieval. During its formative period and even after the struggle for independence from Spain, Catholicism in Latin America never underwent the systematic standardization that was brought about by the Council of Trent elsewhere in the Catholic world. North American Catholicism, for example, was largely dominated by clergy drawn from European ethnic groups who immigrated to this country along with their people in the nineteenth century and who were inspired by the norms and centralized pastoral practices of Tridentine Catholicism. In contrast, Hispanic Catholics, except perhaps those from large cities, have never been historically so influenced. The first period of evangelization of Latin America antedates the Council of Trent; and even after the decrees and norms established by the council were promulgated in Europe, their implementation was both slow and sporadic, even into the nineteenth century. There was also a chronic shortage of clergy during the entire colonial era; a shortage that persists to this very day. This was due largely to the widespread policy of the Spanish ecclesiastical authorities to deny ordination to Hispanic candidates, even if that meant large segments of the population would be without priests. Thus, as Allan Deck and others have pointed out, "the sense of Catholicism and Church order that was transplanted onto the Latin American continent was fundamentally medieval, although features of the dramatic baroque period were soon to manifest themselves in the preaching, architecture, and religious pageantry promoted by the missioners. These approaches reflected a less standardized kind of Catholicism than that which the Council of Trent was to embrace and promote in Europe."[5]

Herein lies the difference between Hispanic popular religion and the devotionalism of the Catholic immigrant groups who came to the United States. Because it adhered more strictly to the spirit of the Council of Trent, the devotional life of most of the European immigrant groups, while sentimental, emotional, and privatistic, was regulated by the clergy, who were instrumental in its revival during the nineteenth century.[6] Latin America never had a history of such clerical oversight, both because of a lack of native clergy and a policy toward popular religion that was much more laissez-faire on the part of the Church. This was especially true in the rural areas, and it is from these areas that the majority of Hispanics come who move to the United States. This factor has had far-reaching consequences on the religious worldview of Hispanics in the United States, who, in cases of necessity, have nurtured their faith and their religious-cultural identity principally through the symbols and rituals of their popular religiosity and without the benefit of clergy. This particular form of religiosity tends toward personal, affective expressions of human relationship with the Transcendent personified in the Suffering Jesus, Mary, and the saints, as opposed to the more doctrinally "correct" version of Catholicism of the European immigrants. It is also perfectly consonant with the emphasis on personal identity based on human relationships of which Paul Wadell speaks in his essay in the present volume on the ethical world of the Hispanic.

Hispanic Liturgy and Popular Religion Before Vatican II

But what of the Liturgy in this context? As we have noted, the Catholicism brought by the Iberian missioners was essentially that of medieval

Spain. By definition, the Liturgy, as the official prayer of the Church, could only be celebrated by clerics. Since these clerics were either Spaniards or descendants of Spaniards, the Tridentine reform of the Mass naturally took hold in Latin America, even if Church order and pastoral practice remained pluriform and medieval for centuries. Thus, while there was a standardization in liturgical practice due to the diffusion of the printed *Missal of Pius V* and the other official liturgical books, this standardization took place within a culture that was essentially oral and nonliterate.

Moreover, since the *Rituale Romanum* of 1614 was not made obligatory in the same way as the *Ordo Missae,* the way the other sacraments were administered continued to vary a great deal from one region to another in Latin America. This diversity is well reflected even today in the various explanatory rites employed during the marriage ceremony, which vary from one region of Latin America to another: the giving of the *arras,* the joining of the couple with the lasso or rosary, the exchange of prayer books, the use of specially embroidered cushions upon which the couple kneels, and so on. The relatively little importance placed on confirmation in Latin America, except in the larger cities, also reflects this essentially medieval approach to the sacramental economy of the Church, which had clearly viewed confirmation as a very secondary sacrament.

This diversity, however, also entered into the Rite of Mass itself. The liturgical myth often voiced in classrooms and from pulpits prior to Vatican II that "one could go anywhere in the Catholic world and the Mass would be celebrated the same way" is called into question by the liturgical experience of Latin America. While the Latin prayers and ritual movements of the priest remained the same and were strictly enforced by the sanctions of Canon Law, the peripheral embellishments that accompanied the Rite of Mass varied considerably from anything found in the *Missal of Pius V.* This was true all over the Catholic world but was especially characteristic of the Latin American approach to Liturgy.

It was these embellishments, inspired by a love for the dramatic, that found pride of place in the celebration of the Eucharist in New Spain, especially during the celebrations of the great feasts of the Church year. The Christmas custom of beginning Midnight Mass with the placing of the statue of the Christ Child in the crêche *(la acostada del niño);* the dramatic reenactment of the Last Supper on Holy Thursday, with "apostles" specially dressed and seated at a table in front of the altar throughout the Liturgy; the practice of going to church to give the *pésame* (expression of condolence) to the statue of the *Dolorosa* (the Sorrowful Mother) during Good Friday (sometimes by saying the rosary); the procession of the joyful *encuentro* (encounter) of the statues of the Virgin Mary and the Risen Christ in front of the Church before Mass at Easter, all speak of the flair for the dramatic that helped make the liturgical celebrations of the Church accessible to the people. However, they also naturally tended to overshadow what was deemed the essential part of the Liturgy by the "official" theology of the Church. In short, what the official Church understood it was doing at liturgical celebrations was often quite different from how the people experienced these same celebrations. While this situation was not unique to Latin America, the gulf that separated the official (clerical) understanding of the meaning of liturgical celebration and that of the people was especially wide in Hispanic countries.

The Liturgical Reform of Vatican II and Latin America

The reform of the Liturgy mandated by Vatican II was largely inspired by the pastoral goal of returning the Liturgy to the people; of making the celebrations the prayer of the whole Church and not of just the clerical few. The "full, conscious, and active participation" of all Christians gathered for worship "demanded by the very nature of the liturgy" (*Sacrosanctum conciliun* 14) was the cornerstone of the liturgical movement both before and after the council.

The principal means used by the Church in promoting this liturgical renewal was the thorough revision of the liturgical books of the Roman Rite: the Sacramentary, Lectionary, the rituals for celebrating the other sacraments, the Rite of Funerals, and the Liturgy of the Hours. A Latin *editio typica* of the revised rites was issued by the Holy See after teams of experts in liturgy, theology, history, and canon law spent years recasting them in light of the mandate received from the council. These rites were then translated into the vernacular languages by teams appointed by the various national conferences of bishops, who in turn sent these translations to the Holy See for final approval.

As Annibale Bugnini, the secretary of the *Consilium* for implementing the reform pointed out, the experts who were engaged in liturgical revision were guided by certain "guiding principles" *(altiora principia)*, some of which were more general and "directive" *(orientativi)*, such as the desire to promote participation of the assembly. Others were of a more strategic variety which he termed "operational" *(operativi)*, such as the move to the vernacular languages and the heightened importance given to the Word of God in the celebration of all the sacraments.[7]

Among these operational principles, however, was the conscious attempt by the various teams of experts to return to the simple, austere, classical shape of the Roman Liturgy. This principle was inspired not by archeologism but by a concern that the rites "express clearly the holy things they signify and that the Christian people, as far as possible, are able to understand them with ease and to take part in the rites, fully, actively, and as befits a community" (SC 21). Article 34 of the constitution more fully describes this operational principle based on the *gravitas* and *sobrietas* of the classical Roman Rite: "The rites should be marked by a noble simplicity; they should be short, clear, and unencumbered by useless repetitions; they should be within the people's powers of comprehension and as a rule not require much explanation."

Having reviewed the objectives and goals of liturgical reform in broad strokes, and keeping in mind some of the characteristics of Catholicism as it developed in Latin America, I believe that it is easy to see some of the reasons why liturgical renewal was never a matter of high priority in Hispanic countries. Prescinding from the crushing political, economic, and social problems in Latin America, which undoubtedly played a decisive role in establishing pastoral priorities both in Latin America and among Hispanics in this country, the liturgical reform itself, as presented in the *editio typica* and duly translated by the various Spanish-speaking bishops' conferences, failed to stir up much enthusiasm among the faithful for a variety of reasons. I would suggest three reasons why the liturgical reform was often received with indifference in Latin America: (1) the reform was initially based more on the revision of books than actual liturgical practice; (2) it was influenced by a certain rationalistic worldview not shared by the majority of Christians in Latin America; and (3) guidelines for adapting the rites were largely inattentive to popular religion, which was and is the principal medium of the cultural/religious expression of most Hispanics.

Liturgical Reform as Repristination of the "Roman Genius"

The way the reform of the Liturgy was promoted by Vatican II represented a real novelty in the history of the Church. Never before in the history of the Roman Rite had the worship of Christians been substantially reworked and reoriented by *committees* of scholars and pastors. It is true that the Roman Rite underwent attempts at simplification in the seventh century under Gregory the Great and was supposedly returned to its original "Roman Genius" under Gregory VII in the eleventh century. But because these reforms were undertaken without the knowledge of the tradition available to scholars today, they were basically exercises in editing out doubtful material rather than reworking the ritual patterns that had been long established. This is also the case of the *Missal of Pius V* in 1570, which was basically a standardization of the medieval Order of Mass, shorn of the abuses common in the period before the Reformation.

The liturgical reform of Vatican II, however, was produced in a "scientific" fashion by scholars who were guided by a more thorough knowledge of the history of the Liturgy as well as the theological and liturgical principles that undergird worship. First and foremost, the Liturgy of Vatican II is a scholarly *recovery* of the ancient worship practice of the Church with the pastoral goal of *reorienting* the Church's understanding of Liturgy by promoting the "full, conscious, and active participation" of the faithful.

To its credit, the council realized that the liturgical reform would not take place without extensive catechesis of both the clergy and the faithful. Various articles in the Constitution on the Sacred Liturgy called for just such education (SC 14–19) as well as for the establishment of diocesan or interdiocesan liturgical commissions composed of those "eminent" in liturgical matters to regulate the "pastoral liturgical action" of the diocese (SC 44). That the constitution opened the door to liturgical pluriformity and adaptation of the worship of local Churches (SC 37–40) also reflects its awareness of the diverse cultural contexts in which the reform was to take place.

It should be noted, however, that most of the time and energy in this, the first stage of liturgical reform, was spent on the translation of the *editio typica* of the liturgical books. Because of this emphasis on the implementation of the *official* Liturgy of the Church through the revision of the rites contained in the liturgical books, it can be argued that the liturgical reform of Vatican II had much the same impact on worship in Latin America as that which took place after the Council of Trent. The *clergy* changed the official rites while the *people* maintained both the peripheral dramatic embellishments of the Liturgy and their own *religion casera.*

This emphasis on official liturgical books seems to be continuing with the recent publication of the so-called *texto unico* or *texto unificado* of the Mass (1988). This retranslation of the Sacramentary was the product of collaboration between representatives of episcopal liturgical conferences of Spanish-speaking countries (the United States included) and has been made obligatory for the celebration of the Mass in Spanish. While offering substantial improvements over previous Spanish-language Sacramentaries through the addition of the Swiss synodal Eucharistic Prayers, new prefaces, and blessings, the *texto unico* also illustrates a certain centralizing tendency that seeks to standardize the new Liturgy following a Eurocentric model throughout the entire Spanish-speaking world. Despite the international collaboration that went into its compilation (and perhaps because this effort was spearheaded by the Spanish Church), it reflects very little of what the major Latin American pastoral documents of Medellín and Puebla have said about Liturgy and popular religion.[8]

Because of this emphasis on liturgical reform through the promulgation of official liturgical books (which do not take into account the particular challenges posed by popular religion), it could even be argued that the gulf between the official Liturgy and the religiosity of the people continues to widen. The Liturgy, celebrated exactly as it is presented in the first translation of the *editio typica* or even in the new *texto unico,* is essentially an artificial repristination of the classical Roman Genius characterized by simplicity and abstraction. One could not imagine two characteristics of worship more antithetical to popular religious expression, especially that of Latin America.

Rationalism in Liturgical Renewal

Another characteristic of the liturgical reform that also inadvertently made the renewed Liturgy less appealing to Hispanics is a certain tendency toward rationalism that went beyond even the simplicity and sobriety of the classic Roman Genius. Since the vast majority of those scholars involved in revising the rites of the Church were European (or at least educated in Europe), the *editio typica* of the reform exhibit a decided disease with ritual practices that could possibly be construed as magical or shamanistic.

The blessing of baptismal water at the Easter Vigil is a particularly good example of this tendency. This rite was simplified by the redactors of the new Sacramentary in such a way as to do away with, or make facultative, the traditional symbolic association of blessing and fertility, which, although dating from the early Middle Ages, images the font as not only tomb but womb of the Christian. This interpretation is very traditional and firmly grounded in the writings of the patristic period. The presidential gesture of dividing the water of the font with the flat of the hand in the form of a cross while praying for the Holy Spirit to "fertilize" the water through the mysterious incorporation of divinity *(arcana sui numinis admixtione fecundet)*, the graphic image of the font as "the immaculate womb of the divine fountain" *(immaculato divini fontis utero)*, the various signs of the cross exorcising the water, the blessing of the water by breathing upon it three times, the plunging of the paschal candle with the epicletic prayer, and the *admixtio* of oil after the plunging, all illustrated a mimetic "fertility rite" with which the redactors of the new Sacramentary were obviously uncomfortable.[9] It is interesting to note that this squeamishness about sexuality also extended to references to fertility in the presidential prayers of Ritual Masses for the Scrutinies.[10]

While there were perfectly valid pastoral and theological reasons for simplifying this rite,[11] one wonders if the reform occasionally went too far in expunging dramatic ritual elements that communicate the message of the gospel. It is precisely such elements that, if properly enacted, speak to the Hispanic worldview; a worldview less influenced by rationalism and fear of the "superstitious" and "magic" than that shared by Europeans and North Americans. And it is this worldview that is expressed in Hispanic popular religion. In listing the positive aspects of popular religion in Latin America, *Puebla* points to the ability of popular religion "to express the faith in a total idiom that goes beyond all sorts of rationalism (chant, images, gesture, color, dance), . . . (3:2)." This leads me to suggest that the liturgical reform overlooked an important way to better integrate liturgical prayer with popular religion because it was largely dominated by scholars whose worldview was necessarily shaped by a certain tendency toward a rationalism born of the European philosophical tradition—a rationalism not shared by most Hispanics. It also helps to explain why the official rites, despite the best of intentions on the part of the scholarly committees who revised them, excited relatively little enthusiasm in Latin America.

The Liturgical Reform and Popular Religion

From its inception many of the leaders of the early liturgical movement saw popular devotions as one of the stumbling blocks standing in the way of true liturgical reform. They felt that much of the Catholic religious imagination was distracted by the nonessential aspects of the faith so emotionally celebrated in popular devotions and that the Liturgy, the true prayer of the Church, had become an inaccessible source of spiritual nourishment for the faithful. If the Liturgy were returned to the people, if the faithful were given a means of expressing themselves in the official worship of the Church, they would have a diminished need for the overly sentimental, individualistic, and theologically inaccurate manifestations of popular piety that were prevalent at the turn of the century.

An aspect of devotionalism that the movement opposed with the most vehemence was its individualism and subjectivism, which fostered a "me and Jesus" spirituality. Leaders of the movement, especially those in the United States, advocated the restoration of the liturgy to its proper place in the life of all Catholics as a powerful antidote to an individualism that tended to overlook the communal dimensions of the Christian life and the responsibility of the church as a whole to be engaged in the work of building up the reign of God. William Busch, a leader of the movement, sums up the antipathy of many of his colleagues to devotionalism in a letter to the editor of *Commonweal* written in 1925:

> Undoubtedly, there is something amiss in the present quality of Catholic spirituality. Our devotional life, and hence our whole mentality as Catholics, is individualistic, and the chief reason for this is to be found in the examination of our prayer books. The individualistic character of modern prayer literature cannot fail to impress itself upon our life and to dim our social vision. But the official liturgical prayers of the church, which we do not use, or which we use so privately and mechanically as not to count, are filled through and through with that very spirit for which you are so justly pleading. We have lost that sense of Christian neighborliness and of the kingdom of God on earth which the liturgy teaches.[12]

While most leaders of the liturgical movement before the council did admit that devotionalism had a legitimate place in the spiritual life of Catholics, that place was to be clearly secondary to the Liturgy.[13] This is basically the position eventually taken by Vatican II's Constitution on the Sacred Liturgy, which, while admitting that "the Sacred Liturgy does not exhaust the entire activity of the Church" (SC 9), also announced the need for ecclesiastical oversight in extraliturgical prayer. In continuity with previous legislation dating from the period of the Council of Trent, this document is quite explicit in calling for hierarchical control over popular devotions:

> Popular devotions of the Christian people are to be highly endorsed, provided that they accord with the law and norms of the Church, above all when they are ordered by the Apostolic See. Devotions proper to particular Churches also have a special dignity if they are undertaken by mandate of the bishops according to customs or books lawfully approved. But these devotions should be so fashioned that they harmonize with the liturgical seasons, accord with the sacred liturgy, are in some way derived from it, and lead the people to it, since, in fact, the liturgy by its very nature far surpasses any of them (SC 13).

Given the historical relationship between the official Liturgy of the Church and Hispanic popular religion, it is easy to see that this attitude of the liturgical reform reflected in the constitution would cause problems both in Latin America and among Hispanic communities in the United States. There is no denying that there are points of contact between the devotions of which the constitution speaks and Hispanic popular religion. But as I have stated before, a fundamental error is made in equating this kind of devotionalism with Hispanic popular religion. In many ways, we are speaking of two different phenomena.

Unlike the devotionalism of the pre–Vatican II European and U.S. Churches, Hispanic popular religion is not based on prayer books or the printed word but on oral traditions passed on from one generation to the next. Even more importantly, the exaggerated individualism characteristic of the devotionalism before the council does not seem to predominate in Hispanic popular religion. On the contrary, most of the expressions of piety so dear to the hearts of Hispanics are strongly anchored in a context of *communal* struggle for identity, both religious and cultural. While it is sentimental and at times theologically unbalanced and even syncretistic, expressions of popular piety usually underscore the connectedness of people and events with the sacred, the relational nature of all life and the power that governs it rather than an individualistic relationship with the divine. This aspect of the communal nature of Hispanic popular religion is noted by *Puebla* in its list of the positive aspects of the people's religion.[14]

Thus it is easy to see why the liturgical reform, with its concern to "put devotionalism in its proper place" simply succeeded in driving a larger wedge between the official prayer of the Church and the religious life of the people—a religious life and worldview that is fundamentally promoted by popular religion.

The Road Ahead: Liturgical Reform and Hispanic Popular Piety

What can be done to bridge the chasm between the liturgy and the Hispanic popular religion sketched in the preceding pages? One concrete step that would go a long way in reconciling the two aspects of Hispanic religious life seems to be obvious: liturgists and pastoral agents working in the Hispanic community need to reevaluate their attitudes toward popular religion. Rather than seeing it as a distortion of "orthodox Christianity," it needs to be taken seriously as a *locus theologicus* in developing strategies for evangelization among Hispanics and for celebrating the faith within the Liturgy. It cannot simply be dismissed as an aberrant cultural element to be eliminated once proper catechesis has taken place.

This is not to say that all expressions of Hispanic popular religion are equally good reflections of the gospel and should be incorporated helter-skelter within the Liturgy, following a kind of *piñata pastoral* that is sometimes passed off as "inculturation." What is needed is a serious dialogue between the Liturgy and Hispanic popular religious expressions, to the mutual enrichment of both. *Puebla* has called for just such a dialogue, which it proposes as the basis for inculturating the Liturgy in a Hispanic context:

> We must see to it that the liturgy and the common people's piety cross-fertilize each other, giving lucid and prudent direction to the impulses of prayer and charismatic vitality that are evident today in our countries. In addition, the religion of the people, with its symbolic and expressive richness, can provide the liturgy with creative dynamism. When examined with proper discernment, this dynamism can help to incarnate the universal prayer of the Church in our culture in a greater and better way (*Puebla* 3,4.e).

What are the concrete implications of such a dialogue here in the United States? I would suggest that first of all, in preparing Liturgy in a Hispanic context, it is necessary not only to consider the norms enunciated in the official liturgical books but to be attentive to the rites and practices of popular religion. These practices may often appear to be at odds with the theology of worship proposed by the Church. A good example of this is the intense Marian piety of most Hispanics, which was succinctly expressed by the U.S. bishops' *National Pastoral Plan for Hispanic Ministry* in 1987 and which states that "the Hispanic people find God in the arms of the Virgin Mary."[15] It is true that the U.S. bishops' document *Environment and Art in Catholic Worship* seems to discourage the placement of permanent images in the worship space because they distract the attention of the worshipers from the primary liturgical symbols: the assembled community itself, the ambo and the altar (EACW 100, 101). However, this norm must be evaluated in light of the intense identification of Mexicans, for example, with *Our Lady of Guadalupe.* In such a community, it could be argued that the placement of this *Virgencita* in full view of the assembly is entirely appropriate, since *Guadalupe* sums up both the faith and the cultural identity before God of those gathered to celebrate the Eucharist. Rather than being a distraction from the liturgical action, she enhances and focuses it. Clearly, those engaged in liturgical ministry among Hispanics need to be wary of a "liturgical fundamentalism" that would cause them to reject out-of-hand the elements of popular religion that they themselves do not fully understand or appreciate.

This "cross-fertilization" between popular religion and Liturgy must go in the other direction as well—to the *religion casera* of the people. In fact, this is probably the more important place to begin. Parish pastoral and liturgical outreach ought to concentrate on how to support and enrich the practices of popular religiosity in the home by helping to imbue already traditional devotions with a rootedness in the Scriptures and in the signs and symbols of the liturgical tradition of the Church, which they often lack. Rather than ignoring or ridiculing these practices, a positive but critical evaluation of them by the Church's "religious professionals" would go a long way in healing the centuries-old gulf that separates them from the "official Liturgy."

Conclusion

The relationship between Hispanic popular religion and the official worship of the Church is both complex and, at times, problematic, especially for non-Hispanics. It seems clear, however, that unless an honest dialogue between these two aspects of Hispanic Catholicism takes place, the liturgical reform mandated by Vatican II will continue to have minimal impact on the religious life of Hispanics in the United States and elsewhere. A failure to take Hispanic popular religion seriously as a vehicle for evangelization compromises profoundly the Church's ability to speak to Hispanic religious experience and to celebrate that experience in the Liturgy.

Notes

1. I use the term *Anglo* in this essay to refer to non-Hispanics who constitute the social mainstream of the Catholic Church in the United States: those who are in positions of power and dominance in the Church. I realize that while it is a handy label, it is also an oversimplification of the complex nature of non-Hispanic U.S. Catholicism. Many Poles, for example, still maintain popular religious practices in this country. I also realize that the term Hispanic is misleading, but I use it along with *Latino* to refer to the diverse national groups in this country who trace their origins to Central or South America.

2. See Justo L. González, "Voices of Compassion," *Missiology* 20 (1992) 163–73.

3. See J. Vicens Vives, *Historia social y económica de España y América* (Barcelona: Editorial Vicens-Vives, 1977) 364–74; Allan Deck, *The Second Wave: Hispanic Ministry and the Evangelization of Cultures* (New York: Paulist, 1989) 41.

4. On Our Lady of Guadalupe see Virgilio Elizondo's *La Morenita: Evangelizer of the Americas* (San Antonio: Mexican American Cultural Center, 1976) 49–53; Jody Bryant Smith, *The Image of Guadalupe: Myth or Miracle?* (New York: Image, 1984).

5. Deck, *The Second Wave*, 55. For a comparison with nordic Christianity see Virgilio Elizondo, *Christianity and Culture* (San Antonio: Mexican American Cultural Center, 1975) 124–28, 156–57. For a fascinating discussion of the perdurance of the medieval worldview in Latin America as represented in religious folk art, see William Worth, "Arte Popular Cristiano," *Religiosidad Popular: Las Imágenes de Jesucristo y la Virgen María en América Latina* (San Antonio: Mexican American Cultural Center, 1990) 7–14.

6. See Jay Dolan, *The American Catholic Experience* (New York: Doubleday, 1985) 231.

7. Annibale Bugnini, *La riforma liturgica (1948–1975)* (Rome: Edizioni Liturgiche, 1983) 50–59.

8. For a description of the changes made by the *texto unico* in the Rite of Mass, see Julian López y Manuel Carmona, eds., *Comentarios al nuevo ordinario de la misa y a las plegárias eucaristicas: Orientaciones para la catequesis y el uso litúrgico* (Madrid: Coeditores Litúrgicos, 1988).

9. Alex Stock, "The Blessing of the Font in the Roman Liturgy," David Power and Mary Collins, eds., *Blessing and Power*, Concilium 178 (Edinburgh, T & T Clark, 1985) 43–52.

10. See my discussion of the opening prayer for the Mass of the Second Scrutiny where the protasis of this prayer was altered from *"Ecclesiam tuam spiritali fecunditate multiplica"* to read *"Ecclesiam tuam spiritali iucunditate multiplica,"* thus editing out the reference to fertility essential to the coherence of the text, in *The Ritual Masses of Baptism in the Missal of Paul VI* (Editions Saint-Viateur: Rome, 1988) 159–73.

11. See Balthasar Fischer, "Die Intentionen bei der Reform des Erwachsenen und Kindertaufritus," *Liturgisches Jahrbuch* 21 (1971) 65–75.

12. William Busch, "Letter to the Editor of Commonweal, 1925," quoted in Kathleen Hughes, ed., *How Firm a Foundation: The Voices of the Early Liturgical Movement* (Chicago: Liturgy Training Publications, 1990) 54.

13. See Louis Bouyer, *Liturgical Piety* (Notre Dame: University of Notre Dame Press, 1955) 243–56.

14. Among the positive aspects of popular religion, *Puebla* notes "an awareness of personal dignity and of solidary brotherhood; . . . an ability to celebrate the faith in expressive and communitarian forms" (*Puebla* 3:2).

15. *Origins* 17 (December 10, 1987) 46.

Afterword

Has the dialogue been rejoined? The question does not admit a straightforward answer. First of all, the conditions have changed greatly in four and a half centuries. The encounter does not come in the immediate aftermath of the trauma of conquest. To be sure, as Paul Wadell points out in his contribution, the *conquista* remains the defining character of the Hispanic narrative about its identity. But there is now a long history of encounter—often violent—between parties of unequal strength, fraught with misunderstanding, but also one that has created deep, rich, and vibrant cultures. The parties to the dialogue have also changed. The Anglo interlocutors are more willing to admit their ignorance and their need to listen, even though they continue to fall short in their efforts. The Hispanic partners represent a variegated tapestry of histories and cultures, brought together under the sometimes dubious epithet of "Hispanic" to designate the ethnicizing experience of Spanish-speaking peoples—those long resident within the boundaries of the United States as well as peoples from Latin America and the Caribbean. And the purpose of the dialogue has changed as well: now its goal is to help non-Hispanics understand what the theology and experience of Hispanics means in its own contexts and what it offers to the rest of the Church.

The conduct of the dialogue is also different this time. Here Hispanics take the lead, describing their history and current reality. In the original forum, there was an opportunity for questions that led to revisions in order to make the presentations more intelligible to a wide variety of audiences. The term "Hispanic" took on more destiny in the telling of these stories, as the distinctive elements of each of the four major cultures presented had the chance to speak. The Anglo theologians in the second part of the dialogue were all accompanied by Hispanic mentors. All the chapters were also subjected to a lively discussion with Hispanic and Anglo participants together. Both forums were conducted in English, which unavoidably gives a certain shape to the conversation. But both forums also gave the opportunity to hear themselves speaking and to receive immediate feedback on how their communication was received by a diverse group of listeners. These forums represented a kind of *encuentro,* with some common features with those national events described by Ana María Pineda in her presentation. They involved both speaking and listening. Not quite dialogues in the fullest sense (for the Anglos made no presentations about their reality and only indirectly about their theologies), yet a very human exchange nonetheless. Perhaps even more important than anything that was actually said, they created an atmosphere and environment out of which a long-term, ever-deepening dialogue might occur.

So it would appear to this observer (and participant in the forums) that the dialogue has been rejoined: not under the conditions or terms of that first attempt (for both conditions and terms made dialogue ultimately impossible), but under conditions more suited to dialogue and terms more conducive to it. And it would be hoped that such dialogues might continue. For the different cultures that make up the United States Hispanic reality, it was an opportunity to think about how to present themselves and what issues most needed to be brought to the attention of the whole U.S. Church. For some of the theologians, it was a first exploration into the cultures and lives of Hispanic communities. For others, it was an opportunity to deepen that connection. All in all, it suggested a way of addressing more adequately the needs of Hispanic communities and appreciating more acutely their richness. And it might even offer a pattern that might be used in engaging other cultures present in the U.S. Church today.

Beyond process and engagement, was anything else learned in the dialogue? One could make a catalogue of the various themes that were addressed, both in the presentations on the four cultures and in the theological reflections. These would no doubt be commonplace knowledge to the Hispanic interlocutors and be already in the awareness in greater or lesser degree to the Anglo participants. Rather, it might be more useful to note some distinctive contributions that do not just illuminate Hispanic realities but address larger issues for doing theology at all today in the United States. Here are five such contributions that struck this Anglo, both in participating in the forums and in the rereading of the presentations.

Mestizaje and Cultural Belonging

Both Moises Sandoval and Dominga Zapata make much of the blending of peoples that make up Mexico and Puerto Rico respectively. For the racial theorists of earlier in this century (and surviving still in reactionary movements), such mixing was miscegenation or mongrelization. In Hispanic circles, however, this mixing was seen differently. Rather than bringing out exaggerations or weaknesses of the groups mixed, such mixing created a new people. Mexican philosopher José Vasconcelos (1882–1959) spoke of "la raza cósmica" as a new cosmopolitan race that would provide a synthesis of the races that had flowed into it. Virgil Elizondo speaks of "mestizaje," the mix that creates a new people. He finds a parallel in the Galilee of Jesus' time, when Jesus' own environment was a crossroads of peoples.[1]

The thinking of Vasconcelos or Elizondo find little credence with racial purists, but does find considerable resonance with students of globalization and with the postmodern, postcolonial cultural theorists. Both of these groups are trying to take stock of what is happening to the world today and how those global and cultural processes are affecting identity and awareness for peoples.

Students of globalization—the homogenization of the world through a single capitalist market network, electronic communications, science, and the extension of United States cultural artefacts—see a twofold process going on. On the one hand, there is a tremendous homogenization brought on by the shared networks just alluded to. Internet reaches around the globe, as do telecommunications. Denim jeans and athletic shoes constitute a common cultural costume. As one observer has put it, we are becoming "McWorld."

On the other hand, there is a countermove afoot. This resists homogenization by emphasizing local particularity. Local cultural distinctiveness is reasserted, leading to a reclaiming of ethnic identities. This seems to give local, manageable contour to the endless sweep of the globalizing processes.[2]

The postmodern and postcolonial reading of culture goes hand in glove with what the globalization process is perceived to be doing. It attends to the migration of peoples that leads to extensive diaspora communities that become "ethnicized," that is, assert cultural distinctiveness in order to survive in alien environments yet change ineluctably at the same time. Culture in these settings is not the self-enclosed meaning system imagined by nineteenth-century anthropologists. Rather, it is an open flow, a stream that runs alongside other streams, and communities find themselves participating in several streams at the same time.[3]

The experience of *mestizaje* and of the refugee communities of which Carlos Córdova and Guillermo Fernández-Toledo speak represent a kind of globalized and postmodern-postcolonial history *avant la lettre*. The long history of coming to terms with *mestizaje* will be instructive as theologians try to come to terms with a multicultural Church, not just in a dominant culture/minority culture model (similar to the colonial model of center and periphery) but in a way that shows how all of these cultures are changing in each generation and are changing one another. How, too, people are made to feel to belong in a *mestizo* culture is something that other cultures in the United States might learn from Hispanics. Donald Senior touches upon the theme of hospitality in the foreword. Hospitality becomes a key category in the theology of a multicultural church.[4]

Narrativity, Tradition, and Community

Paul Wadell proposes in his presentation that whereas Anglo ethics typically begins with a definition of human nature, Hispanic ethics would begin with a narrative of the experience of being a conquered people. At one time such narrative approach to ethics would have been relegated to the periphery as the product of a "nonliterate" people incapable of producing a more sophisticated, analytic ethics.

The situation has changed. In a growing disillusion with the universalizing pretensions of the modernist project, and under the press of awareness of cultural variability around the planet, it becomes harder and harder to accept universalizing statements about human nature. Postcolonial thinkers are especially suspicious that the universals are but the cultural particulars of the West writ large. Similarly, the Enlightenment's dismissal of tradition as a source of authority now runs up against the reassertion of the cultural particularity noted above. All of this has led to a revaluing of both distinctive communities and the narratives by which they transmit and transform their traditions. Narrativity is thus no longer the preserve of predominantly oral peoples but becomes the hallmark of self-conscious cultural communities deepening their own identities.

Wadell himself makes some of these connections in his presentation, notably to the work of Stanley Hauerwas. Communitarian thinkers of varying stripes could be added to this list.[5] Such approaches do not respond to the need to find some common means of discourse in a world that is more consciously diverse and potentially fractious, but they do cultivate the voices of communities that contribute to the chorus of a multicultural society. Most likely no new common discourse will be found until each of those voices finds itself and has the opportunity to be heard. Narratives of slavery, of exile, of being refugees, and of seeking opportunity will find their places alongside the narratives of being conquered of Hispanic peoples and the narratives of the dominant culture. In listening to Hispanic narratives we discover models for discerning and shaping those narratives in other communities, both as a way of strengthening them and discovering their ethical values and commitments.

A New Practical Theology

Under the influence of praxis-based liberation theologies in Latin America and as a result of the disaffection with academic theologies too distant from the life of the Church, there has been a movement in recent years in the United States and in some countries of Europe to create a new practical theology. This new practical theology is not the same as the older Protestant practical theologies or the Catholic pastoral theologies, all of which tended to be applications of theoretical insights to practical situations. Rather, the new practical theology, like the praxis-based theologies of liberation, sees practice and theory as mutually informing each other. Practice, therefore, is changed by theory, but theory is also changed in the encounter with practice. Such a practical theology is not only "closer to the ground" in engaging the lives of believers, but it also provides an important check on theory itself.[6] It calls into question the objectivist stance of theory over against practice and exposes presuppositions sometimes not otherwise evident.

Barbara Reid's presentation on biblical interpretation begins an exploration of these issues as it moves beyond traditional historical-critical approaches to seek out more engaged readings of the Bible. But these insights are especially highlighted in Gary Riebe-Estrella's presentation on theology. The essay actually brings together the longer Hispanic and Latin American reflection on this manner of doing theology and the needs of a practical theology suited to United States realities today. Such a practical theology not only is congenial to American empiricist and pragmatic traditions; by engaging communities at the level of their practices it gives them clearer voice in the manifold of cultures in order to work with other cultural streams.

Popular Religiosity and Liturgical Reform

Popular religiosity is a topic a number of the presentations addressed, since it appears as such a distinctive feature of Hispanic cultures. Mark Francis takes it up in terms of the liturgical reforms of the Second Vatican Council. A point he makes is that the liturgical reform has not had the same effect in Latin America because of the different history and experience of the peoples of that region.

A greater sensitivity to popular religiosity is a theme sounded frequently in recent years. But how it is to be situated with the liturgical reform continues to be a matter that needs greater theoretical attention. The entire reception of Vatican II by the peoples of Latin America, while enthusiastic and serious, shows up something of the inherent limitations of that ecumenical council.

In retrospect, it becomes clearer that the Second Vatican Council was called principally to deal with the problems of the modern world. "Modern" here refers to the increasingly secular societies of Western Europe, North America, and Australia. The reforms, wittingly or unwittingly, had these societies in mind. While the message of Vatican II has important things to say to other parts of the world, its investigations did not engage those societies so completely. It is not for nothing that the CELAM conferences of Medellín and Puebla seemed to capture the imaginations of Latin Americans more than Vatican II—although they never lost respect for that great council.

Popular religiosity stands as a reminder that there are fundamentally different ways of being religious—and being faithful—in a public, communal manner. The postconciliar reading of the proper restoration of the Roman Rite was done largely with an eye to secularized societies. But these too undergo continuing change. The American town meeting in New England may have been something of a rough correlate for public gathering in basilicas, but even the meaning of public gathering continues to change. Some have suggested that the town meeting has been replaced by the TV talk show. Keeping in mind the public forms of popular religiosity keeps us focused upon the inculturation task that is ever before us.

Being Church

Both John Linnan's and Ana María Pineda's presentations focus upon meanings of being Church in Hispanic communities. Linnan addresses especially the small ecclesial communities in two locations and speculates about how they are Church. Pineda discusses pastoral formation for working within the Hispanic experience of Church.

A temptation for the outsider is to see Hispanic ecclesial expressions as somehow the exceptions to the general (or generic) sense of the renewed, post–Vatican II Church. They may be actually being juxtaposed to particular United States understandings of Church, growing out of the experience of the nineteenth and twentieth centuries. This was an experience that, from the time of the Third Council of Baltimore, predicated a parochial school system, which, in turn, required larger parishes as a financial base. The immigrant experience made urban parishes the cultural center of the neighborhood as well. What should a culturally mainstream *and* multicultural United States Church look like? Again, the Hispanic experience is not simply an exception that somehow has to be rhymed with the rule. It presses us to question what we thought was the norm. Or, in Gary Riebe-Estrella's words in his presentation, a move from differentness to otherness.

A dialogue rejoined? In the final estimation, yes. It takes on a complexity that was not first so imagined but reveals a richness unforeseen—not just of Hispanic contributions (although certainly that) but of new possibilities for theology and ministry in the United States Church as a whole.

Robert J. Schreiter, C.PP.S.

Notes

1. For Vasconcelos, see Roberto S. Goizueta, *"La Raza Cósmica?* The Vision of José Vasconcelos," *Journal of Hispanic/Latino Theology* 1 (February 1994) 5–27. For Elizondo, see his *Galilean Journey* (Maryknoll, N.Y.: Orbis, 1983).

2. See, among others, Jonathan Friedman, *Global Identity and Cultural Process* (Thousand Oaks, Calif.: Sage, 1994).

3. See, for example, Paul Gilroy, *The Black Atlantic: Modernity and Double Consciousness* (Cambridge: Harvard Univ. Press, 1993); Homi Bhabha, *The Location of Culture* (London: Routledge, 1994).

4. For a survey of some of the issues, see Robert Schreiter, "Multicultural Ministry: Theory, Practice, Theology," *New Theology Review* 5 (August 1992) 5–19.

5. For example, Amitai Etzioni, *The Spirit of Community* (New York: Simon & Schuster, 1993).

6. See, for example, Randy L. Maddox, "The Recovery of Theology as a Practical Discipline," *Theological Studies* 51 (1990) 650–72.

Contributors

Part One: Hispanic Realities and Ministry Today

A native of New Mexico, MOÍSES SANDOVAL is the editor of *Revista Maryknoll* and the editor-at-large of *Maryknoll,* the monthly magazines of the Catholic Foreign Mission Society of America. A historian as well as an award-winning journalist, Mr. Sandoval is the author of *On the Move: A History of the Hispanic Church in the United States* and the editor of several other historical works on the history of U.S. Hispanics in the Church.

CARLOS B. CÓRDOVA holds a doctor of education degree with emphasis in multicultural education from the University of San Francisco. Currently, he is associate professor of La Raza studies at San Francisco State University. He is a native El Salvadorean and has specialized in the sociocultural anthropology of Mexico and Central America. His recent research includes the history of Central American migrations of the Bay Area since the early 1900s.

DOMINGA ZAPATA, S.H., is a native Puerto Rican and has been actively involved in Hispanic ministry in the United States both on the regional and national level. Currently she is the Hispanic American consultant in the Chicago Archdiocesan Office of Ethnic Ministry. She holds an M.A. in theology from Mundelein College in Chicago.

GUILLERMO FERNÁNDEZ-TOLEDO holds an M.A. in theology from St. Vincent De Paul Regional Seminary. Currently, he teaches at Belen Jesuit Preparatory School as well as at the Southeast Pastoral Institute (SEPI) in Miami. He is a lecturer in theology at St. John Vianney College Seminary and collaborates with the Archdiocese of Miami Lay Ministry Program and the Office of Worship and Spiritual Life.

Part Two: Hispanic Realities and Theology

BARBARA E. REID, O.P., holds a Ph.D. in biblical studies from The Catholic University of America in Washington. She is associate professor of New Testament at Catholic Theological Union. Her scholarly interests are in

Luke-Acts and feminist hermeneutics. A former Spanish teacher, she is also interested in Hispanic ministry. Recent articles of hers can be found in *Biblical Research, The Bible Today,* and *New Theology Review.*

GARY RIEBE-ESTRELLA, S.V.D., is a Mexican American, a Divine Word missionary, and the founder of Casa Guadalupe, el Seminario del Barrio. He was director of the NCCB Project XIII on Hispanic vocations and formation. He holds an S.T.D. in pastoral theology from the Pontifical University of Salamanca, Spain, and is assistant professor in doctrinal theology and Hispanic ministry at Catholic Theological Union.

JOHN LINNAN, C.S.V., is adjunct associate professor of doctrinal theology at Catholic Theological Union, where he has served since 1978. Educated at the University of Louvain, he has specialized in ecclesiology and historical theology.

PAUL J. WADELL, C.P., is professor of ethics at Catholic Theological Union. He holds a Ph.D. in ethics from the University of Notre Dame. He is the author of *Friendship and the Moral Life, The Primacy of Love: An Introduction to the Ethics of Thomas Aquinas* and several articles in moral and spiritual theology.

ANA MARÍA PINEDA, R.S.M., is a native El Salvadorean. She has worked extensively in the process of Hispanic ministry and the *Encuentros* in the United States. She is associate professor of pastoral theology and director of Hispanic ministry at Catholic Theological Union. A member of the Academy of U.S. Catholic Hispanic Theologians (ACHTUS), she holds an S.T.D. in pastoral theology from the Pontifical University of Salamanca.

MARK FRANCIS, C.S.V., is associate professor of liturgy at Catholic Theological Union. He holds a doctorate in liturgy from the Pontifical Liturgical Institute of St. Anselm, Rome. His special interest is in the inculturation of worship, and he has contributed articles on this topic to periodicals such as *New Theology Review* and *Liturgy 90.* He is author of *Liturgy in a Multicultural Community* (The Liturgical Press, 1991) and is co-editor of *Living No Longer for Ourselves: Liturgy and Justice for the Nineties* (The Liturgical Press, 1991).

ROBERT SCHREITER, C.PP.S., is professor of doctrinal theology at Catholic Theological Union. He holds a Theol. Dr. from the University of Nijmegen. He is author of the widely acclaimed *Constructing Local Theologies* and editor of the Orbis Faith and Cultures Series.

DONALD SENIOR, C.P., is professor of New Testament studies and past president of Catholic Theological Union. He holds an S.T.D. from the University of Louvain. Noted Scripture scholar, he is author of *The Passion Series* (Collegeville: The Liturgical Press, 1984–1991) and *Jesus: A Gospel Portrait* (Mahwah, N.J.: Paulist Press, 1992).